IMAGES
of America

BOURBON COUNTY
1860–1940

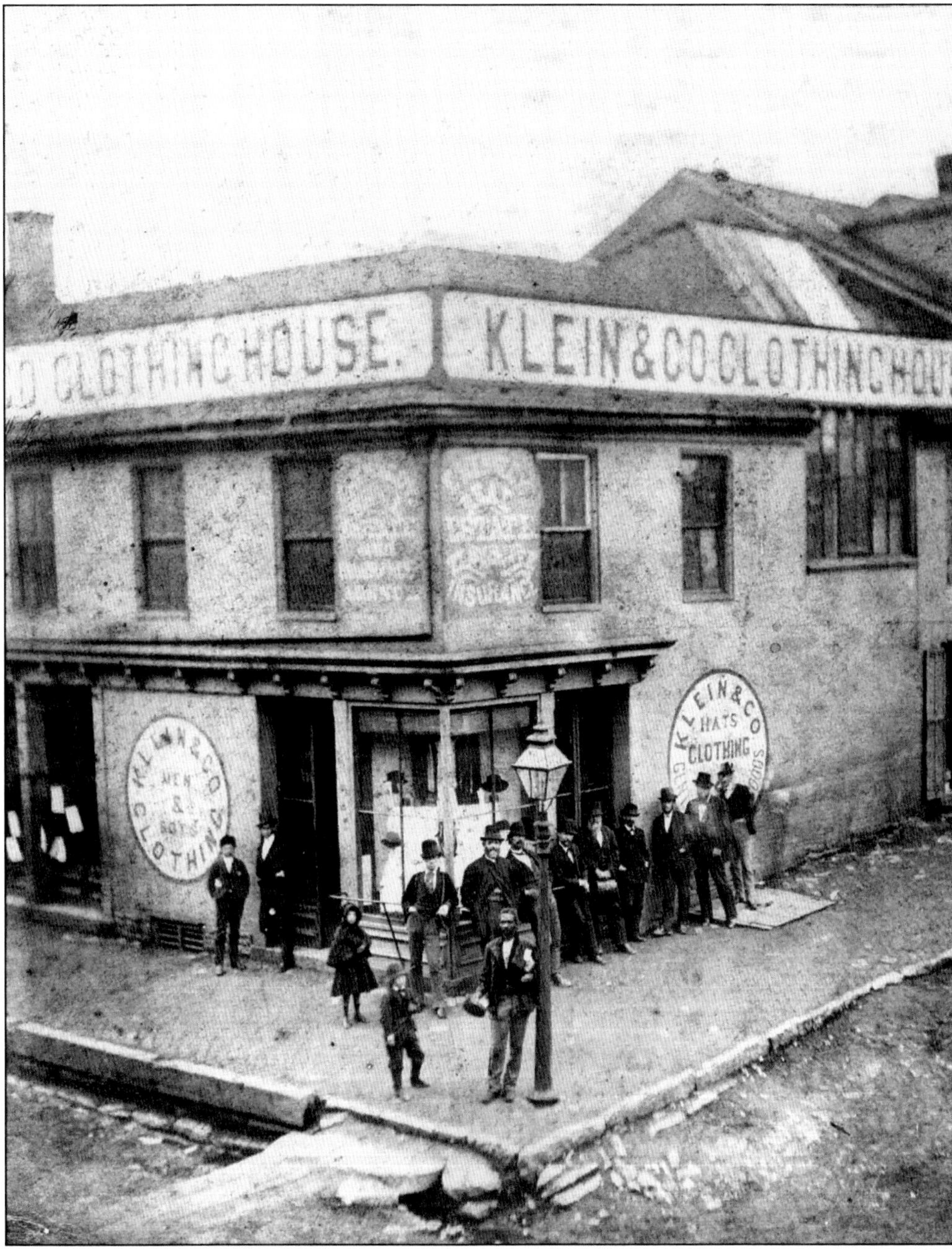

CORNER OF MAIN AND BROADWAY (BANK ROW). Klein & Company Clothing House had a prime location in 1871 where the Kentucky Bank now has its offices. Identified in this old photo (along the wall), from left to right, are Ed Knapp, Jim McClure (in doorway), Moses Koplan, John Atchison, Jown W. Holladay, Charles Klein, John McDaniels, Abe Shire, Charlie Kenney, John Hampton, and Harry Holt. The little girl in front is Jennie Bassford; the little boy is Ike Price; and the black man leaning against the gaslight pole is Tom Brown, "Bell Ringer."

IMAGES
of America

BOURBON COUNTY 1860–1940

Berkeley and Jeanine Scott

ARCADIA
PUBLISHING

ISBN 978-0-7385-0685-2

Published by Arcadia Publishing
Charleston, South Carolina

Printed in the United States of America

Library of Congress Catalog Card Number: 2001087304

For all general information contact Arcadia Publishing at:
Telephone 843-853-2070
Fax 843-853-0044
E-Mail sales@arcadiapublishing.com
For customer service and orders:
Toll-Free 1-888-313-2665

Visit us on the Internet at www.arcadiapublishing.com

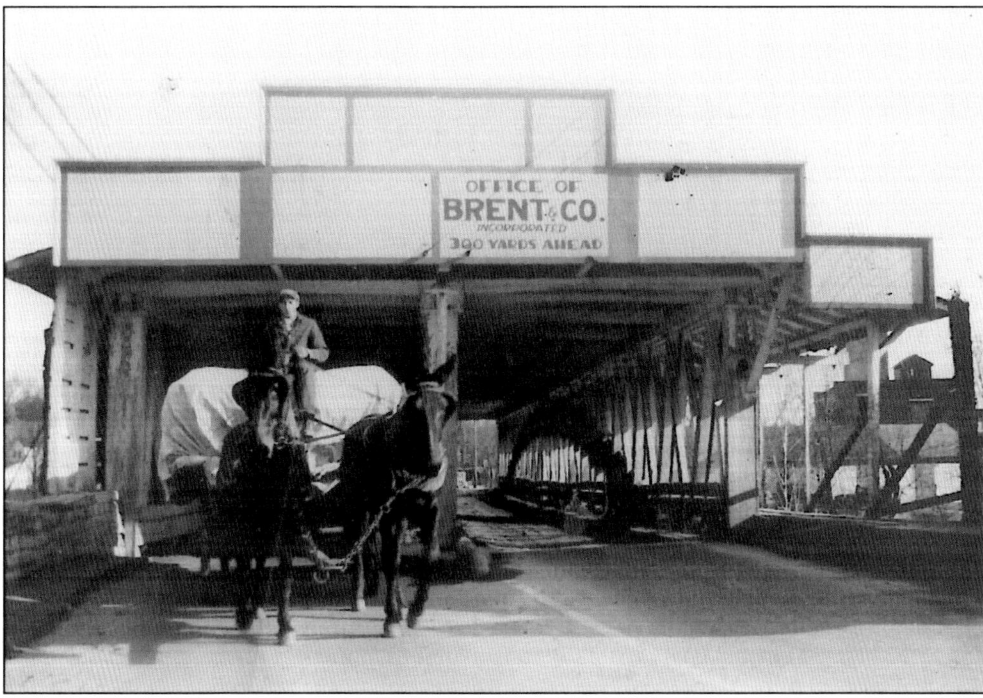

COTTONTOWN BRIDGE SAW A CENTURY OF COUNTY HISTORY. This covered bridge, known as the Cottontown Bridge because it linked the Paris business district with the area where a cotton mill once stood, was a "double-barreled" structure, which spanned Stoner Creek at North Main Street between 1833 and 1933. Lewis Wernwag, a German immigrant who built several bridges in the state and was one of the first to use a cantilevered bridge design, built the bridge. The bridge had two "drive-ways" for vehicles, each 12 feet wide, separated by a partition, as well as a six-foot wide walkway for pedestrians.

Contents

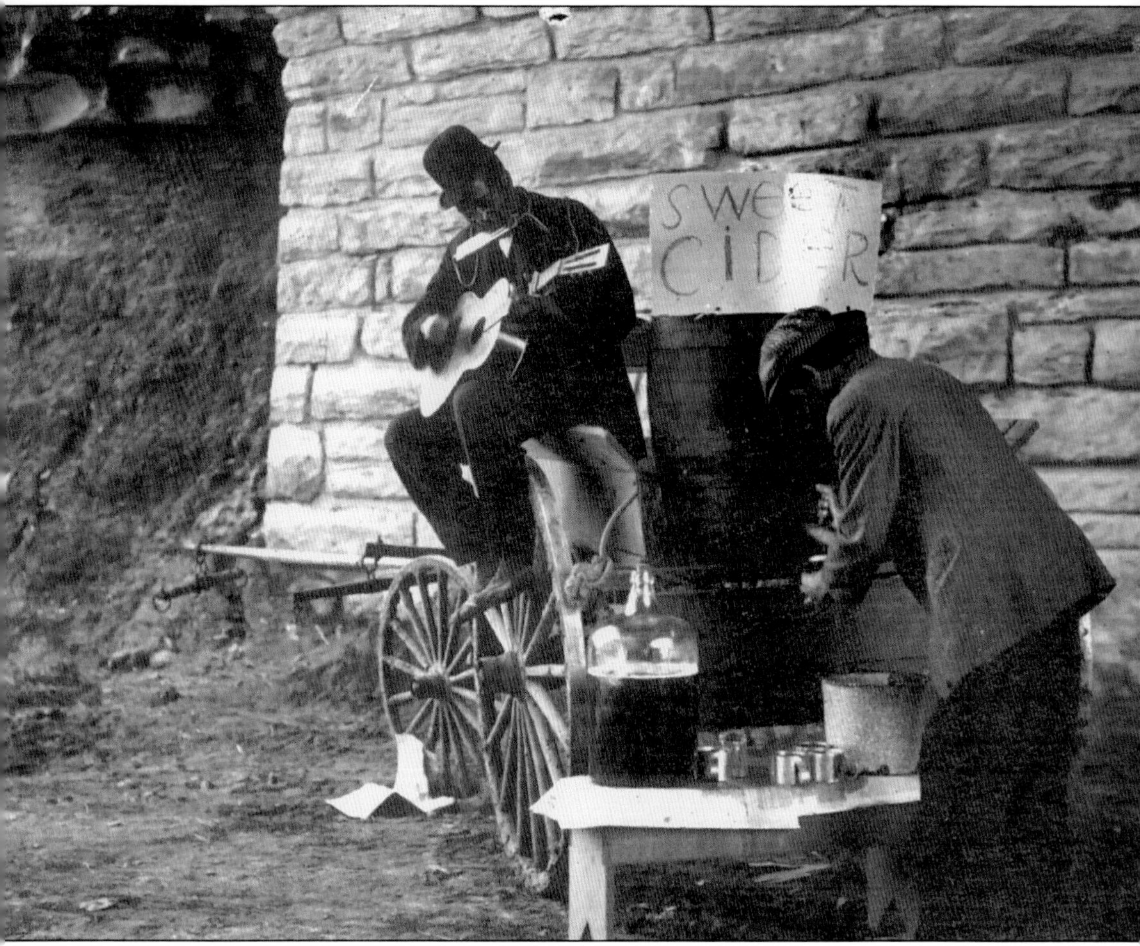

Sweet Cider and Entertainment. This black entrepreneur provided harmonica and guitar music along with tin cups of "sweet cider" to his customers in Paris sometime in the early 1920s. The price he charged for this treat and his name have been forgotten. He is pictured under the railroad bridge that crosses Stoner Creek on the north side of town. (Anyone who remembers something about this picture, or others in this book, is encouraged to contact the authors.)

INTRODUCTION

Images are powerful things—in fact a picture is said to be worth a thousand words. Our purpose was to make this collection of more than 200 images merge together to form a cohesive picture of our subject—much like bits of cloth come together to form a beautiful quilt. This book of Bourbon County photographs and other images made between 1860 and 1940 has a lot of quilt pieces: black and white faces of people young and old; interior and exterior views of buildings long gone or much altered by the passage of time; and photos of rural life and small vignettes of life in a more urban setting.

Residents of the county naturally view their home as special. When you talk to other Kentuckians about Bourbon County and what it represents, you get a less sentimental view of the area coupled with an acknowledgement of its beauty and history. Bourbon County, formed in 1785, was named in honor of the French royal family that supported the United States in its war against England. Originally extending northward to the Ohio River and eastward to the Big Sandy River, it was long ago split into more than 30 counties.

Bourbon County today has an area of 292 square miles in the east-central area known as the Bluegrass Region of Kentucky. It continues to be known for its fertile soil, limestone base, and the many springs and creeks that attracted some of the state's earliest settlers. Many pioneers like Daniel Boone, Michael Stoner, Simon Kenton, and James Smith braved the dangers and rigors of the frontier to populate and "civilize" Bourbon County. By the 1770s, pioneers were establishing stations and homesteads here.

The county seat of Paris began growing almost immediately as early settlers poured into the area. Some of the county's smaller towns and villages, like Millersburg, North Middletown, Little Rock, Clintonville, and Ruddles Mills can also trace their beginnings to this earliest pioneer era. After Kentucky became a state in 1792, Bourbon County became a major political and economic power in the state, contributing a number of statewide leaders including the Commonwealth's second governor, James Garrard, who served from 1796 to 1804.

Agriculture was the natural mainstay of the county's economy. It was a smooth reddish whiskey aged in charred oak barrels, a product of the bountiful corn crops, that insured worldwide recognition for the county's name. Although disputed by a few, Bourbon Countians feel confident that bourbon whiskey was first distilled in their county by one of several early settlers, most likely Jacob Spears. The county continued to be the home of many distilleries right up to Prohibition in 1919.

The usual pioneer crops that provided sustenance and products to sell such as bourbon soon gave way to other agricultural products that dominated the farming and economic life of the county. Hemp, cattle, sheep, bluegrass seed, and tobacco became the primary crops for more than two centuries. Horses of all breeds were developed to a high standard in Bourbon County, and mules were a major export before the arrival of the automobile and tractor.

With a strong and rich agricultural base, the county's towns grew and prospered. The railroads brought increased access to the outside world, as well as a way to transport the county's famous agricultural products to market.

Bourbon County was very representative of the rest of the state when the Civil War tore the country asunder. While dependent on slavery for their agricultural success and generally Southern in culture, most residents were still reluctant to see the Union destroyed. In the end, like the rest of the nation, the county was dragged into a conflict that split the government, community, churches, and families for decades.

After the war, the community reunited against the real and imagined indignities of Reconstruction, and became more Southern in sympathy than before the conflict. Despite the end of slavery, the agricultural and newly developed industrial concerns enjoyed a prosperity that would last until the Depression of 1929. Paris experienced a building and population boom that provided a collection of Main Street buildings still admired today and an ever-growing population of better-educated and wealthier citizens.

Like other communities of similar size in the region, Bourbon County had its share of racial, ethnic, and economic problems. Inequities between the black and white communities reached an extreme during the 1930s as was true in most of America. But somehow the people of Bourbon County found a way to work through problems and conditions began to show slow improvement.

We chose the starting date of 1860 for the book because that is when photography began, providing a variety of images to choose from. Our book ends with 1940 and the beginning of World War II, an event that certainly changed the world and our country.

This book, *Bourbon County: 1860–1940*, does not attempt to tell the complete history of our fascinating, complex, and lovely county. All it attempts to do is offer a photo album that gives a glimpse of what life was like during that period. As no two quilts are alike, so this "crazy" quilt of images is only one of the hundreds of patterns that could have been made using other images of early Bourbon County life.

We tried not to favor any group, family, or community in the county, working with the pictures available to us. Sharp-eyed readers might notice a couple of photographs that fell outside the dates we had chosen, but we felt they were important images to include. We did not dwell on the individual stories of the county, other than in the short chapter titled *Fascinating Faces*; instead, we tried to present images of all kinds.

Searching for photographs and information for this book has reminded us of the importance of maintaining our history, whether it is family, local, national, or global. And by "maintaining" we mean remembering it accurately and respectfully. We owe it to the people who lived that history not to embellish it or change it. And most importantly, not to forget it.

One

The Courthouse Square

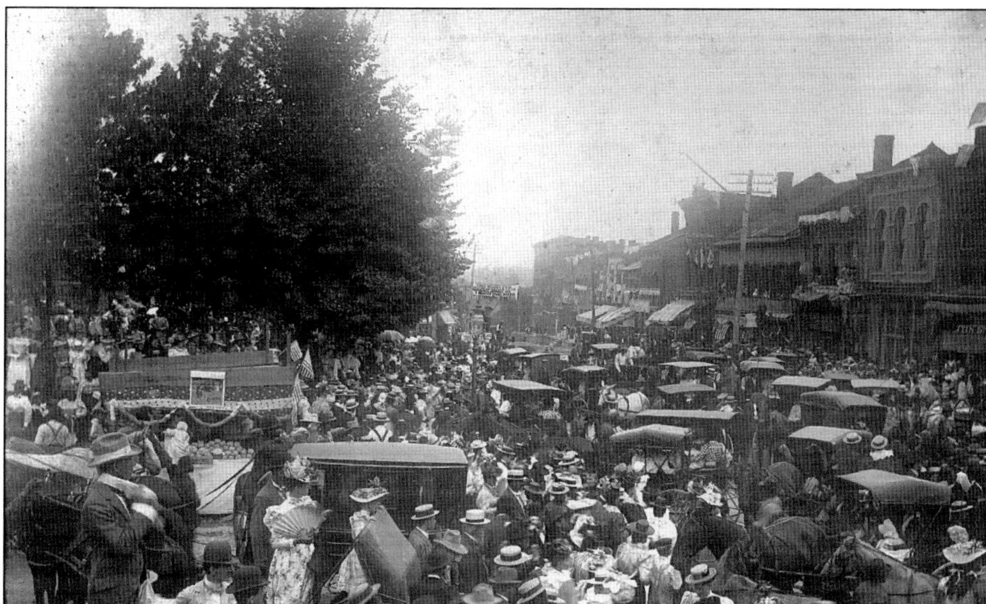

Courthouse Square. Since 1787 when the first frame and log courthouse was built on the hill overlooking Hopewell Spring, the public square surrounding it and all subsequent courthouses have been the site of countless public celebrations and commemorations. The event pictured here was in August of 1899 and was a celebration of the country's victory in the Spanish-American War. A banner stretched across the street seen in the distance promised "Merchants Carnival and A Monster Trade Parade - Balloon, Fireworks, Public Wedding, Etc. Etc."

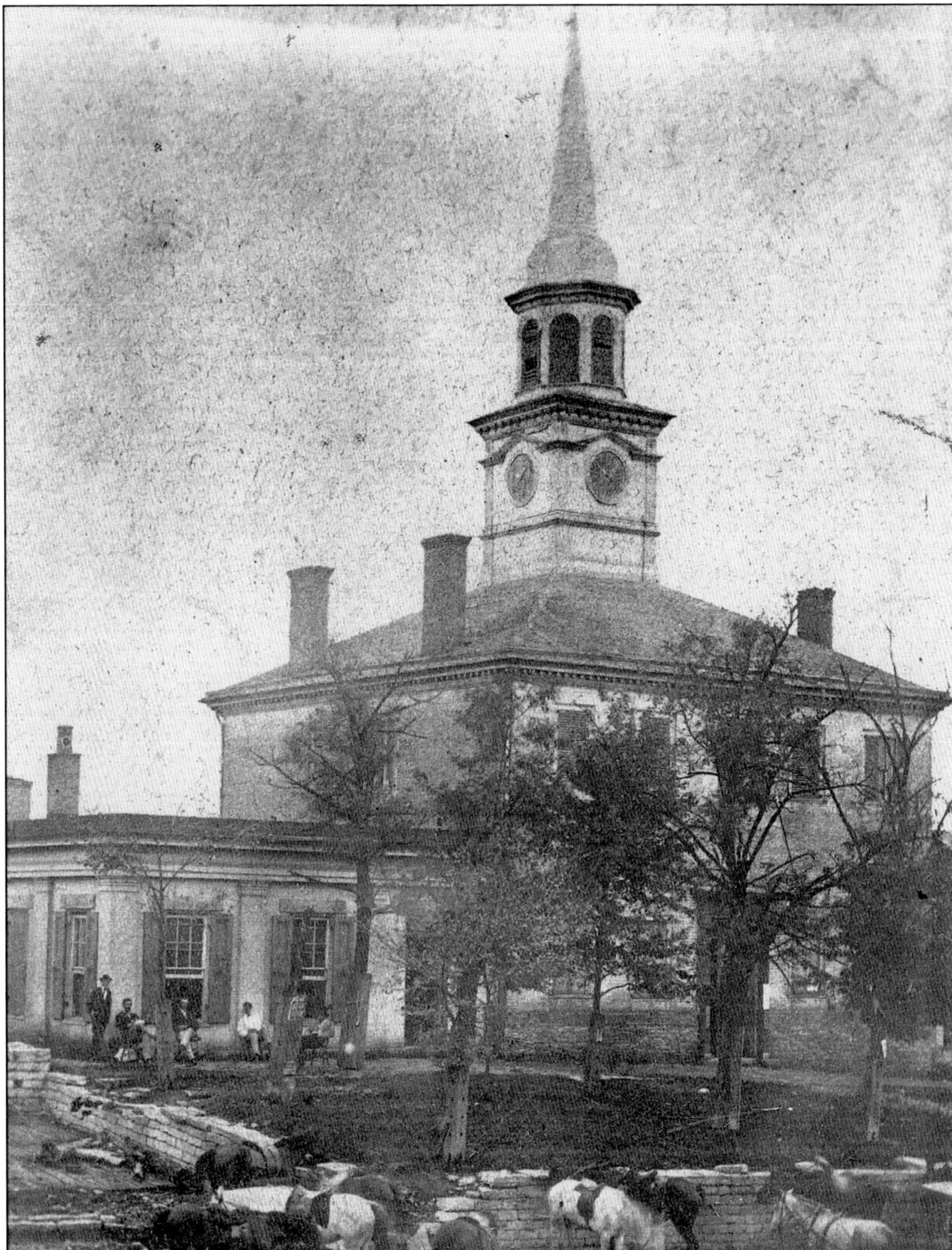

COURTHOUSE, 1799–1872. At the end of the 18th century, Bourbon Countians felt their seat of government should appear as important and grand as any in the state. In February 1797, the Bourbon Fiscal Court ordered that a new courthouse "be built to rival the great stone temple of justice in Lexington." The structure was designed and constructed by renowned builders John and Thomas Metcalf. The magistrates must not have been satisfied with the building's original box cupola as it was replaced in 1816 by the tall spire seen in this early photograph. The new addition was similar to the cupolas on the 1806 Fayette County Courthouse in Lexington and on the Catholic Cathedral in Bardstown.

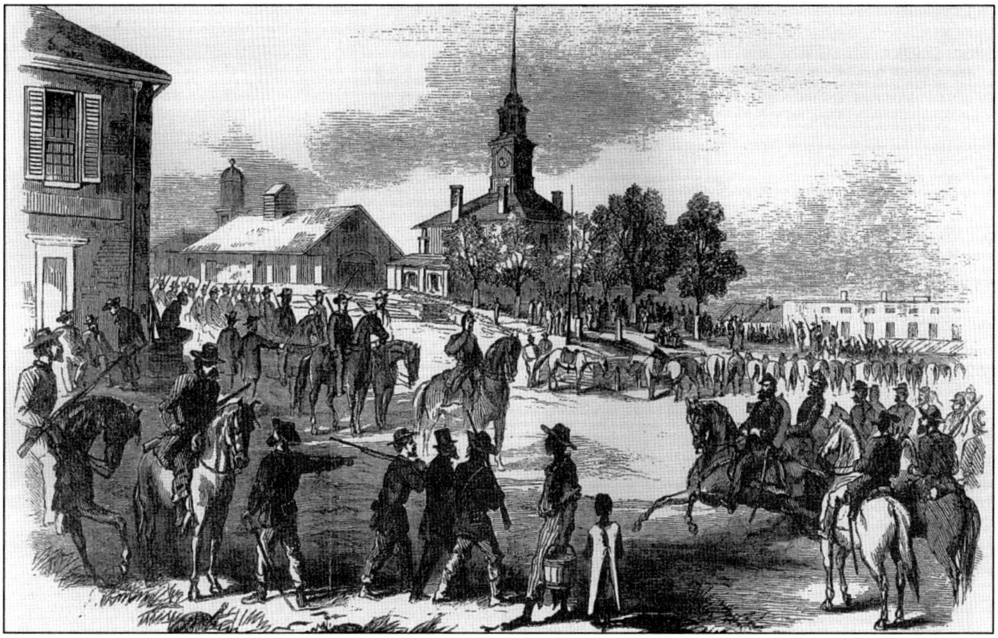

John Hunt Morgan Captures Paris During Civil War. This view of Paris's Courthouse Square appeared in the August 16, 1862 issue of New York's *Frank Leslie's Illustrated Newspaper*. An artist who was in Paris when Confederate Gen. John Hunt Morgan's men captured the city for a brief time made this engraving from sketches. The cutline reads, "The rebel Morgan with his guerillas bivouacking in Court House Square, Paris, Bourbon County, after levying contributions on the inhabitants."

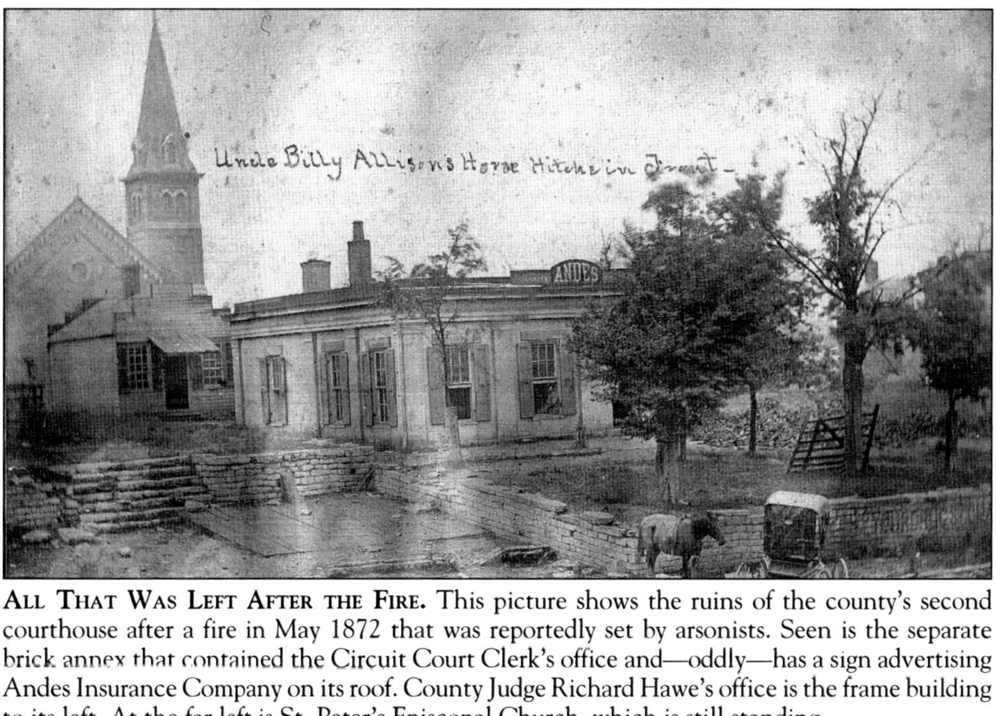

All That Was Left After the Fire. This picture shows the ruins of the county's second courthouse after a fire in May 1872 that was reportedly set by arsonists. Seen is the separate brick annex that contained the Circuit Court Clerk's office and—oddly—has a sign advertising Andes Insurance Company on its roof. County Judge Richard Hawe's office is the frame building to its left. At the far left is St. Peter's Episcopal Church, which is still standing.

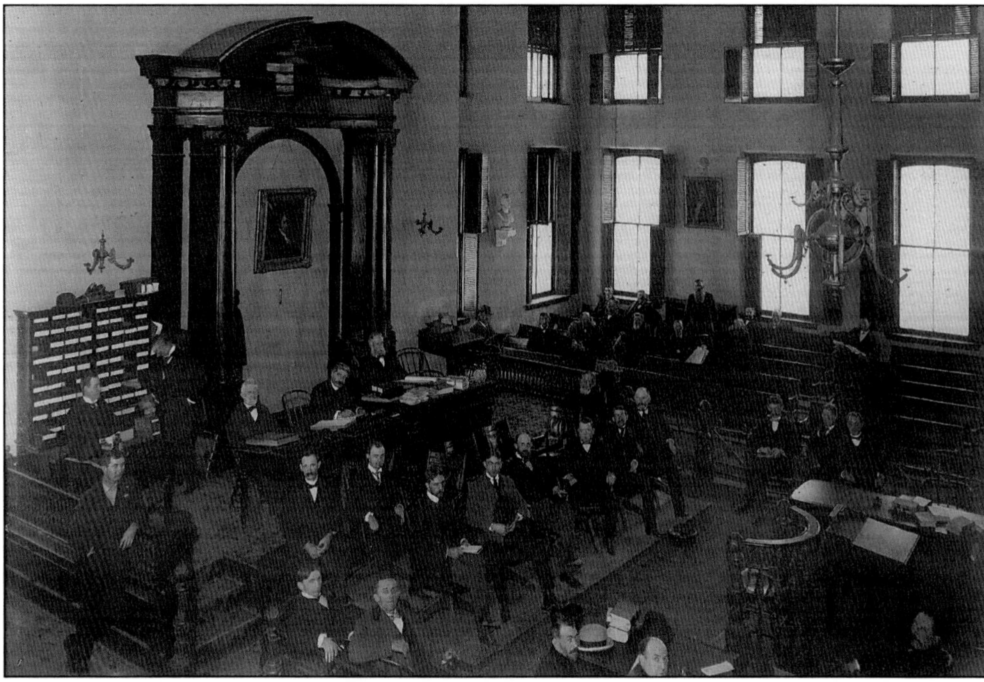

County's Third Courthouse, Built in 1873. The main courtroom in all of the courthouses was the major space in the building. This photo, of what was probably the local legal community, was taken from the balcony. The two men seated at the table in the front of the room are Circuit Clerk Charles E. Butler and Deputy Circuit Clerk F.L. McChesney. The unknown man seated at the table next to them is probably a judge.

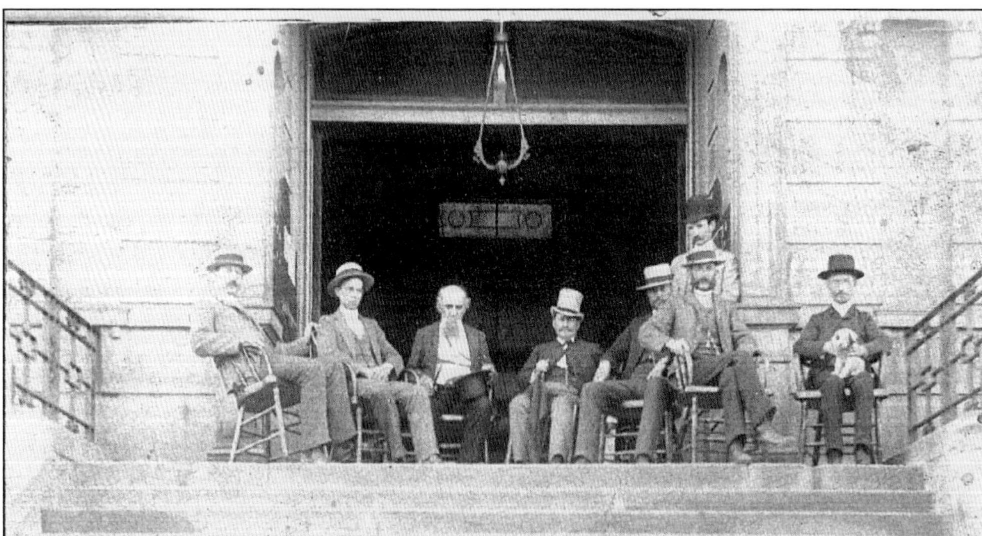

On the Steps of the 1873 Courthouse. These men, identified as local attorneys and courthouse officials, pulled chairs out to the front entrance of the courthouse sometime around the turn of the century for this photo. Pictured from left to right are Tom Lyng, Joe Armstrong, R.H. Hanson, Billy Purnell, Millard Kenney, Bob Talbot (standing), J.S. Smith, and Capt. Pat Miller, holding pet dog.

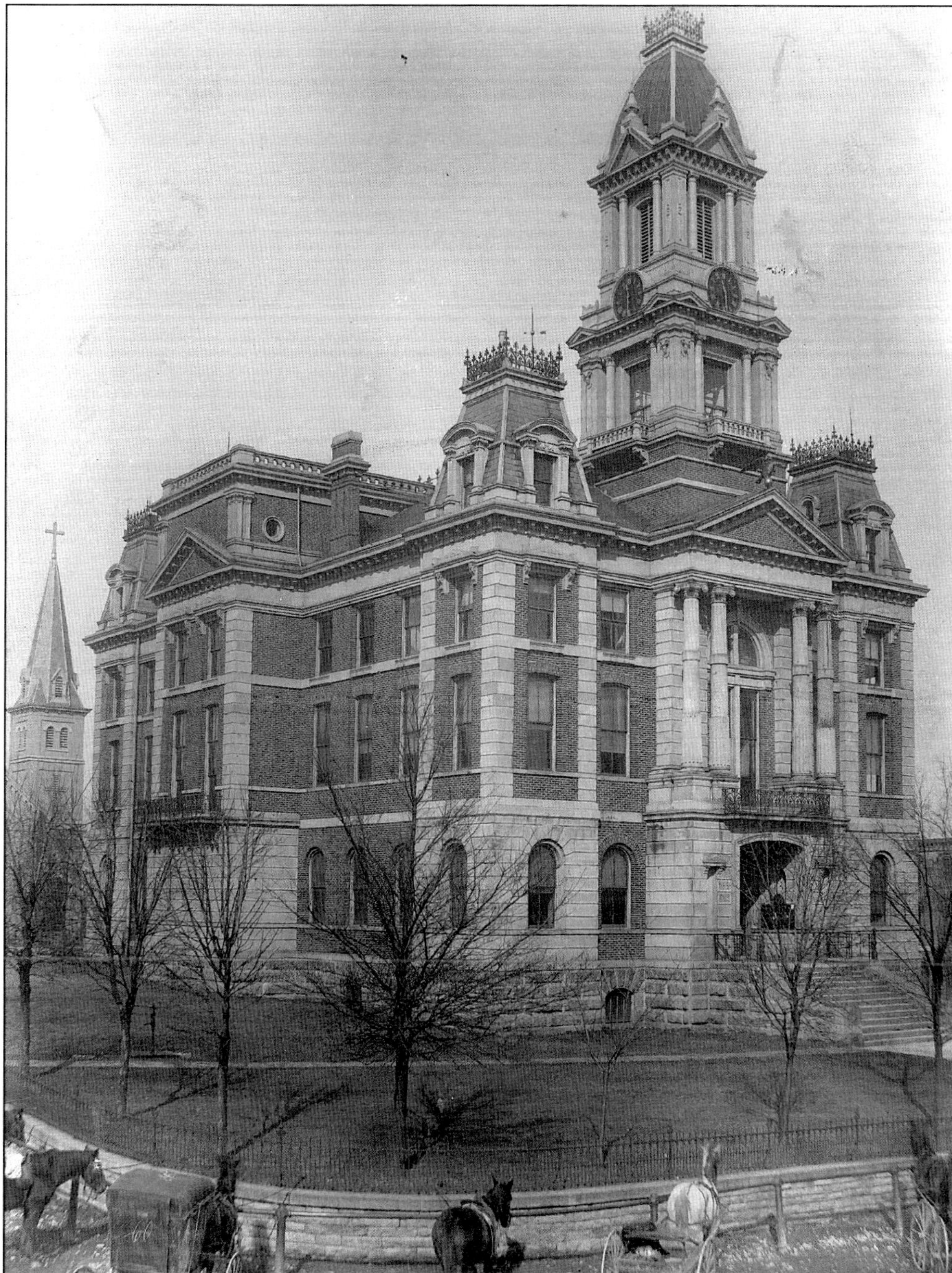

Courthouse, 1873–1901. The courthouse built to replace the one that burned in 1872 was designed to be as grand as its predecessor. The building's imposing clock and bell tower rose 113 feet into the sky. Designed by A.C. Nash of Cincinnati, the French Renaissance–style building cost more than $125,000 and was constructed primarily of brick with iron cornices. It was trimmed with stone from the quarry at Cane Ridge. Mindful of the fate of the last courthouse, planners installed fire and burglarproof vaults for important court and government papers. That foresight proved to be valuable just 31 years later.

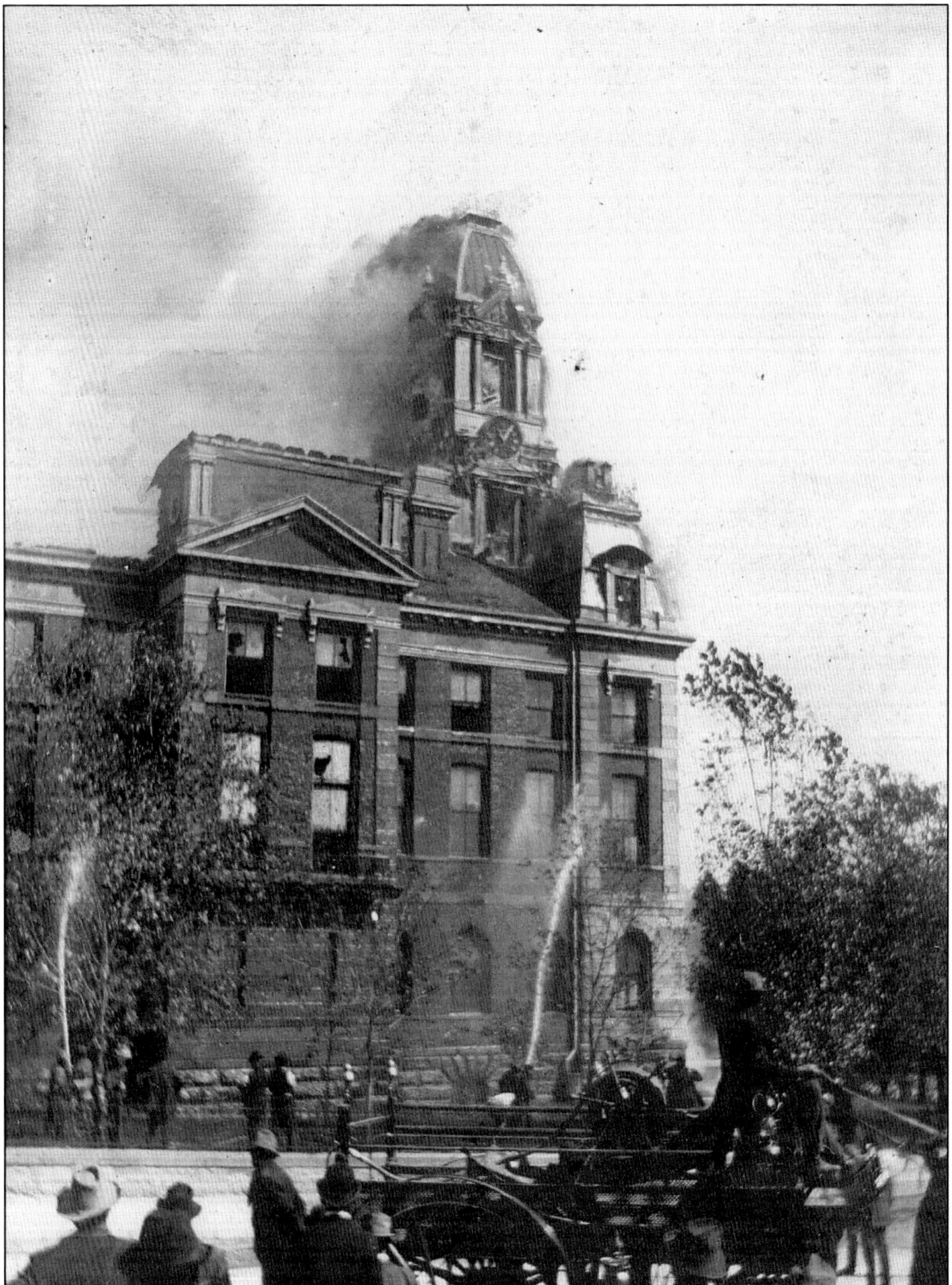

The Fire That Shocked the County. It was a Saturday morning, October 19, 1901, when residents saw flames break through a window of the county's grandest landmark. Strong winds fanned the flames and thwarted the heroic efforts of the firefighters seen in this photo. Weak water pressure and short ladders also hindered their work. Bystanders and courthouse employees rushed to save historic items and move papers into the fire vaults for protection. These efforts insured that Bourbon County has almost complete records of all of its court proceedings.

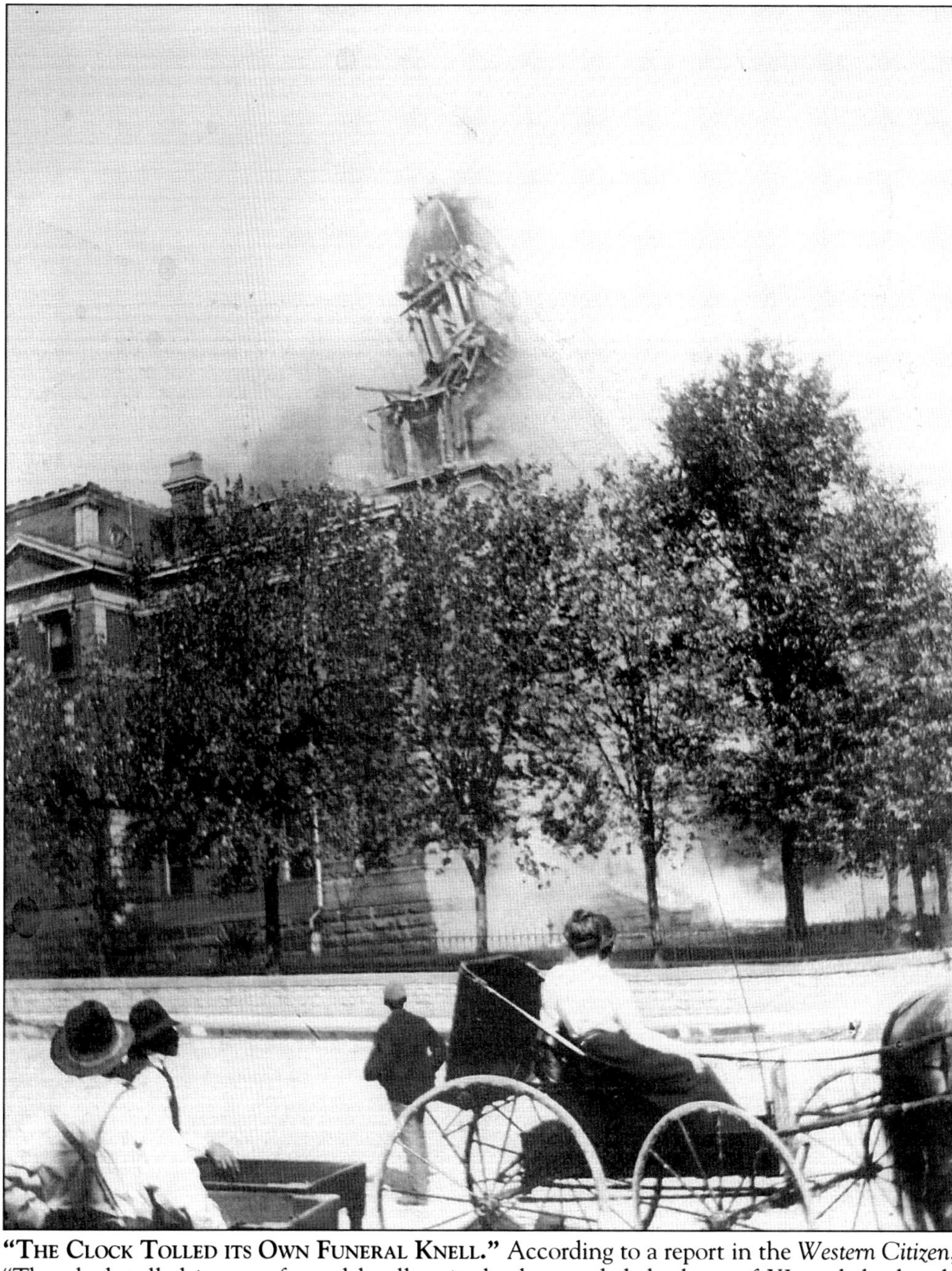

"The Clock Tolled its Own Funeral Knell." According to a report in the *Western Citizen*, "The clock tolled its own funeral knell as it slowly sounded the hour of XI, and the hands marked 11:10 when . . . the stately tower trembled and fell into the seething furnace below." This amazing photo captures that action. Imagine what the lady in the carriage, Miss Kate Alexander, is feeling at that moment.

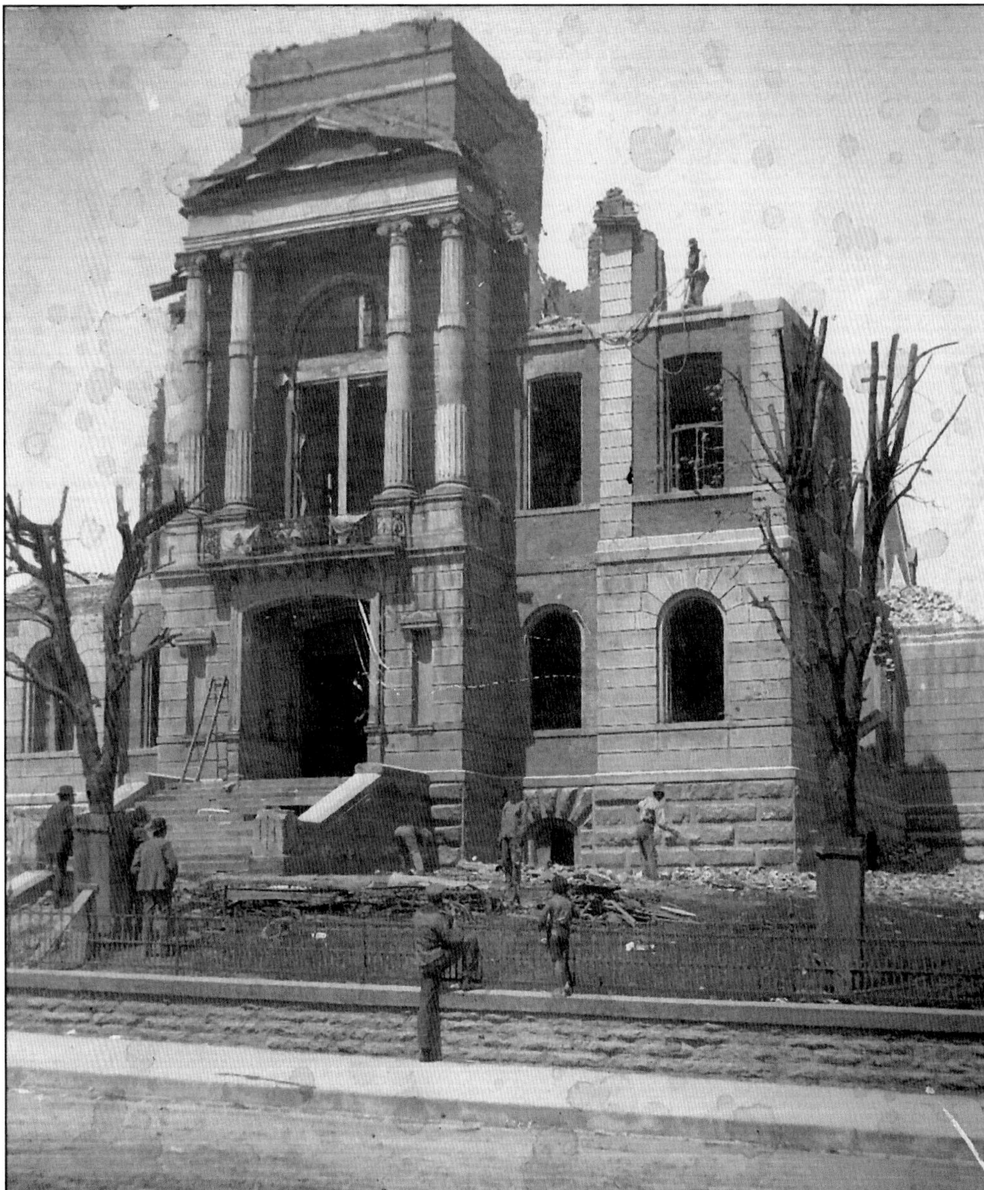

LAST OF THE "OLD COURTHOUSE." The 1901 fire was blamed on defective flues, and officials claimed that only the old slate roof kept the fire from spreading to buildings around the square. The county had to sue the insurance company to receive the $50,000 for which the building was covered. The fire and the costs for constructing the new courthouse caused intense bickering among the county's political factions and their representative newspapers.

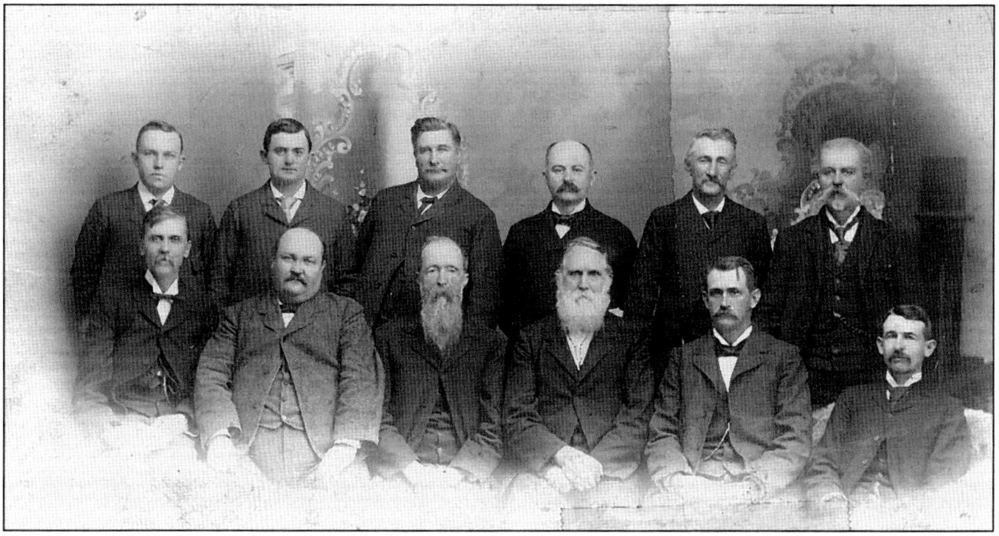

The 1897 Bourbon County Fiscal Court and Officials. This official portrait shows from left to right (seated) Magistrate Ben Stepp, County Clerk Ed. D. Paton, Magistrates S. Lilleston, Porter Jett, Letcher Walters, and Cliff Arnsparger; (standing) Deputy County Clerk Pearce Paton, Magistrates Henry S. Clay and H.C. Smith, County Judge H.C. Howard, and Magistrates E.P. Claybrook and James Stone.

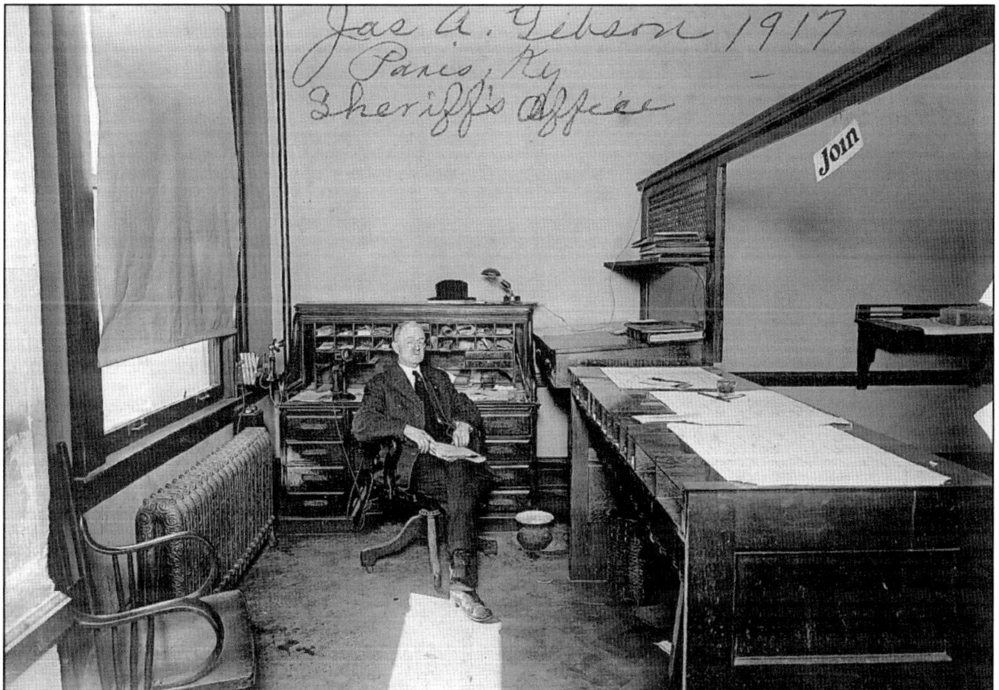

Sheriff's Office in 1917. James A. Gibson, shown in this photo, was probably a sheriff's deputy since William G. McClintock was elected Bourbon County Sheriff in 1917. Gibson is dressed in a suit ,and a bowler hat can be seen on top of the desk—members of the sheriff's department did not wear uniforms until the 1970s. Notice the spittoon, once almost a required piece of office furniture in men's offices

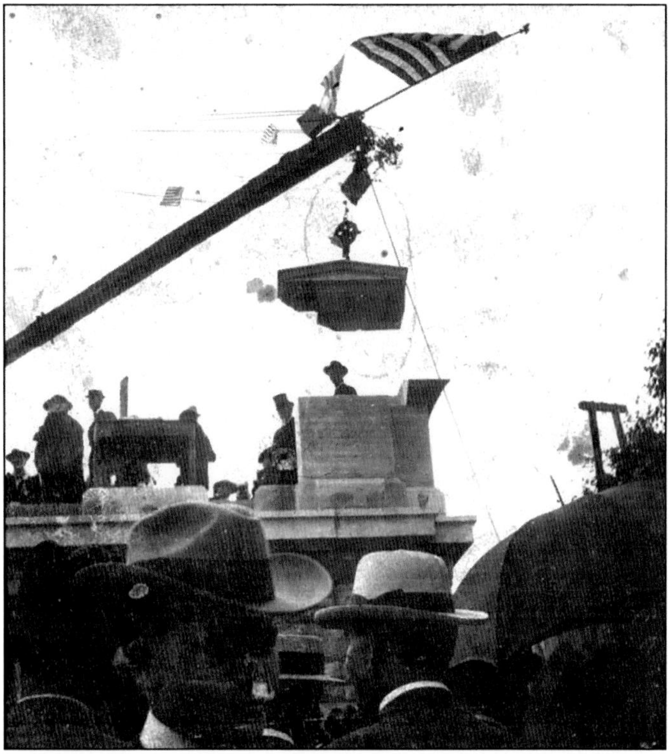

Cornerstone Lowered into Place. With flags flying and members of the local Masonic Lodge in attendance, the cornerstone for Bourbon County's fourth courthouse was lowered into place on June 16, 1903. It would be another two years before the building was completed, furnished, and occupied.

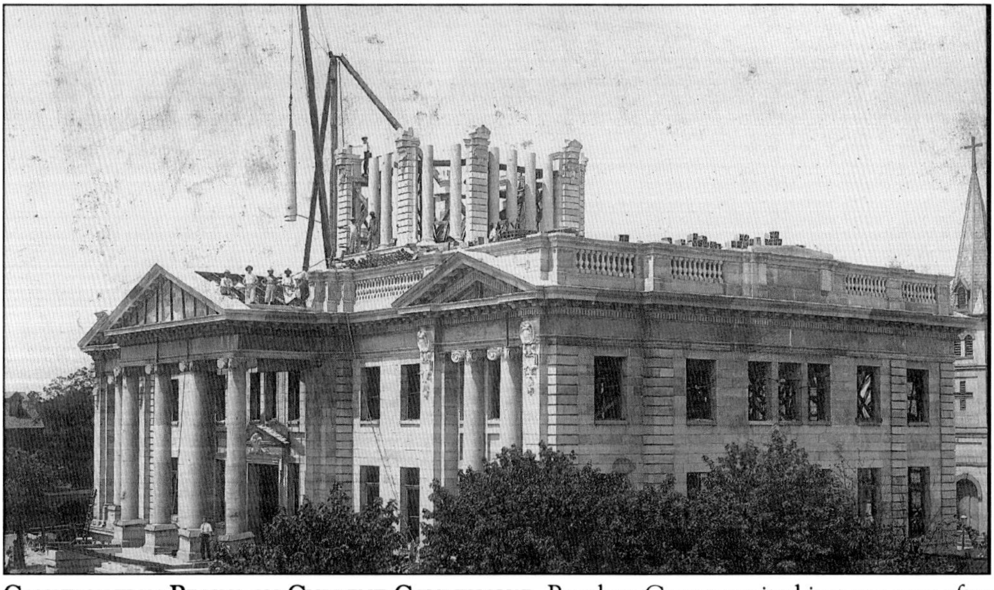

Construction Begins on Current Courthouse. Bourbon County waited just one year after the disastrous fire of 1901 to begin construction on the fourth and current courthouse in Paris. Designed by noted South Carolina architect Frank Milburn, it is fashioned after the United States capitol and provided inspiration for the South Carolina capitol that Milburn would later design. Workmen in this picture are lifting one of the massive granite pillars that support the cupola. Gibson & Crawford of Logansport, Indiana, were the contractors who completed construction at a cost of over $170,000.

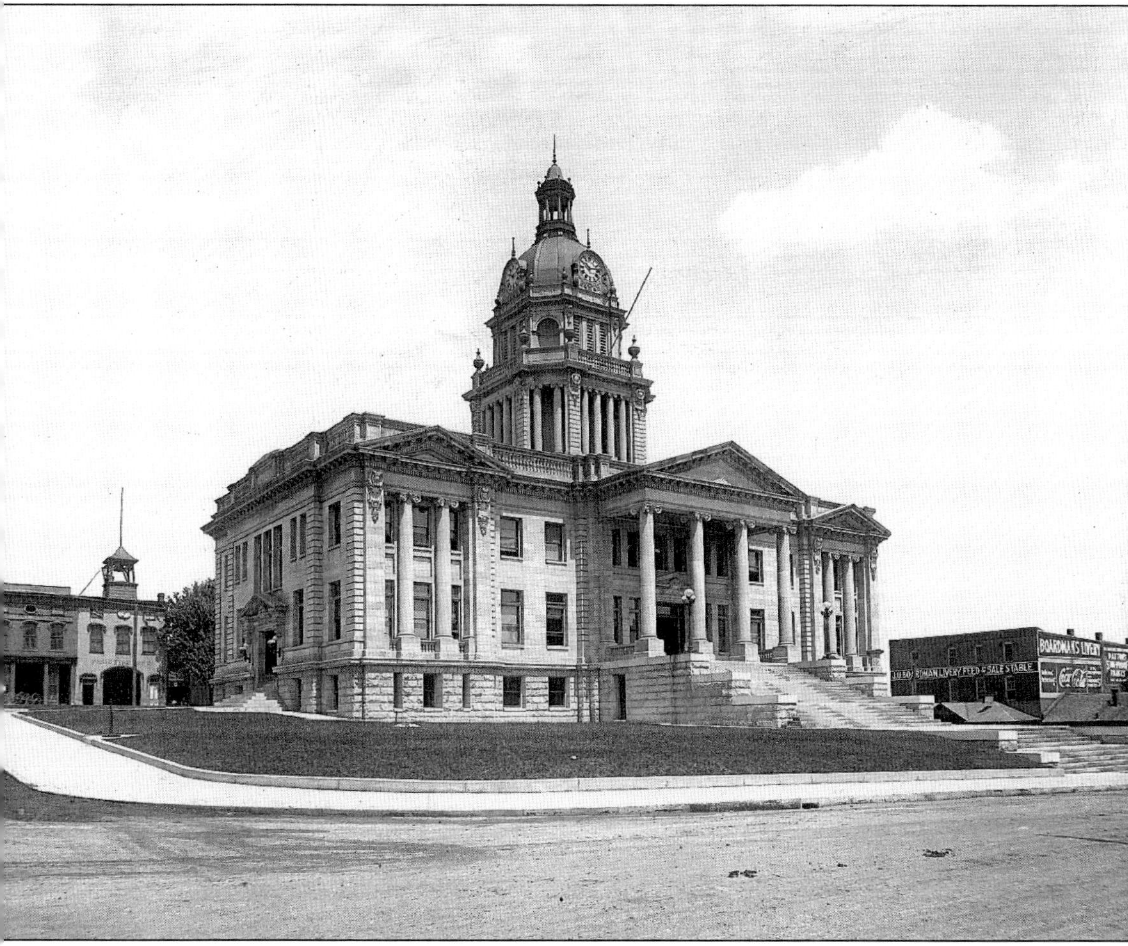

THE CURRENT COURTHOUSE, COMPLETED IN 1905. Constructed of granite from South Carolina and Bedford Stone from Indiana, Bourbon County's much awaited courthouse was finally completed and occupied on June 1, 1905. Lovingly maintained and carefully renovated over the years, it continues to have most of its original interior design and is considered by many to be the finest county courthouse in the state. It was placed on the National Register of Historic Places in 1974.

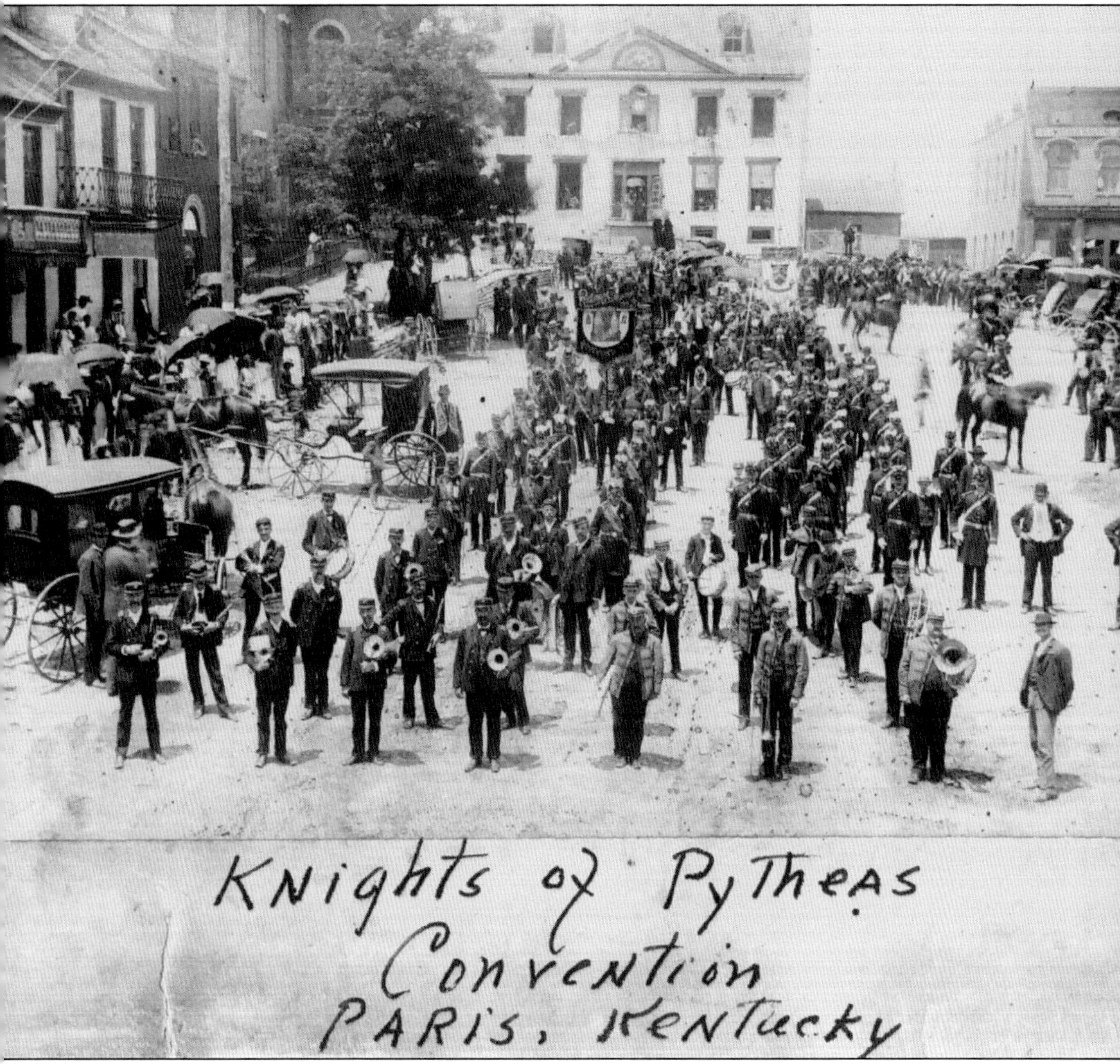

Knights of Pythias Parade. The Knights of Pythias was one of many fraternal and benevolent associations formed after the Civil War. The Paris Lodge was organized on March 17, 1868, with 17 charter members. The Knights of Pythias held their state convention in Paris sometime in the late 1890s and probably filled the town's hotels and boarding houses. Only two Knights of Pythias chapters still existed in the state at the end of the 20th century.

Two

Industry and Agriculture

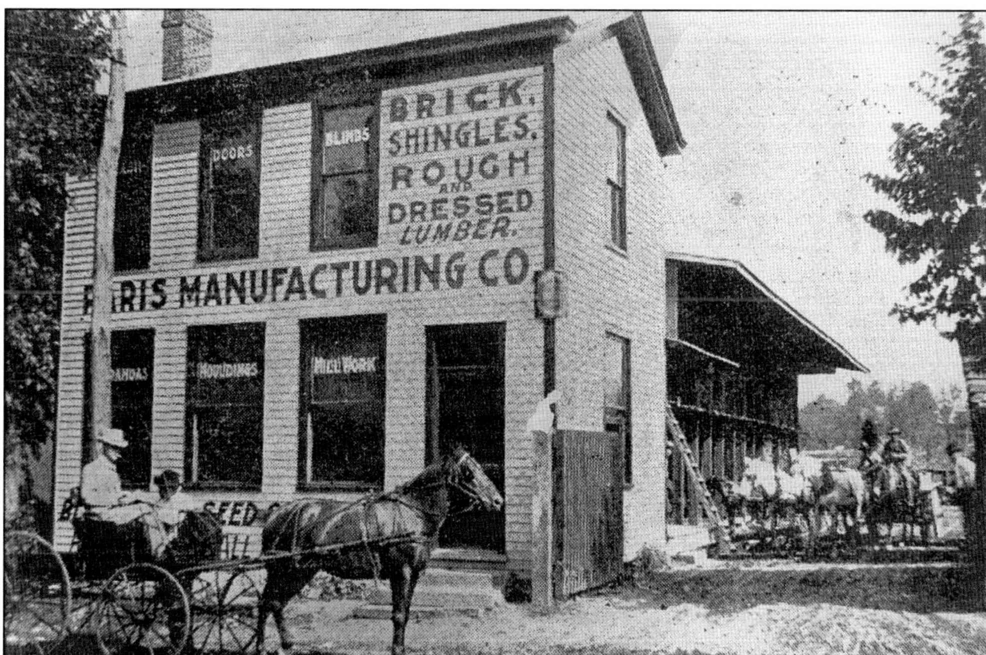

Curbside Service was Available at Paris Manufacturing in 1902. In this photo, one man can be seen loading purchases in a customer's carriage while others can be seen in the background loading wagons with heavier loads of dressed lumber to be delivered. Horsepower — whether a genteel carriage horse or a team of strong work horses—was the only way to move people and materials. This building was located on South Main opposite 15th Street and the yards in the back extended to the railroad tracks.

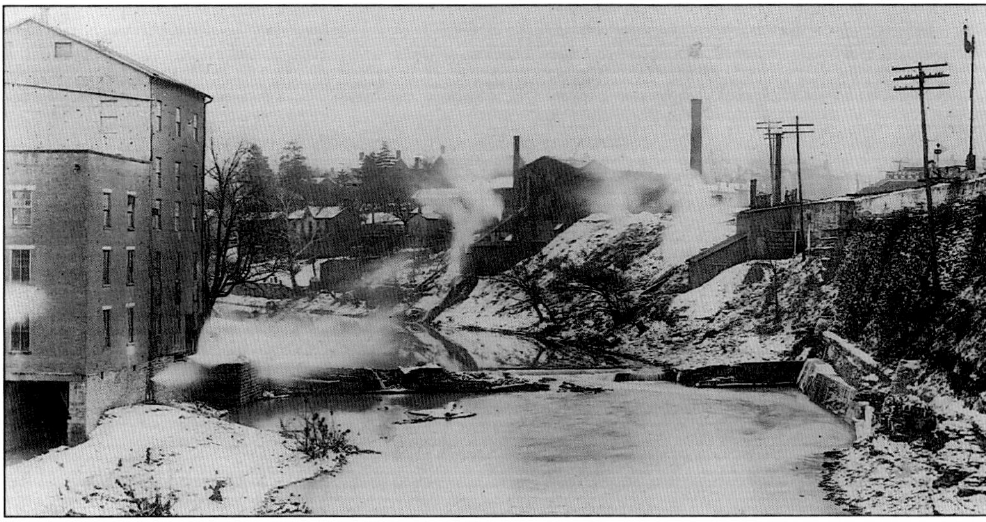

View of Stoner Creek and the Paris Milling Company in Winter. The Paris Milling Company can be seen at the far left. It was reportedly one of the oldest flour mills in the South as Daniel Isgrig built it around 1800 on the site of a former cotton mill. Curiously, the earliest mill was the one that gave its name to that section of Paris—referred to as "Cottontown." Perhaps "Flourtown" did not sound right.

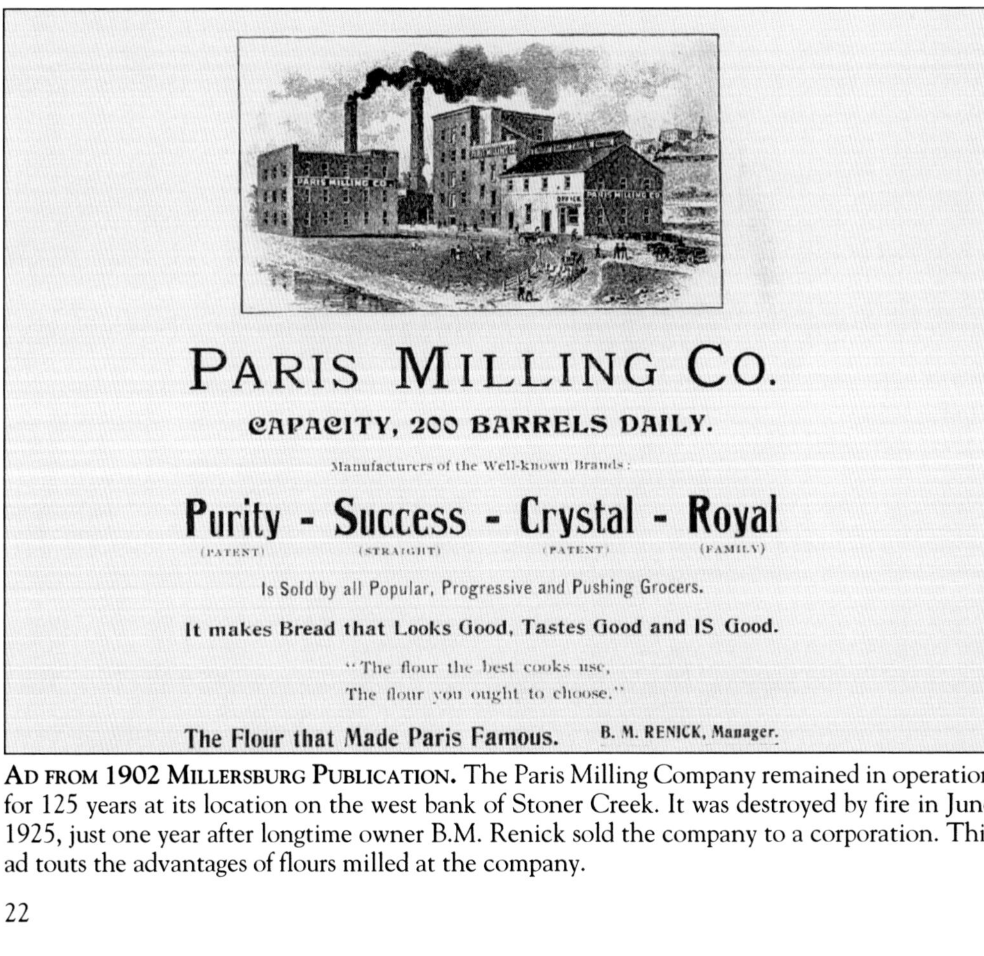

Ad from 1902 Millersburg Publication. The Paris Milling Company remained in operation for 125 years at its location on the west bank of Stoner Creek. It was destroyed by fire in June 1925, just one year after longtime owner B.M. Renick sold the company to a corporation. This ad touts the advantages of flours milled at the company.

July 4, 1906—Special Day for These Construction Workers. That is the date written on the bottom of the photo. Unfortunately, there is no information about where this smoke stack was being installed—just that it was in Paris. As can be seen in the Stoner Creek winter scene photo on the previous page, large smokestacks were common in Paris at the turn of the century.

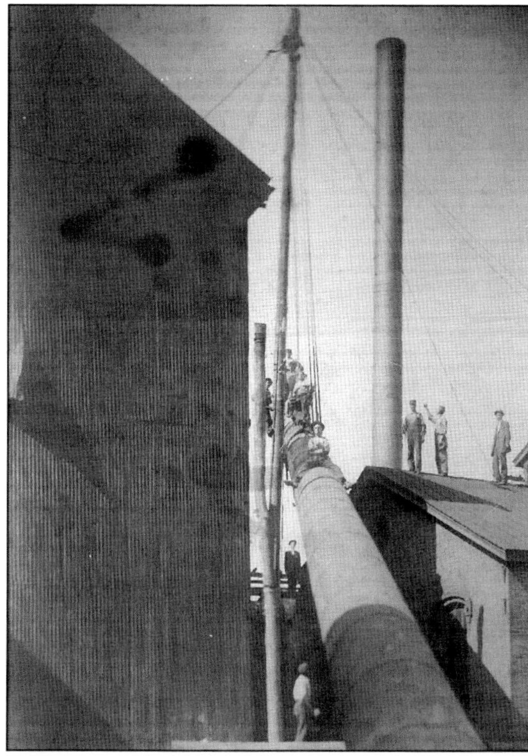

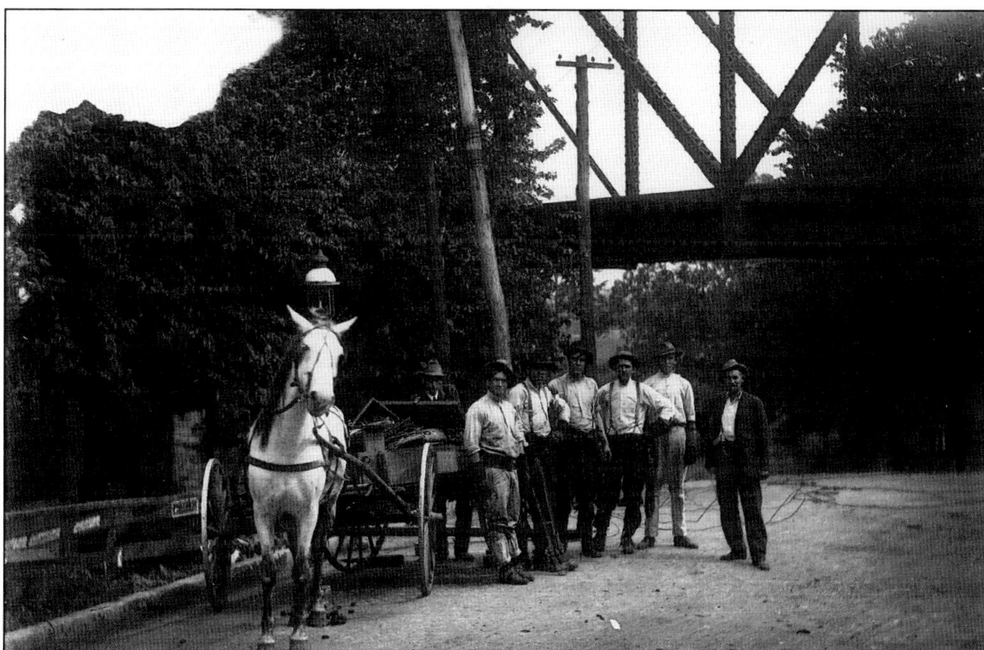

Linemen or Construction Workers Using Horse with Early "Headlight?" It is difficult to tell what sort of workmen stopped work to pose for this picture. One of the most interesting features of the photo is the contraption that the horse seems to be wearing on its head—it looks like it might be a gaslight of some type.

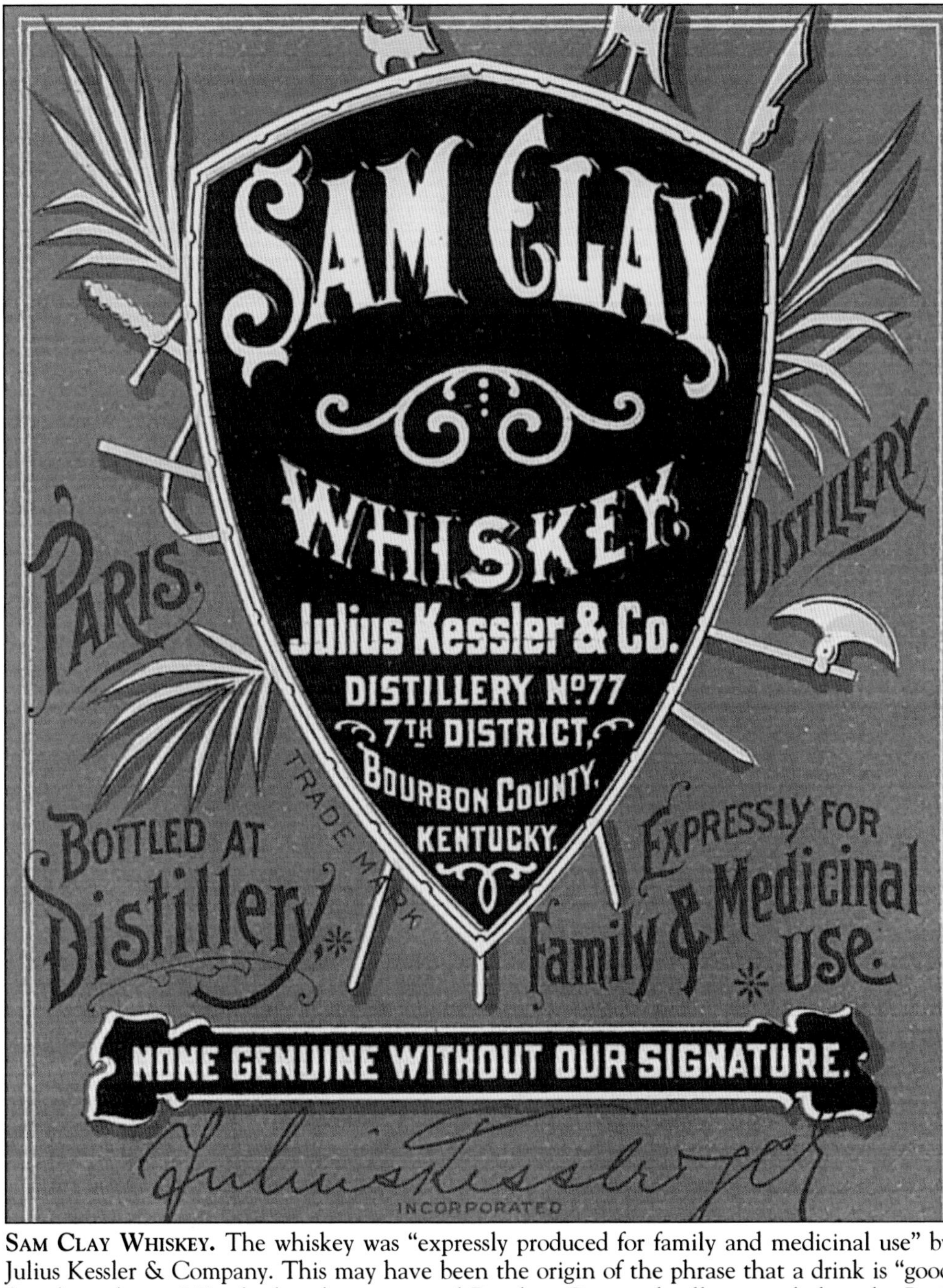

SAM CLAY WHISKEY. The whiskey was "expressly produced for family and medicinal use" by Julius Kessler & Company. This may have been the origin of the phrase that a drink is "good for what ails you." Kessler bought out several Bourbon County distilleries including the Paris Distillery, which produced Sam Clay Whiskey. Although there are some that credit Elijah Craig of Scott County as being the first person to produce "bourbon" whiskey, local history attributes that feat to one of a group of pioneer distillers in Bourbon County including Jacob Spears and Daniel Shawhan. The key seems to be who first began to age the whiskey in charred barrels, which arose from the discovery that the taste of whiskey in barrels accidentally burned was greatly improved.

The Sign of the Peacock For Whiskey—Not NBC. This label from a bottle of Peacock Whiskey indicates that it was made in Paris. The small print on two of the barrels says "sour mash" and "pure rye." The recipe of how much rye and how much malted barley to add to the corn mash that formed the basis of the whiskey ingredients varied from distiller to distiller.

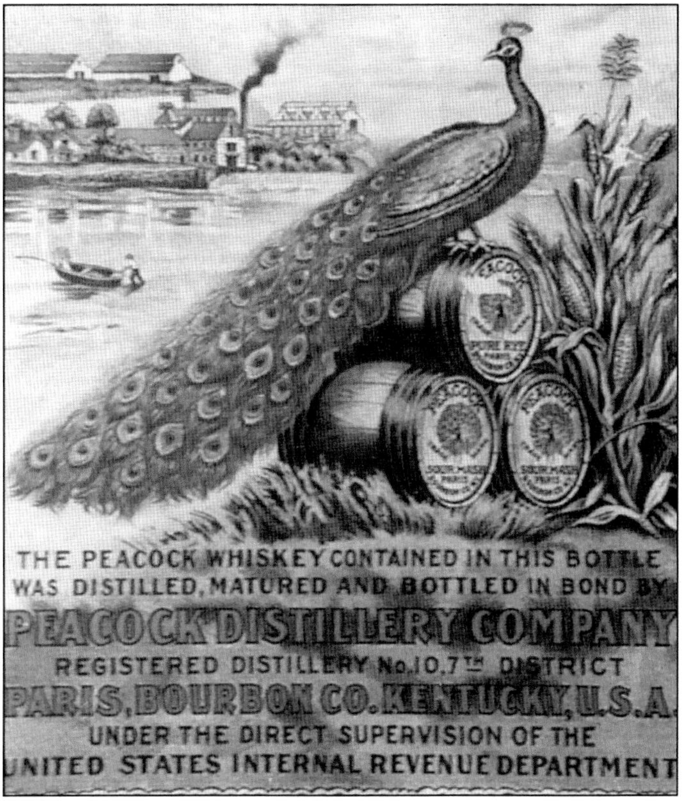

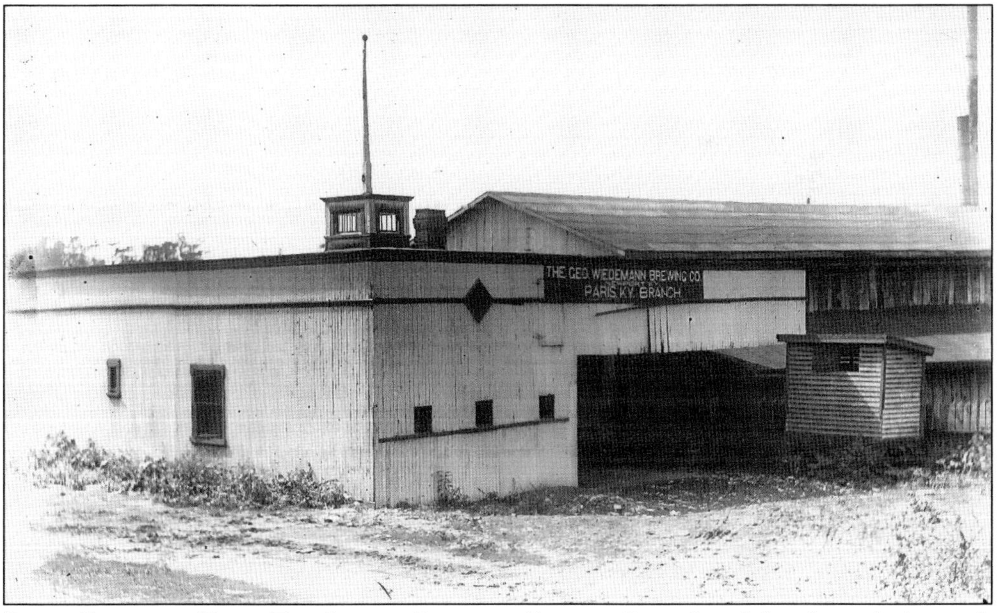

Beer—Preferred Drink For Some in Bourbon County. Even though bourbon whiskey took its name from the county, that doesn't mean that everyone who wanted drink chose bourbon. Beer was a favorite of some of those who patronized the many saloons that are evident on old maps of Paris. The Wiedemann Brewing Company of Newport, Kentucky, obtained a license in 1902 to distribute beer in the county.

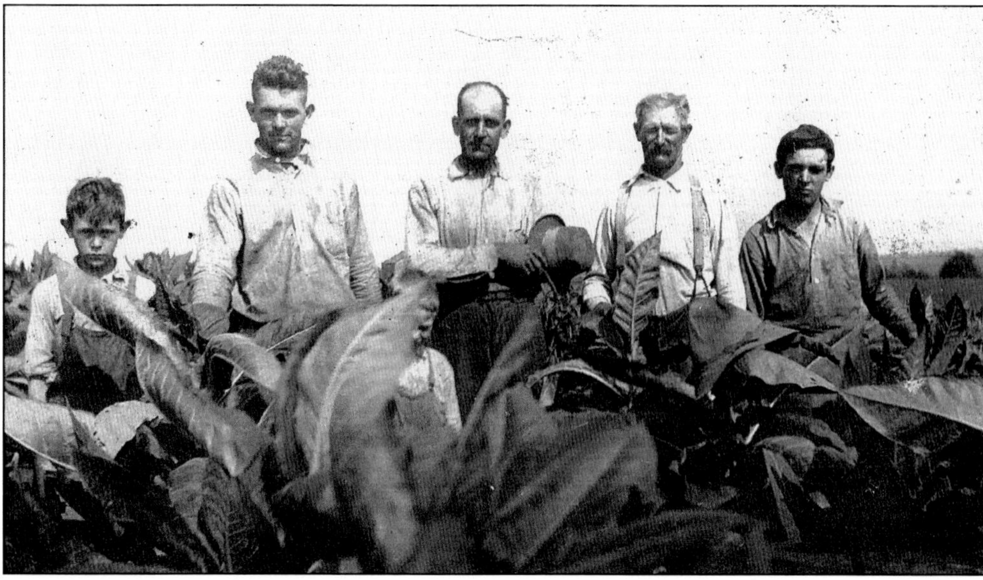

CHECKING OUT THE BURLEY TOBACCO FIELD. Shown from left to right are Charlie Kiser, Theodore Kuster Sr., C.K. Kiser Jr. (partly hidden), unidentified, Charles Kuster, and unidentified. Burley tobacco has been a favorite crop of farmers in Bourbon County for more than 100 years. In 1900, there were 7.2 million pounds of tobacco raised in the county and by 1910 that amount had risen to 11.9 million pounds—more than a 50% increase.

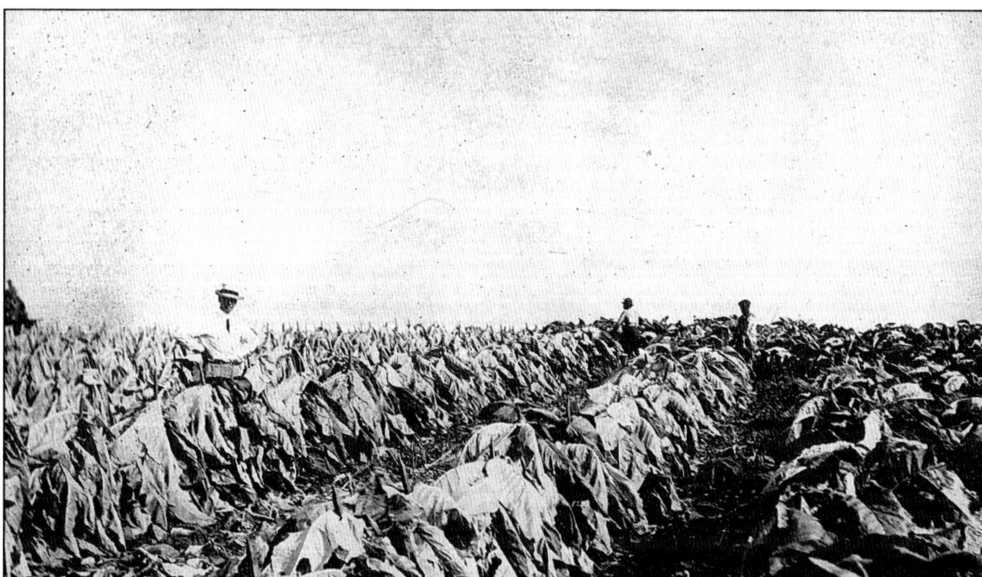

EARLY BURLEY TOBACCO FIELD—CHOPPED AND READY TO CURE IN THE FIELD. James L. Dodge is shown in the foreground of this photo of a field of burley tobacco. Most of the burley plants shown have been chopped off and speared with sharp tobacco sticks. The tobacco was then left in the field to cure naturally. Days later, the sticks with the partially cured tobacco were taken out of the field and "housed" in the rafters of tobacco barns to finish air curing.

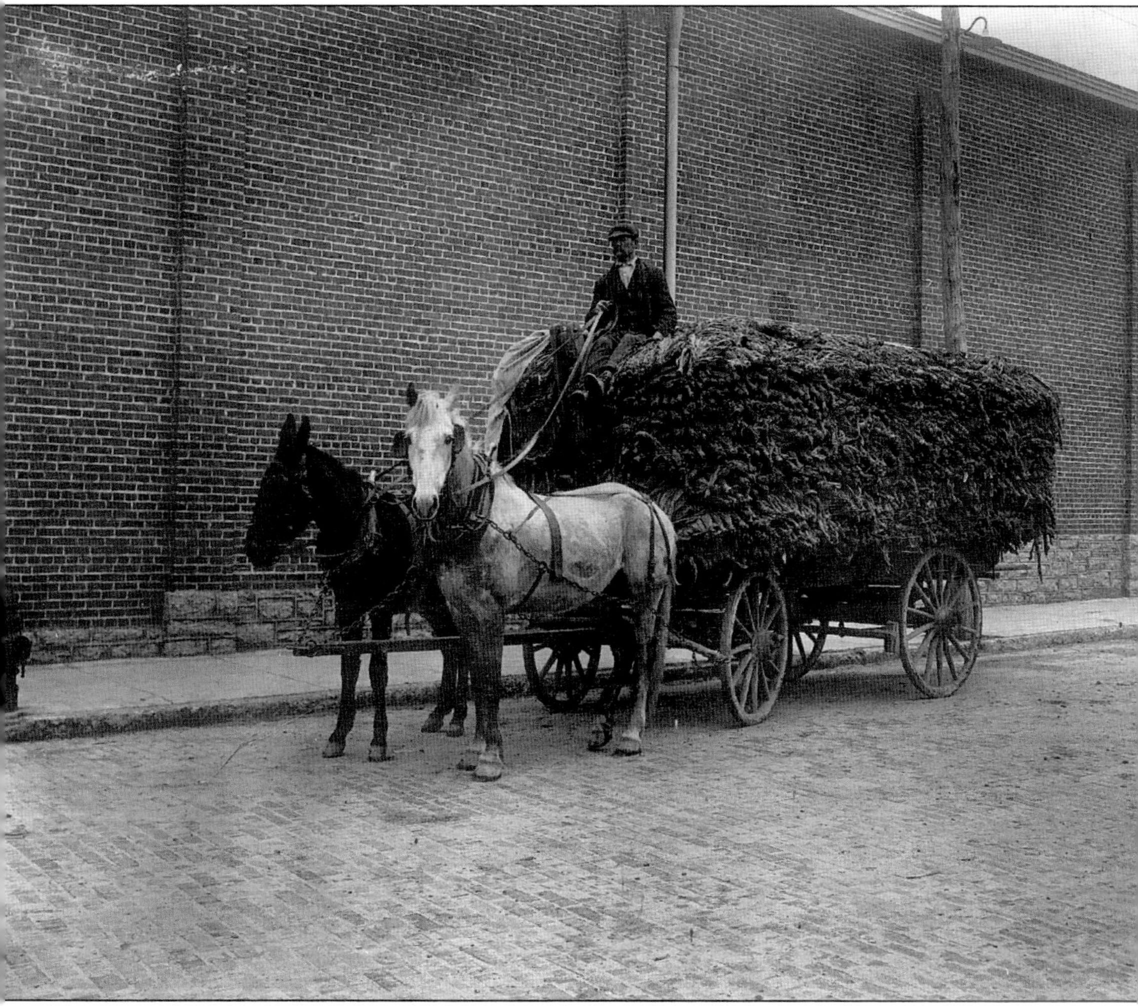

A "KING-SIZED" LOAD OF BURLEY TOBACCO ON ITS WAY TO THE WAREHOUSE. Charles Henry Kuster is shown at the Paris Tobacco Warehouse about 1910 with a huge load of burley tobacco wrapped into "hands," which was how tobacco was sold at market until the 1980s when selling tobacco in bales became the accepted method.

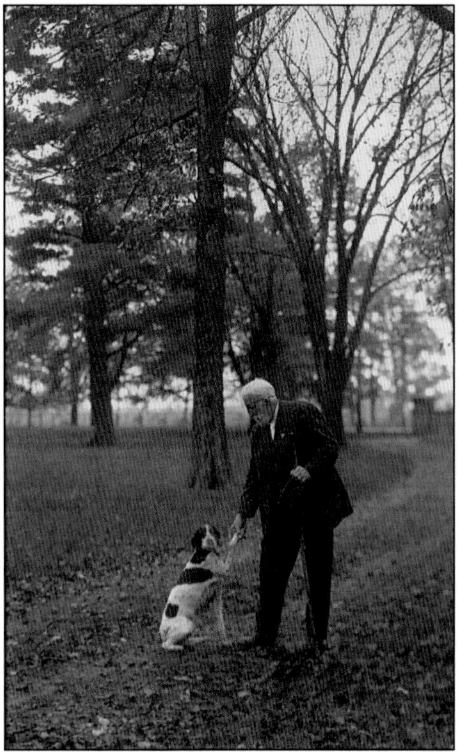

Col. E.F. Clay. He was one of Kentucky's leading Thoroughbred breeders in the late 19th century. Shown here at Runnymede with one of his bird dogs, Colonel Clay and his brother-in-law, Catesby Woodford, formed a partnership in 1876 and established Runnymede Stud. They purchased the imported stallion Billett, who became the country's leading sire in 1883. Among the noted horses sired by Billett was the filly Miss Woodford, who was the first American horse to win more than $100,000.

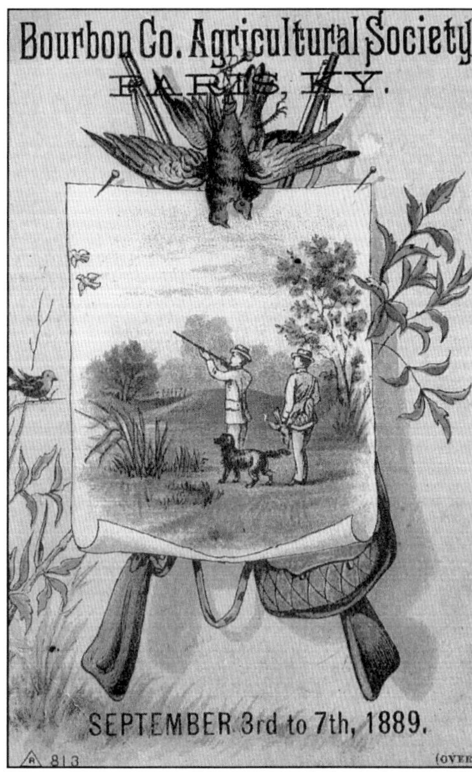

52nd Annual Bourbon County Agricultural Fair, September 3–7, 1889. Two horse races were held each day at the 1889 Bourbon County Fair, including races on Wednesday and Saturday for ponies. Even though these dates indicate that the first Bourbon Agricultural Fair was held in 1837, Mrs. Edna Talbott Whitley wrote that the first Bourbon Agricultural Fair was held at Hornback's Mill in 1819, making it the first county fair held in Kentucky.

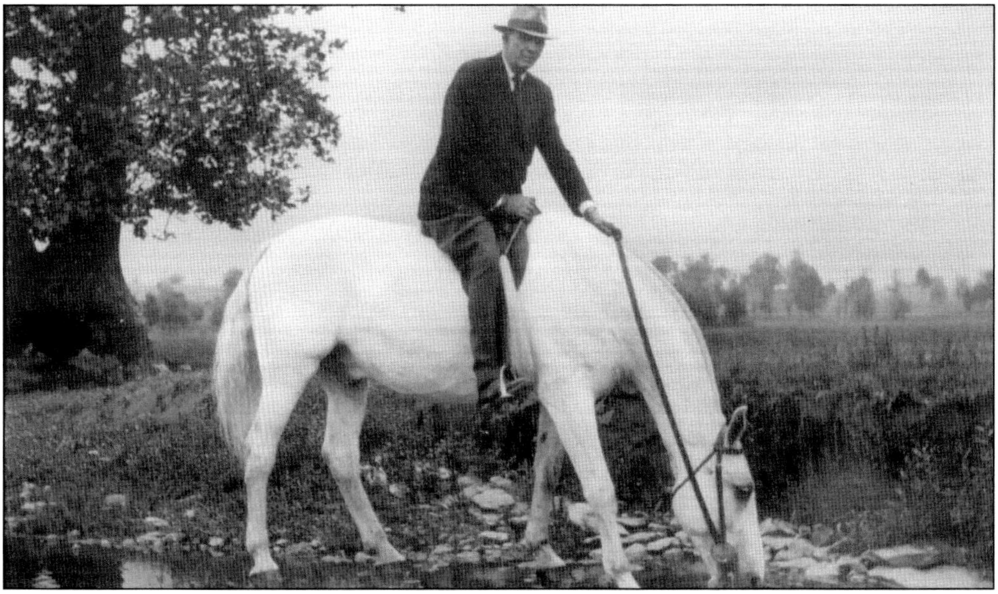

A.B. HANCOCK SR. FOUNDED CLAIBORNE FARM. This photo of Hancock was taken in 1932 at Claiborne Farm, which he founded in the early 1900s. By 1920, Hancock was one of the leading Thoroughbred breeders in the United States. In 1935, '36, '37 and '39, Claiborne Farm was the leading breeder in the country in terms of money won. In 1939, there were 13 stallions standing at Claiborne including Triple Crown winners Gallant Fox and Omaha.

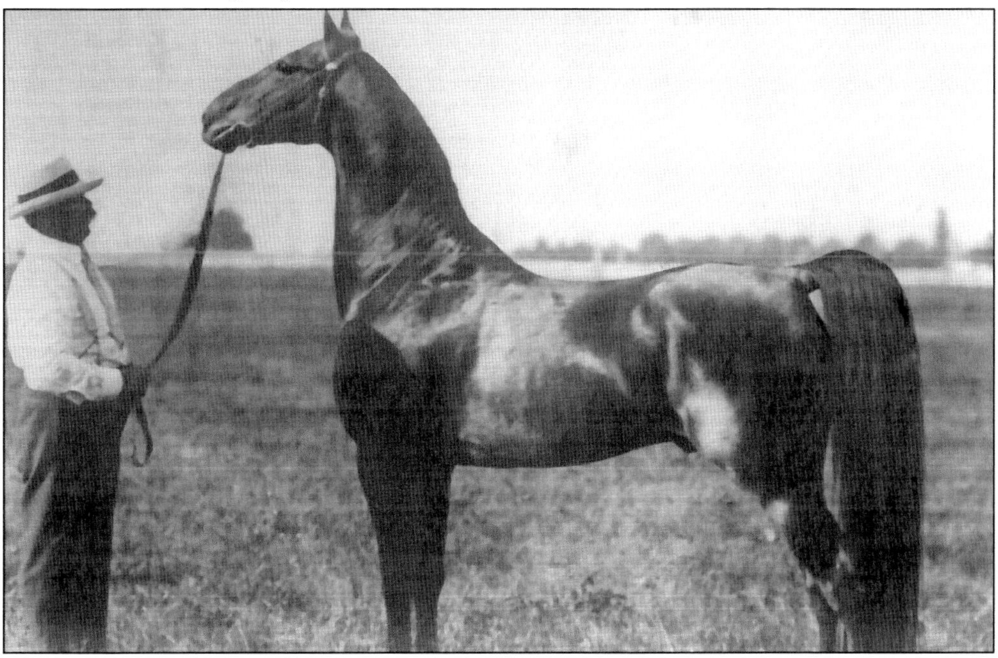

KING CHIEFTAIN WAS PROLIFIC SADDLEBRED STUD IN MILLERSBURG. Sanford C. Carpenter is seen here in 1909 holding his prized Saddlebred stallion King Chieftain, half-brother to the great progenitor of the breed, Bourbon King. Bourbon King was owned by Allie G. Jones of North Middletown. Both stallions were sons of Bourbon Chief, and Carpenter and Jones were great proponents of what became known as the "Chief family."

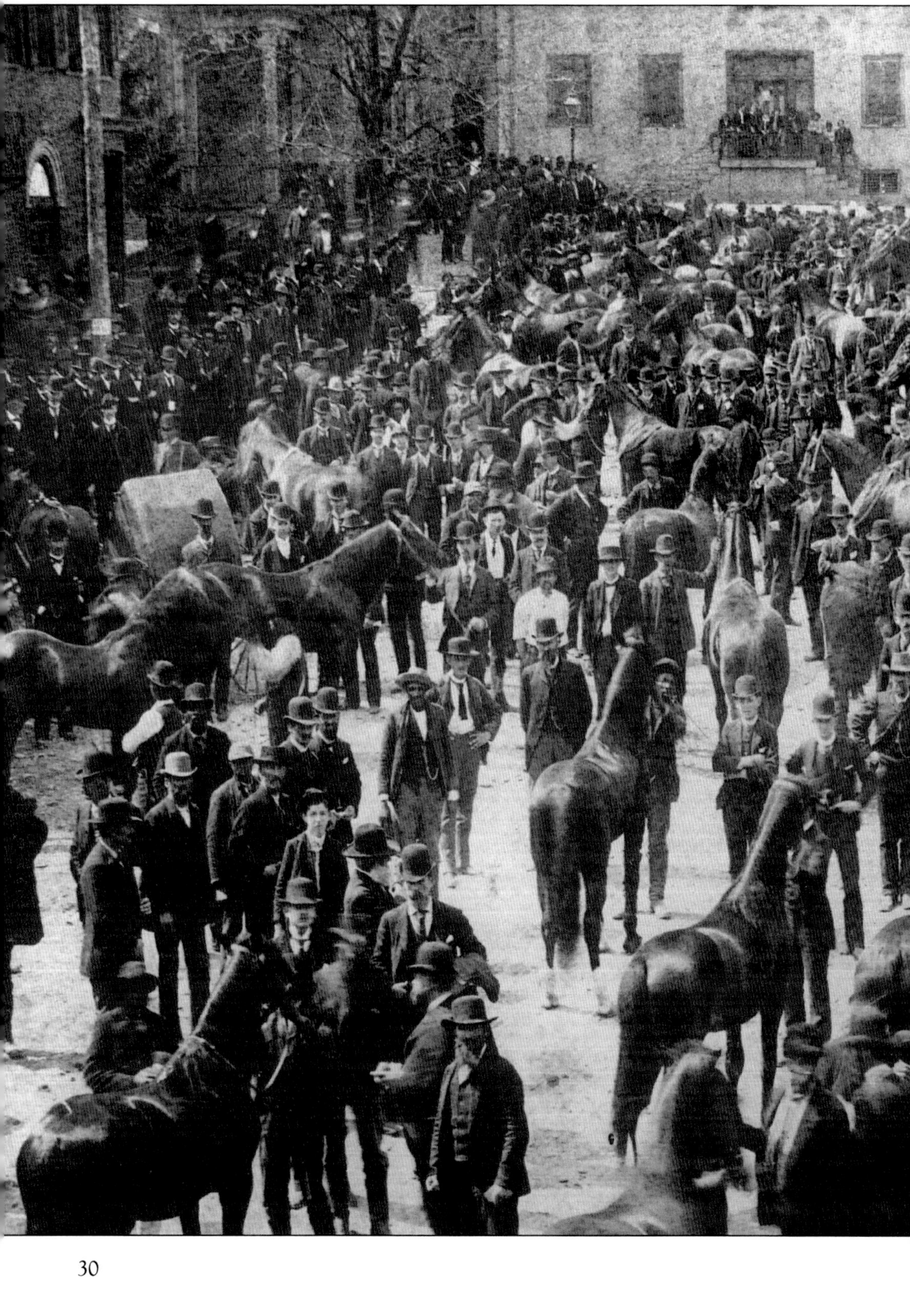

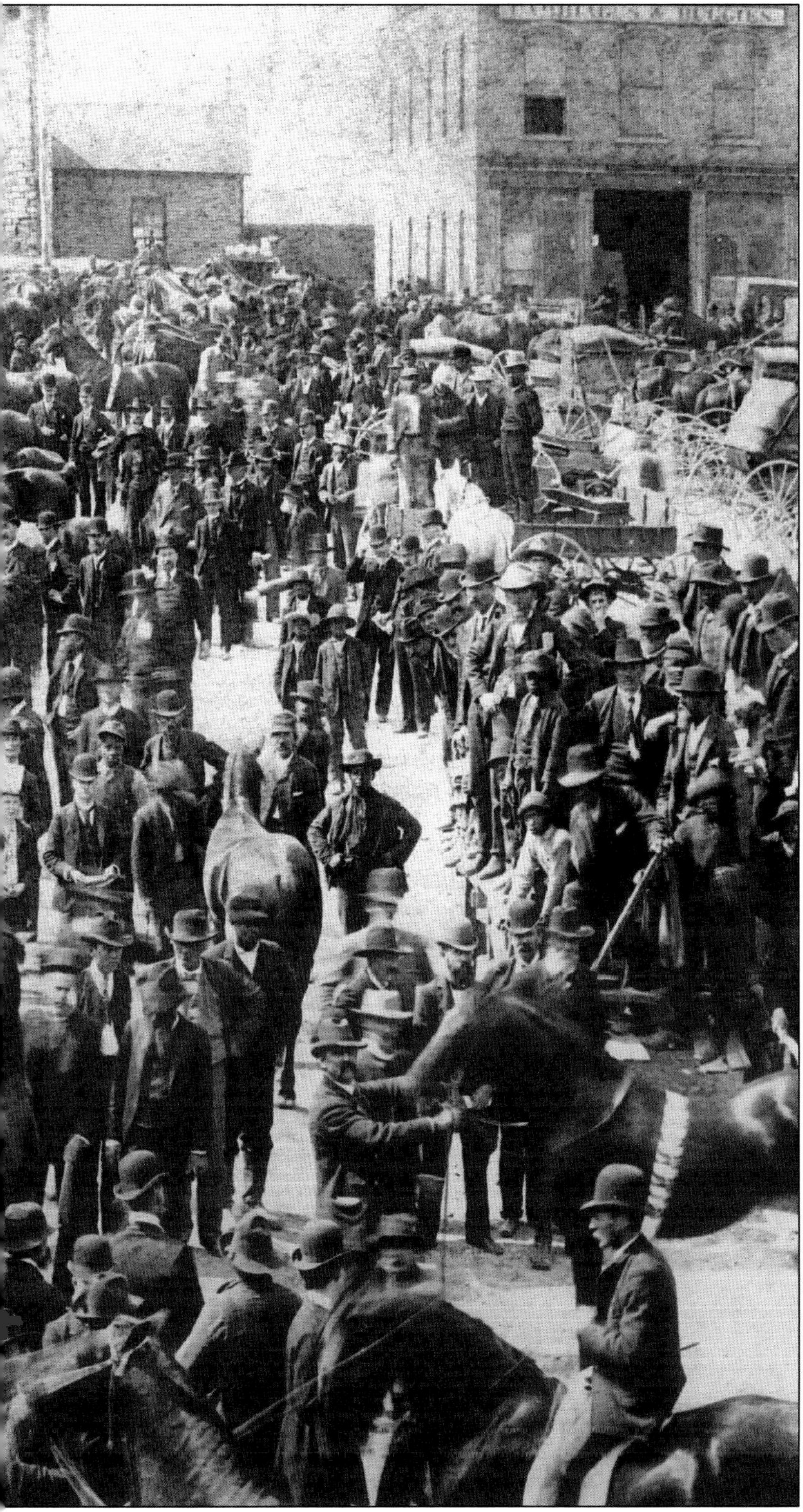

Stallion Day at the Bourbon County Courthouse Attracted a Crowd. Long before the multi-million dollar equine auctions at Keeneland and Saratoga, horsemen bought and sold horses and breeding rights at events like the "Stallion Day" pictured here, probably in the 1870s. Notice the width of the street—rightfully called Broadway during this era. There are so many horses, men, and boys of all sizes and colors frozen in time in this photo that you expect there to have been some movement when you look back at it. Bourbon County horse breeders have long been recognized as some of the foremost producers of Thoroughbred, Standardbred, and Saddlebred horses in the world.

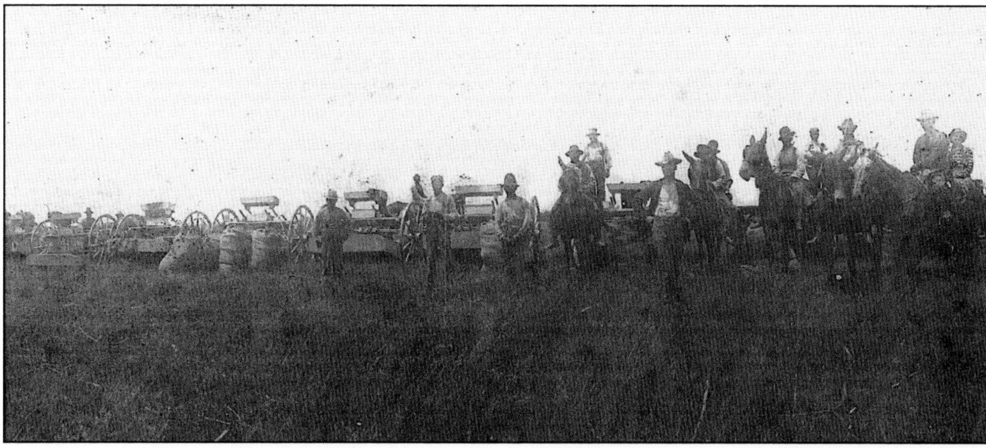

HARVESTING BLUEGRASS SEED. Bluegrass was a preferred pasture grass because of its high nutritional value. Harvesting bluegrass seed yielded thousands of bushels of seeds that were cleaned and processed in Bourbon County and then shipped across the world. In 1939, when the industry was waning because of the competition for pastureland with cattle and Thoroughbred horses, 100,000 bushels of bluegrass seeds still poured through four local cleaning plants.

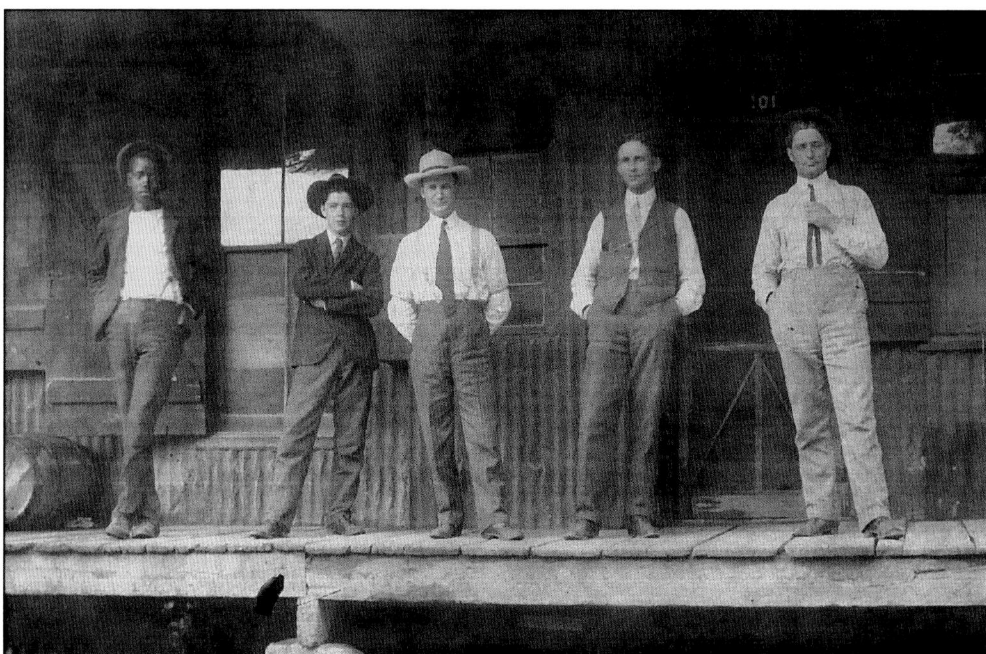

SPEARS NAME SYNONYMOUS WITH AGRICULTURE. Shown from left to right in front of one of the Spears' warehouses are unidentified, Lee Spears, Roe Mansfield, Frank Kiser, and Lon Houston. E.F. Spears and Sons was founded in 1886 by Capt. E.F. Spears, who was a grandson of early distiller Jacob Spears. In 1923, the name of the business was changed to Woodford Spears and Sons. The company dealt extensively in bluegrass seed and hemp.

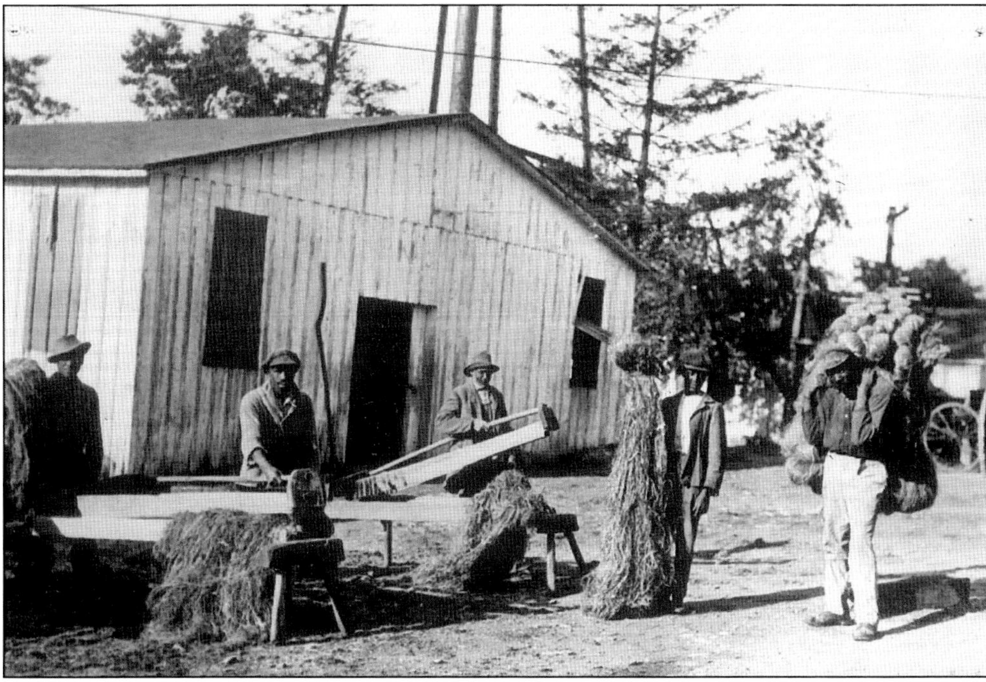

HEMP—AN EXTREMELY LABOR INTENSIVE CROP. Growing hemp was the easy part. The hemp plants were cut by hand and cured on the ground before being stacked in shocks to dry. Later, the hemp was dew rotted and the woody stalks were then broken in a hemp brake. Shown in the photo are hemp brakes, a hand of hemp, and a bundle of hemp along with the some of the hard-working men who performed all of these backbreaking jobs.

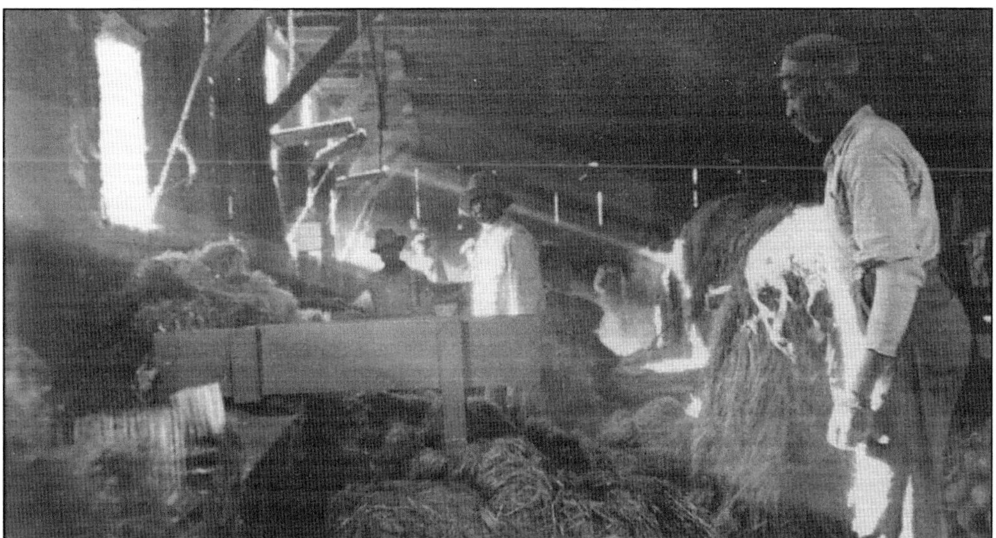

HEMP PRODUCTION. This photo shows the inside of the Spears and Sons hemp factory where the hemp was prepared for utilization as rope or cord. One of the company's last hemp contracts was to supply the hemp for the renovation of the battleship *Constitution* about 1920. Hemp production enjoyed a brief revival during World War II when it was grown again in Kentucky to replace foreign supplies cut off by the Japanese.

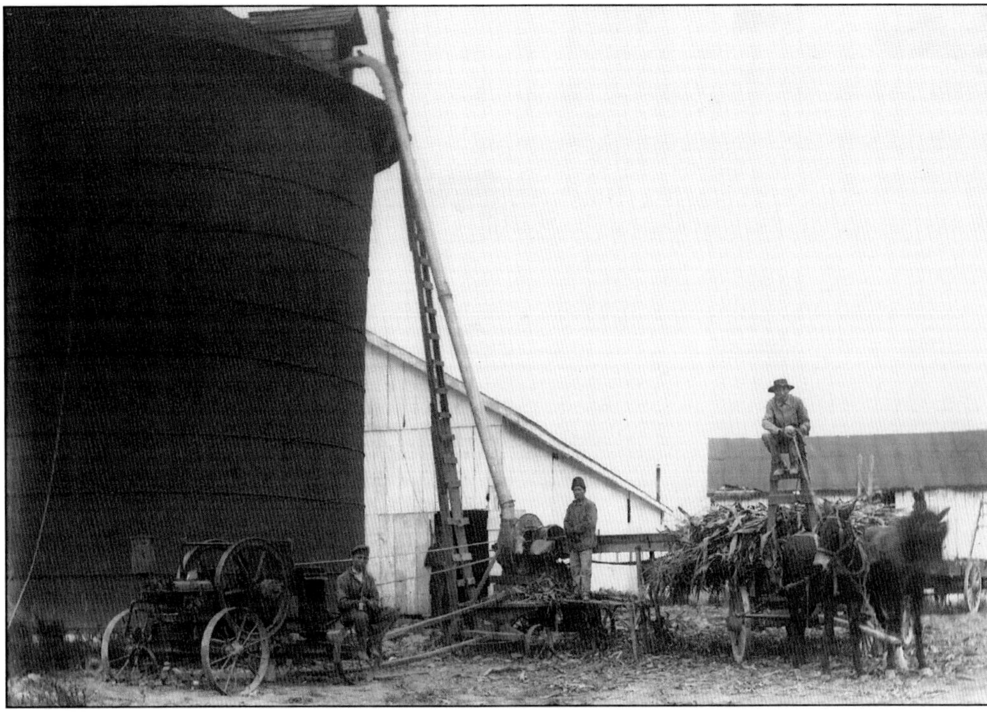

Loading Corn Into a Wooden Silo Using Early Gasoline-Powered Machine. In this photo, the corn is being separated from the stalks and then blown up through the tube into the wooden silo. The young man seated on the wheel of the gas-powered machine is holding an oil can, which he probably used often to keep the machine operating.

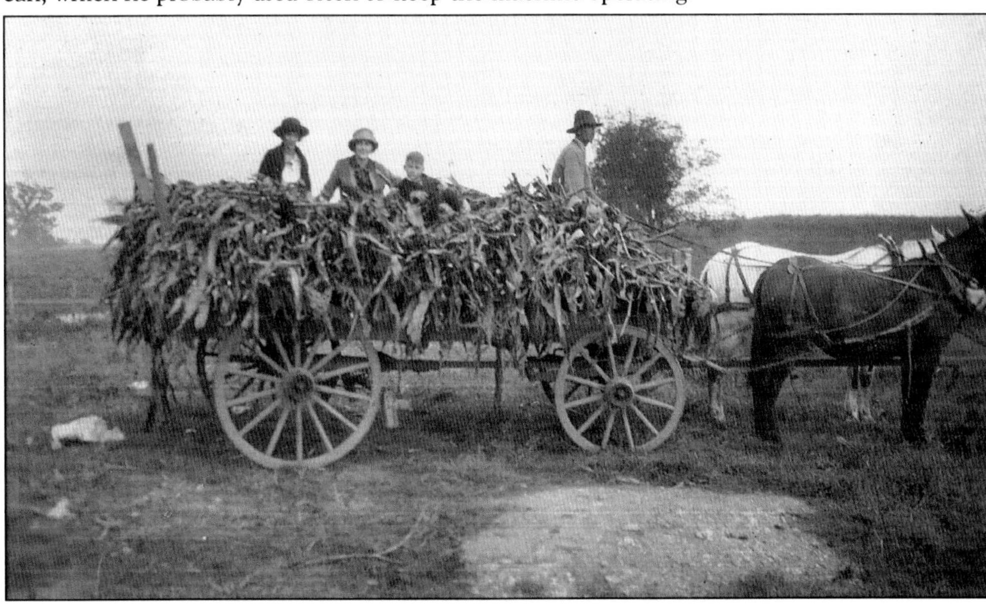

Hauling Fodder Used to Feed Livestock. The two young women and the boy are seated in the wagon filled with fodder ready to be taken to the barn and stored until winter. Corn was an important crop in the county as it could be used as corn meal, as feed for livestock, and as one of the most important raw ingredients for making bourbon whiskey.

Three

Main Street Life

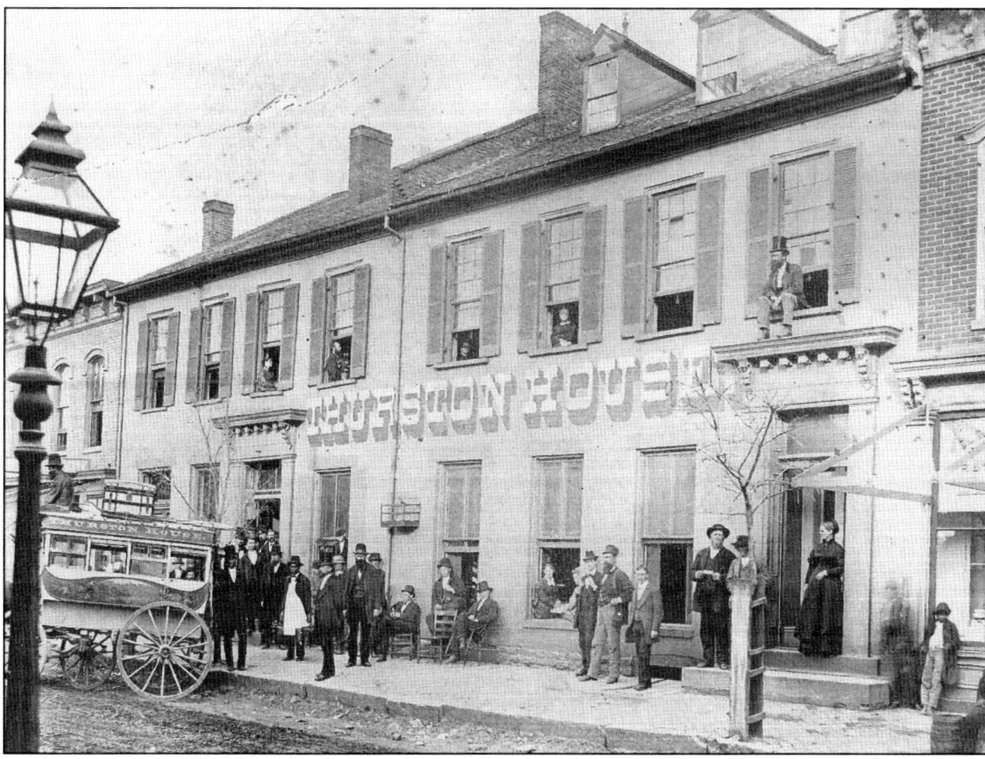

Thurston House Hotel on Paris Main Street. This photo, taken a few years after the Civil War, shows Mrs. R. Griffith (in doorway), a longtime innkeeper in Paris, and some of her contented customers and staff. The Thurston House provided a coach to transfer guests and their baggage to and from the train depot. An ad in 1878, when the establishment was run by her son, John, promised "Good Beds and Good Meals" for just $2 per day. The hotel stood on the site that was later the location of the J.C. Penney store on Main Street.

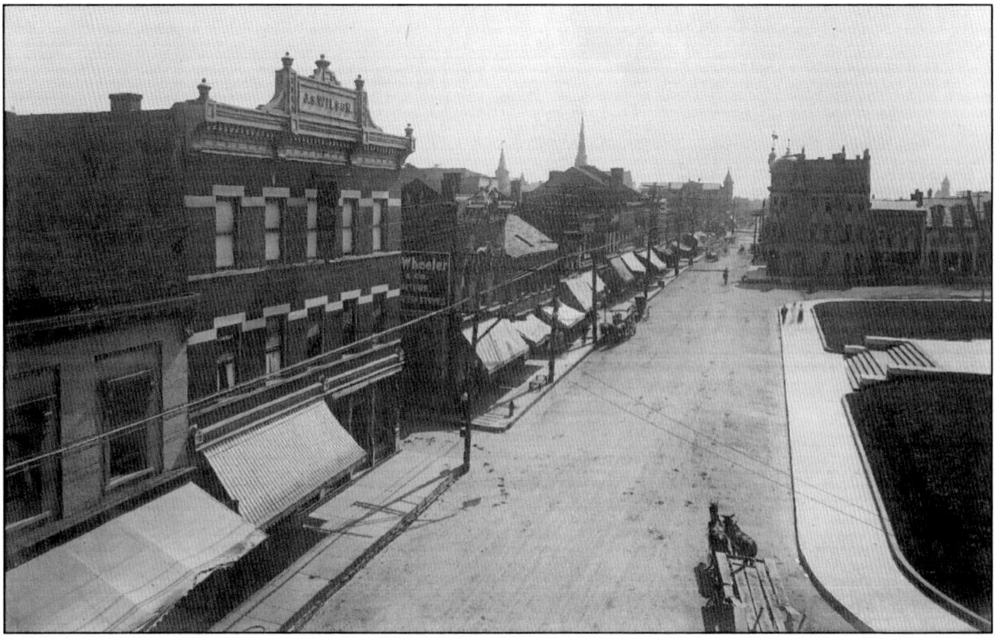

View of Main Street at Courthouse Square Became a Postcard. The photo was obviously taken from an upper story of the Bourbon Hotel on the northeast corner of the square. The large three-story James S. Wilson Building (left-center) was built in 1904–1905. It had an oversized freight elevator that transported carriages and buggies to a second story display room and also housed the George Alexander Bank, which later merged with the Bourbon Bank.

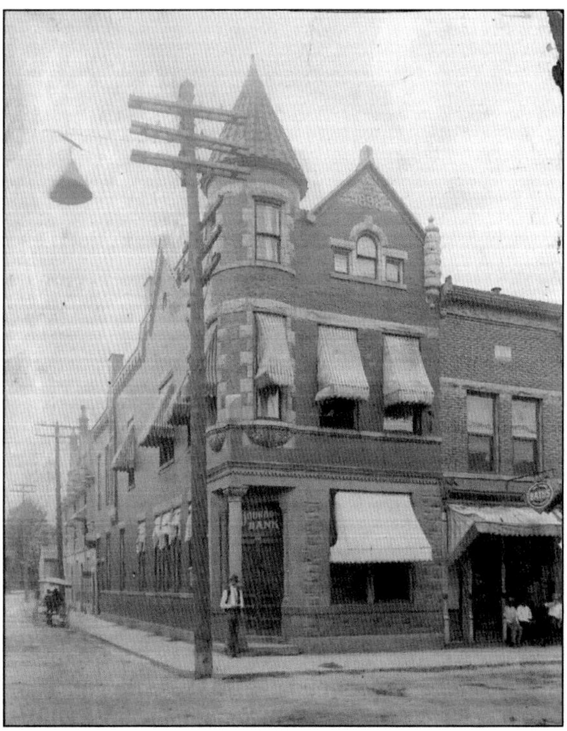

Old Bourbon Bank Building. This excellent building with a corner turret was built in 1898 for the Bourbon Bank, which was established in 1887 by Col. E.F. Clay, Buckner Woodford Sr., and others. It remained a bank building until 1915 when Bourbon Bank merged with Agricultural Bank two blocks away. The building to the right housed the Sanitary Barber Shop that had a sign offering "Baths." Notice the electric street lamp hanging over the middle of the intersection.

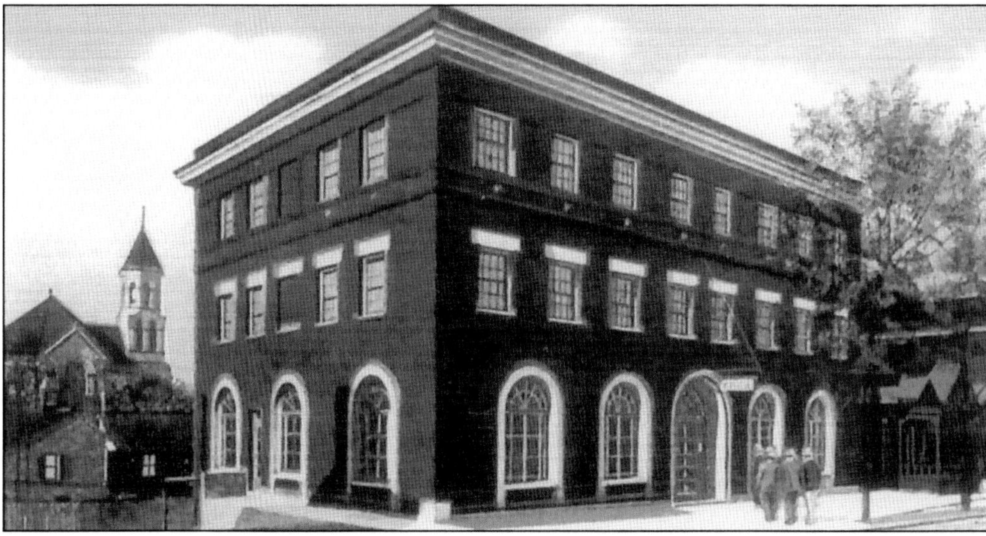

YMCA BUILDING. In 1906 a committee of men first met to consider raising funds to provide activities and a facility for the young men of the county. In 1915, after intensive fund-raising around the county, the three-story Young Men's Christian Association building was opened with "a modern gymnasium, swimming tank and activity rooms." The building is still in use as a YMCA more than 85 years later.

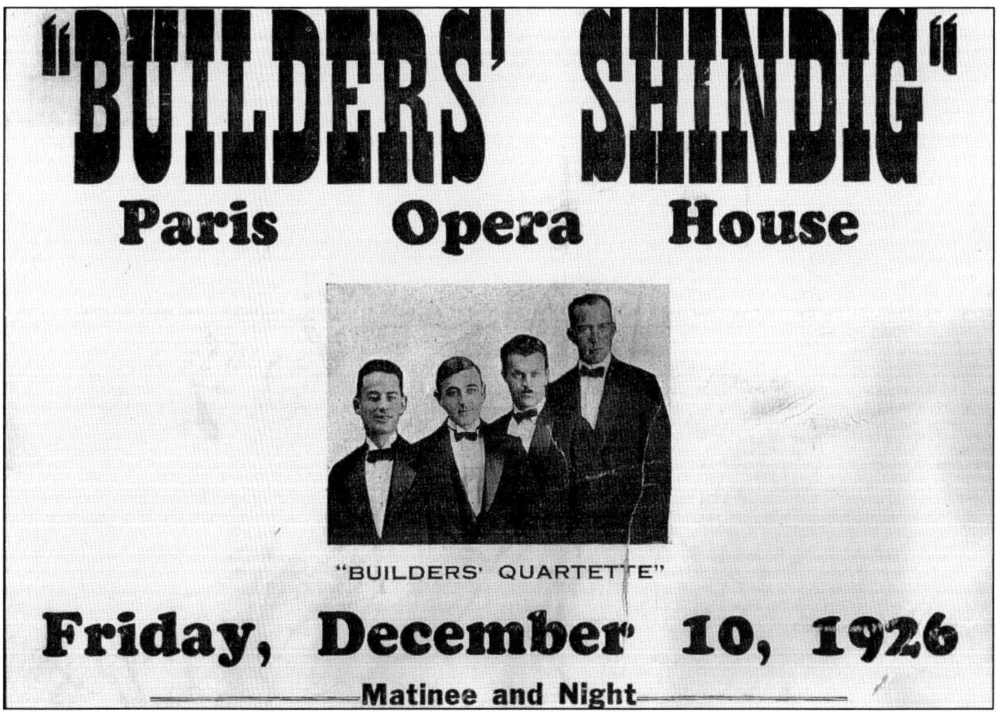

THE "BUILDERS' QUARTETTE." Shown from left to right are Paul Brannon, Hiram Redmond, A.B. Richmond, and Jim "Bigfoot" Thompson. This quartet of local men was a crowd favorite at performances at the Paris Opera House. Live performances ranging from minstrel shows to opera offered entertainment options at the Opera House, which also showed movies when they became popular.

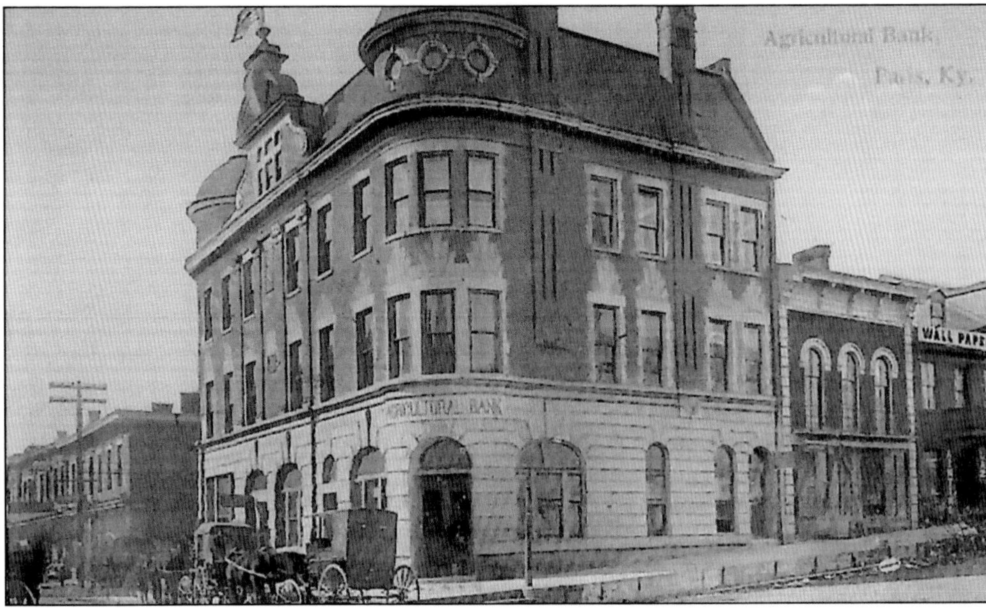

AGRICULTURAL BANK BECAME TODAY'S KENTUCKY BANK. Seen here about 1910, Paris's most photographed corner of Main Street and Ardery Place (once Broadway) contains this neo-Colonial structure built in 1899 for Agricultural Bank. The Agricultural Bank merged with the Bourbon Bank in 1915 and the Bourbon-Agricultural Bank was the first bank in the county with a million dollars in assets. Eventually the bank absorbed other banks in the county, branched out into surrounding counties and became Kentucky Bank.

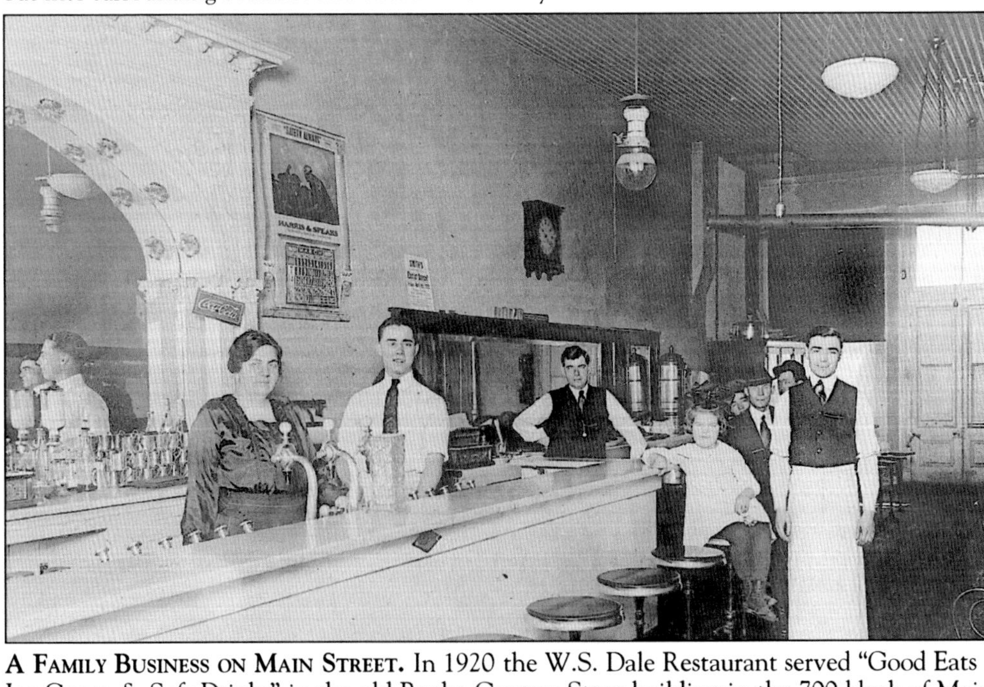

A FAMILY BUSINESS ON MAIN STREET. In 1920 the W.S. Dale Restaurant served "Good Eats - Ice Cream & Soft Drinks" in the old Roche Grocery Store building in the 700 block of Main Street. Pictured (left to right) are Mrs. Gertrude Harris Dale, Harold Shively, William Sheldon Dale, daughter Lillian Dale, customer Mr. Hought, and Bert King.

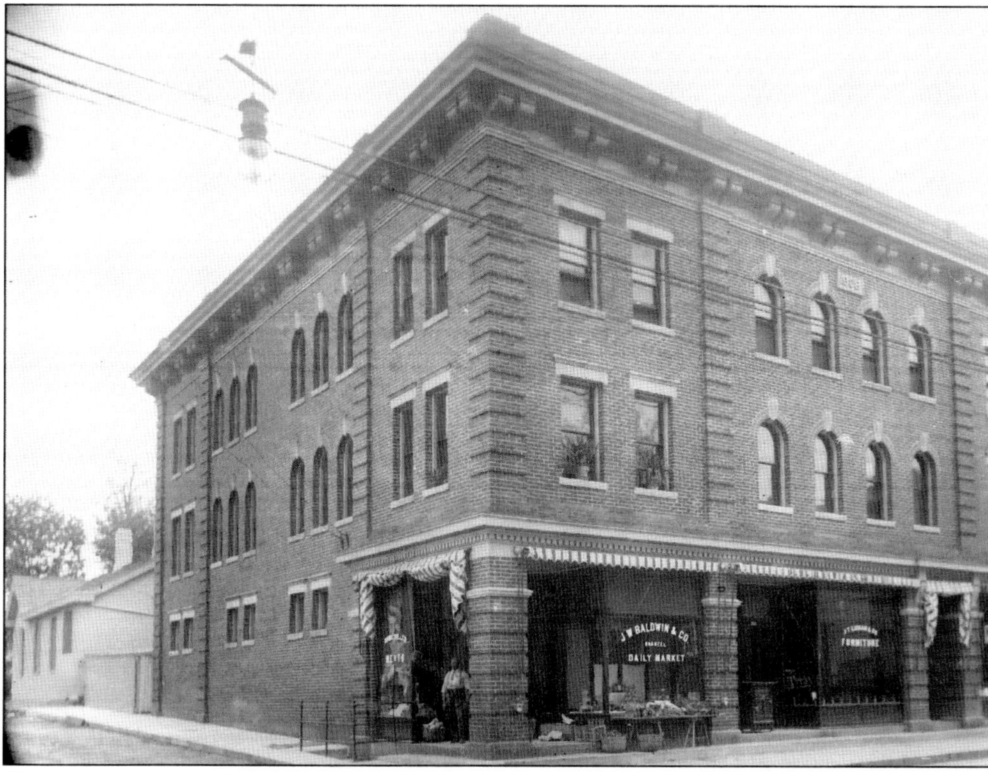

THE ROBNEEL BUILDING. Located at Eighth and Main, this impressive three-story structure was built in 1908 for Robert J. Neely. In 1913–1917, when this photo was taken, it housed the J.W. Baldwin & Co. grocery on the corner and the J.T. Luman & Co. Furniture store next to it. Built around an enclosed atrium, the residential apartments on the upper floors are still in use.

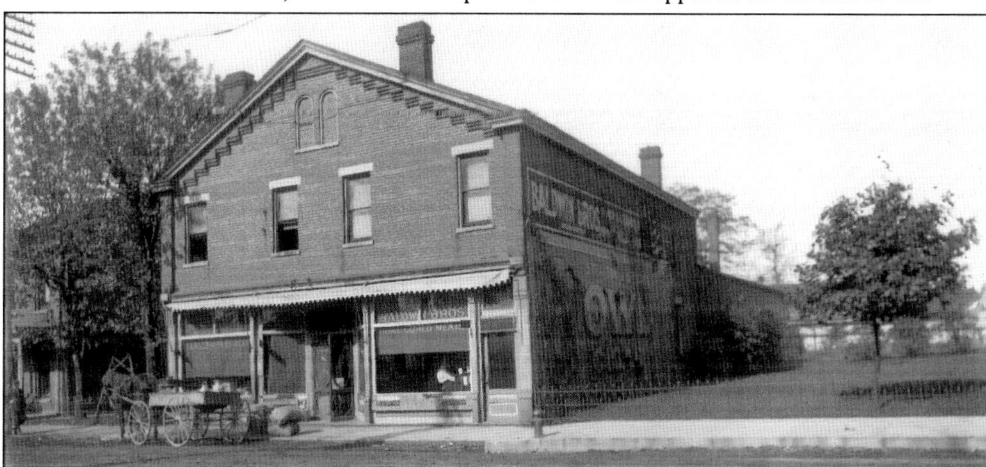

BALDWIN BROTHERS GROCERY ON WEST MAIN IN 1913. This building was constructed sometime before 1886 as a lumber and tobacco warehouse for businessman James M. Thomas. In 1907 it was purchased by Boone and Grover Baldwin and served as one of their grocery stores and a sausage factory. The brothers advertised "You can whip our cream but you can't beat our milk." In 1917 the building was occupied by the Paris Garage, which sold Whippet and Willys-Knight automobiles.

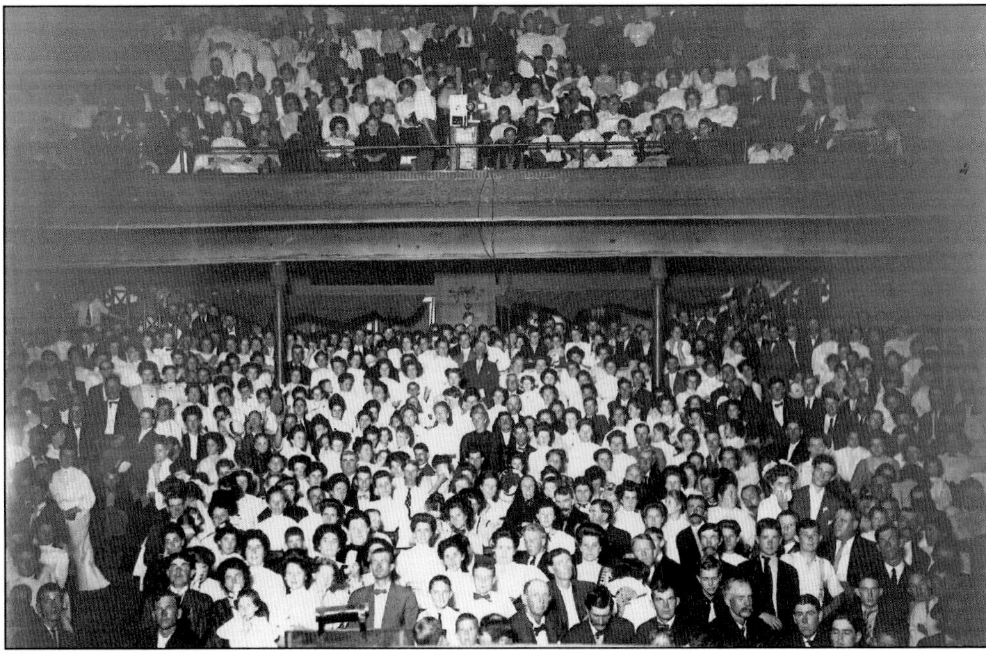

Wedding Night at McMahon & Jackson's Fashionable Vaudeville Theater. Besides vaudeville acts and a silent film, this crowd of Bourbon Countians turned out on the hot Saturday night of August 22, 1908, to see a wedding, or possibly more than one at the Paris Opera House. This was during an age when Saturday night on Main Street in Paris was full of crowds, excitement, and fun!

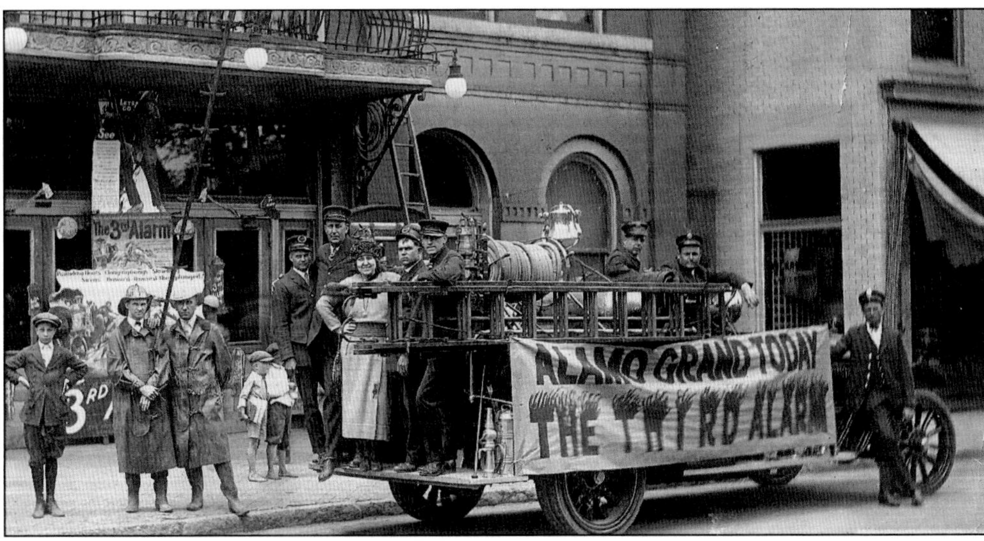

The *Third Alarm* at the Grand. Promoting individual films, even in small towns like Paris, took a lot of creativity and showmanship in the early days of motion pictures. This promotional photo (also on our cover) enlisted the local fire department in advertising the 1922 silent film blockbuster, *Third Alarm*. This film was featured at the Alamo Theatre down the street during the day and at the Paris Grand Theatre at the old Opera House at night.

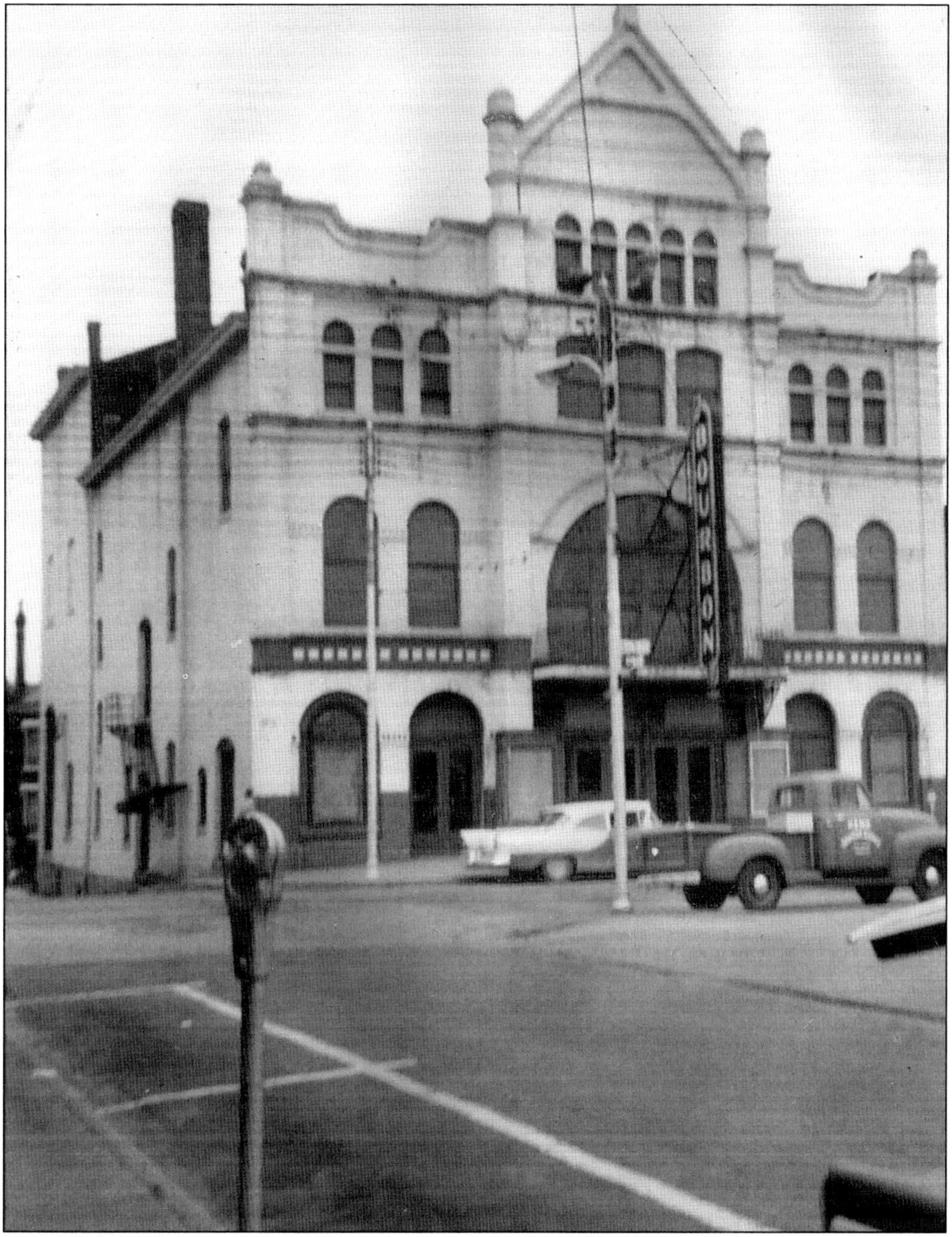

THE PARIS OPERA HOUSE. This grand building was part of the city's big 1890s building boom. Sitting at the corner of Main and Ninth (Cherry) Streets, it was known as the Paris Opera House, the Grand Theatre and finished its life as the Bourbon Theater. It was torn down in the 1960s. In its 70-year existence, it was the scene of many nights of stage and screen entertainment for local citizens. The first performance at the theater was on New Year's Eve, 1890, when about 600 people saw the W.T. Carlson Opera Company perform *The Brigand*. An opening night account described the building in glowing terms: "Everything harmonizes so well that the beholder is filled with admiration. It is the handsomest room of the kind in the state."

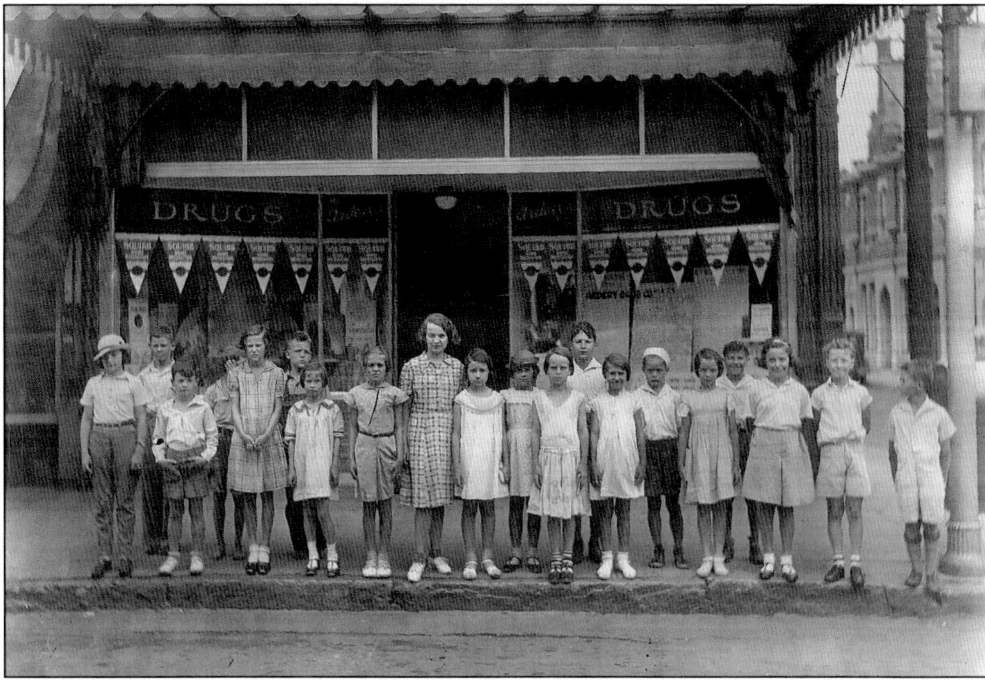

"OUR GANG." What brought out this group of kids to line up in front of the old Ardery Drugstore at the corner of Fifth and Main around 1930 has probably been forgotten. The picture does evoke ideas of what a wonderful playground Main Street must have been when there was such a diversity of sights, stores, and people.

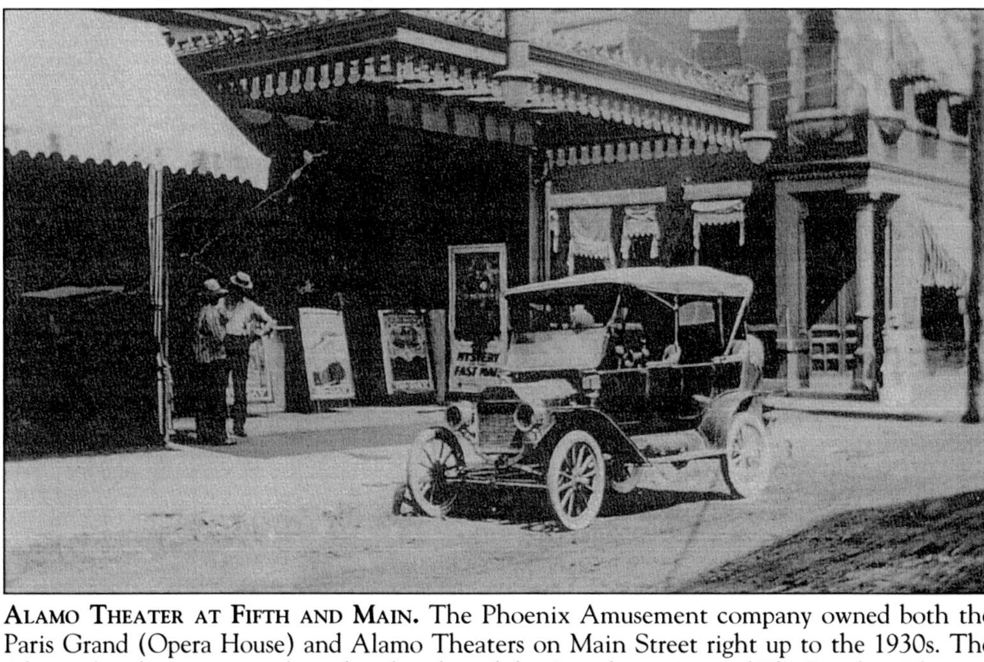

ALAMO THEATER AT FIFTH AND MAIN. The Phoenix Amusement company owned both the Paris Grand (Opera House) and Alamo Theaters on Main Street right up to the 1930s. The Alamo closed sometime early in that decade and the Grand was renamed The Bourbon Theater. Paris regained a second Main Street theater in the 1940s when Schine's Theatre opened at Eighth and Main.

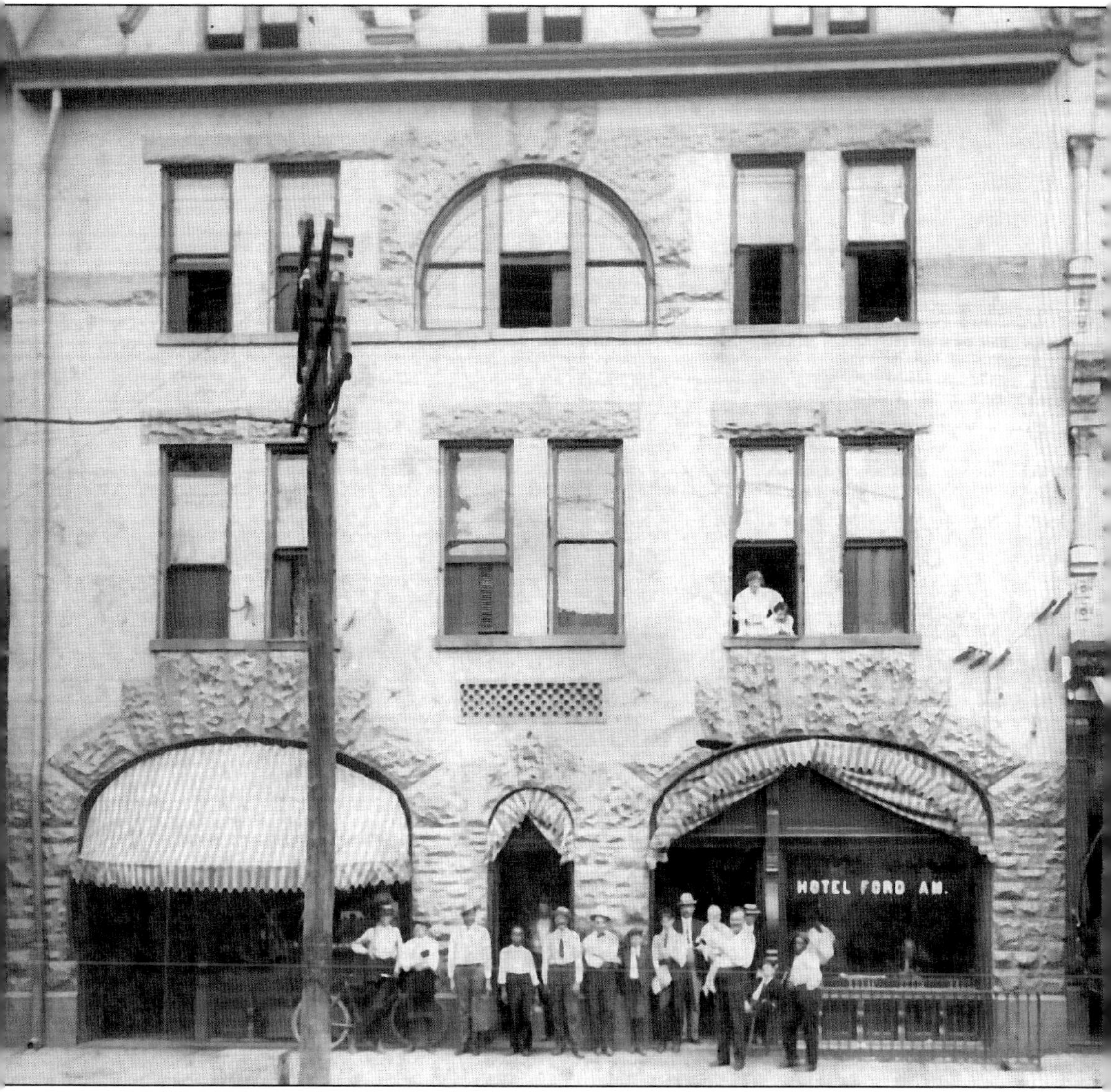

Fordham Hotel. Located on the 500 block of Main Street where the Baldwin Hotel building is now, this "magnificent and commodious" 30-room hotel was built in 1889 by James K. Ford. According to a 1905 article in the *Bourbon News*, it had "all modern conveniences, barber shop and cafe in connection. The dining is as good as can be had in this part of the State. All rooms are newly papered, while neatness and cleanliness is prevalent throughout." The Fordham was destroyed by fire in August 1932 and prominent Paris businessman Boone Baldwin constructed a new hotel on the site, possibly using some of the original structure, in 1933.

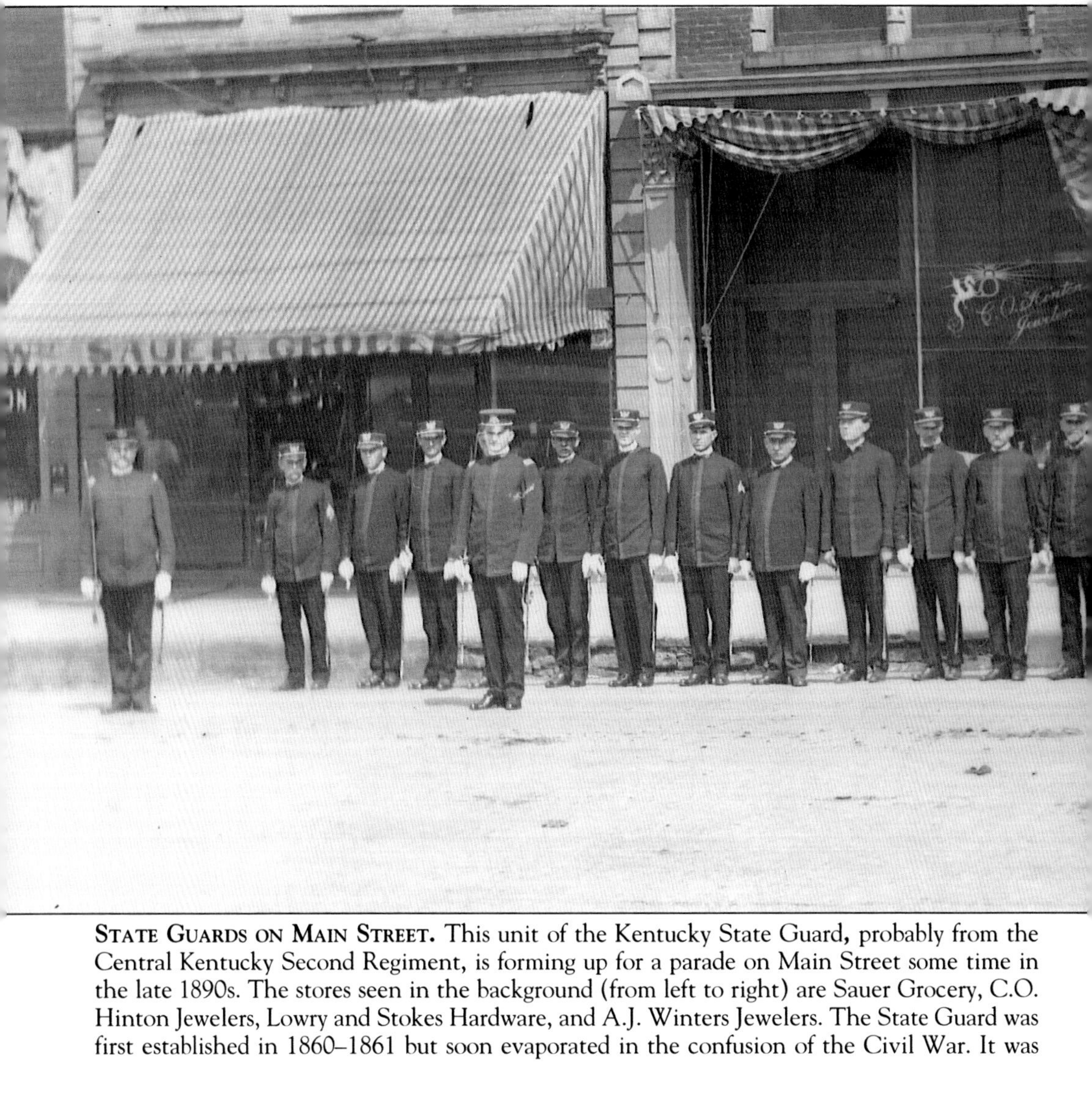

State Guards on Main Street. This unit of the Kentucky State Guard, probably from the Central Kentucky Second Regiment, is forming up for a parade on Main Street some time in the late 1890s. The stores seen in the background (from left to right) are Sauer Grocery, C.O. Hinton Jewelers, Lowry and Stokes Hardware, and A.J. Winters Jewelers. The State Guard was first established in 1860–1861 but soon evaporated in the confusion of the Civil War. It was

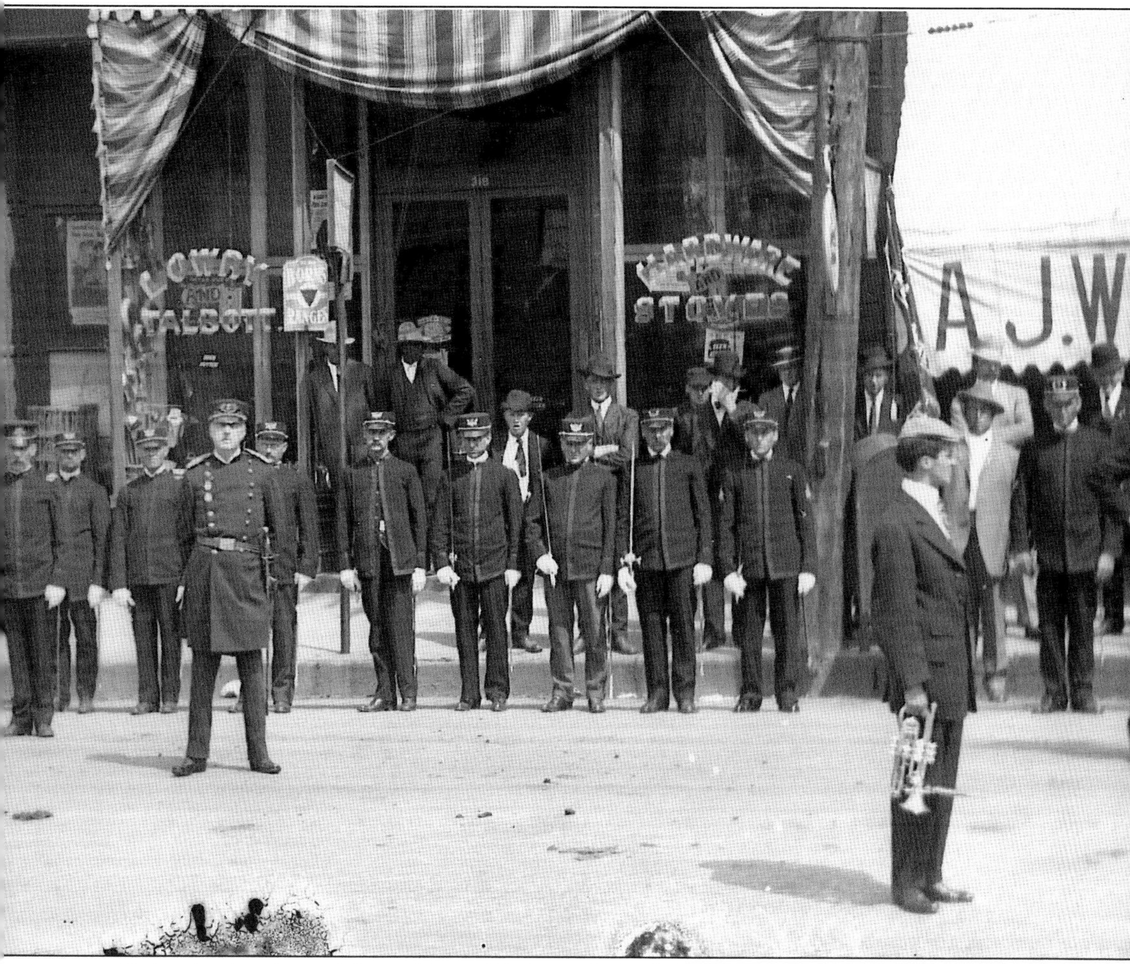

reestablished by the General Assembly in 1878. Poorly funded and equipped, it initially numbered less than 1,000 men and had three regiments headquartered in Louisville, Bowling Green, and Lexington. It had to deal with lynchings, riots, mountain feuds, and coal field disputes. In 1912 it became the Kentucky National Guard, with federal funding and supervision.

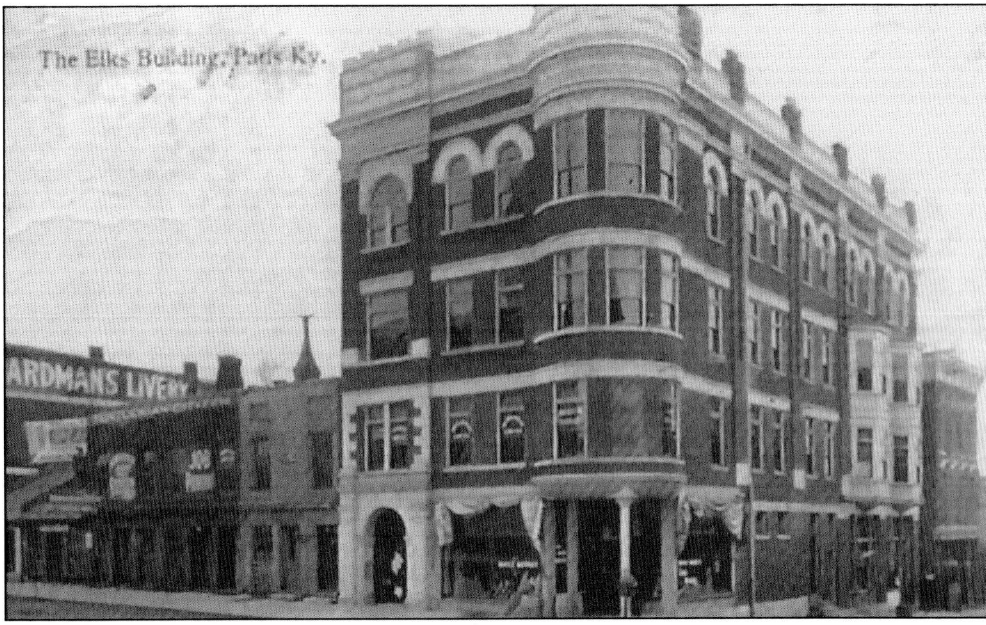

ELKS BUILDING LATER BECAME BOURBON HOTEL. Built in 1901 at the corner of Main Street and Courthouse Square for the Elks Lodge B.P.O.E. 373, the lodge used the third and fourth floors for their club rooms and leased the first two levels for offices and retail space. In 1926 the Elks sold it to the Masons and by the 1940s the Bourbon Hotel had moved from their old building across Main Street to occupy most of the structure.

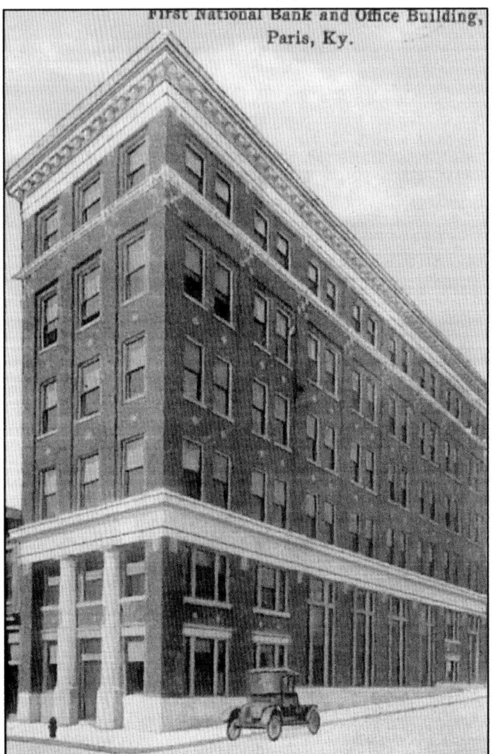

FIRST NATIONAL BANK WAS PARIS'S "SKYSCRAPER." Towering six stories tall at the corner of Fourth and Main, the First National Bank and Office Building was completed in 1915. It was torn down in 1980 and was replaced by a modern structure. This postcard photo shows a car and pedestrian which were obviously added and are out of proportion to the building.

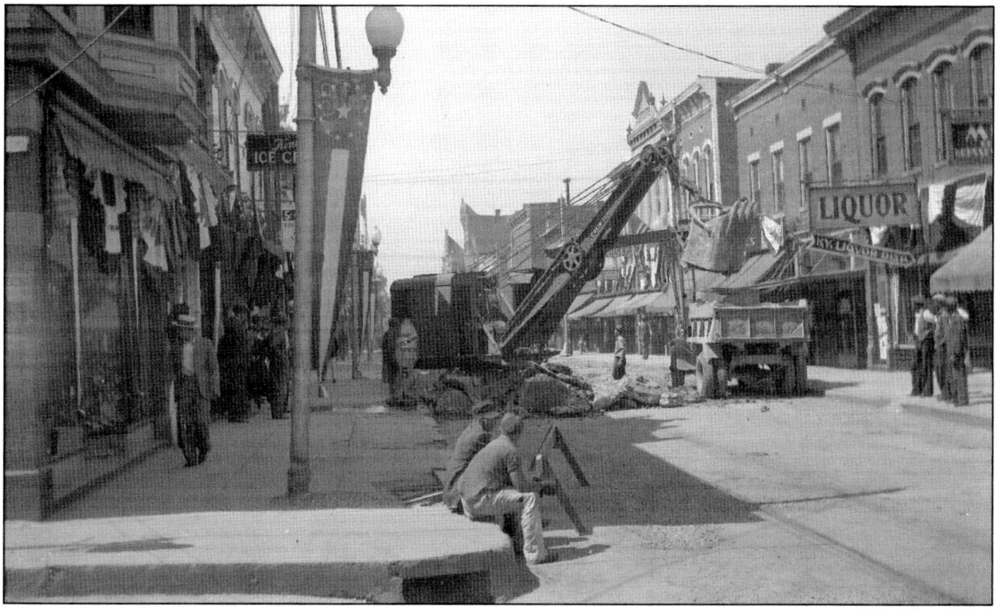

Off with the old—On with the New. Main Street received a facelift in 1936 as a part of the nation's recovery from depression. The old blacktop was torn up and replaced with concrete. The old wooden utility poles were also replaced with steel light posts. This photo was taken at the corner of Sixth Street looking south.

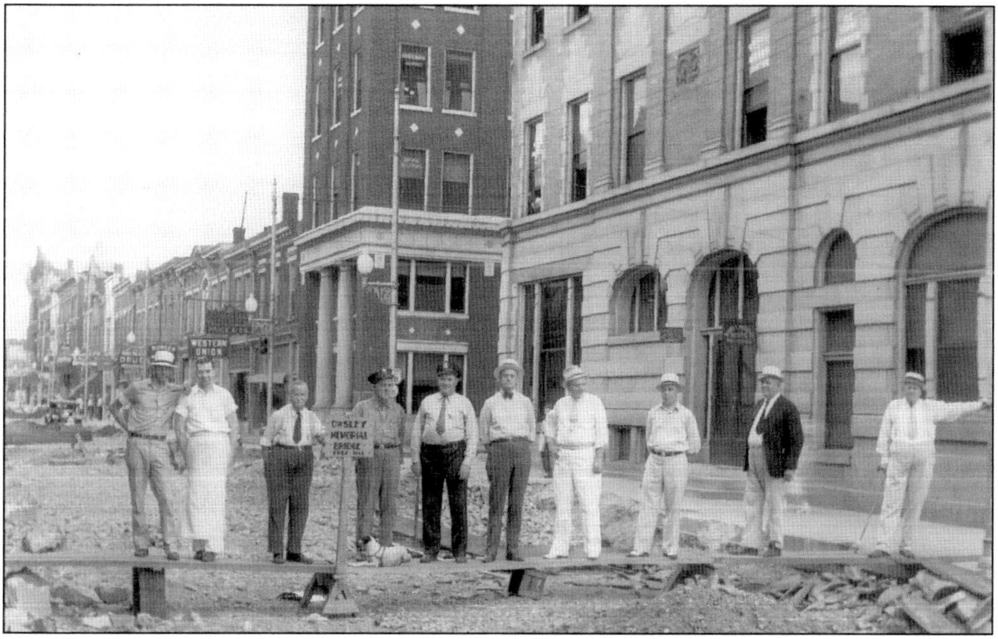

Owsley Memorial Bridge. During the 1936 renovation of Main Street, this questionable pedestrian bridge in front of the Bourbon Agricultural Bank was named for the owner of a popular local restaurant, Grant Owsley (pictured just left of the sign). The only other gentlemen identified are from Owsley's left: fire chief Bud Lancaster; police officer Albert Johnson; and businessman Grant Overby. The neatly lettered sign jokingly reads "Owsley Memorial Bridge—Free Toll."

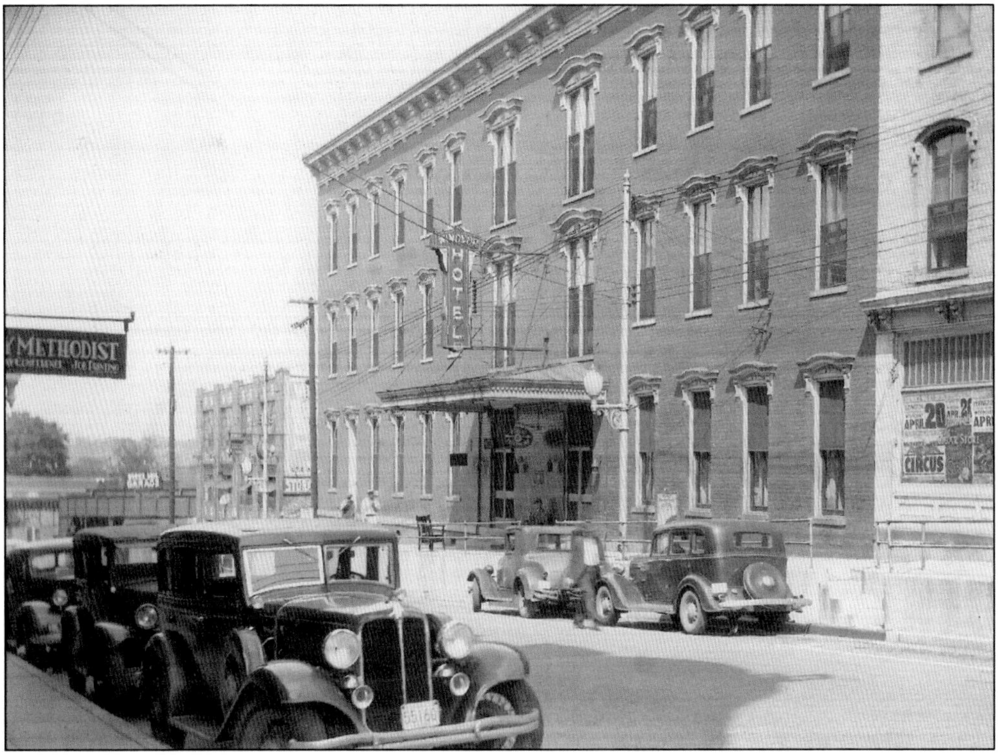

Windsor Hotel—One of Paris's Finest. The 81-room Windsor Hotel stood on a site in the 200 block of Main Street that had held an inn or hotel from Paris's earliest days. In 1854, when it was known as the Bourbon House, the railroad came to Paris and built a depot directly behind the hotel. In 1900 it was sold to a Lexington syndicate that renamed it the Windsor Hotel. It burned in a horrific fire in January of 1945.

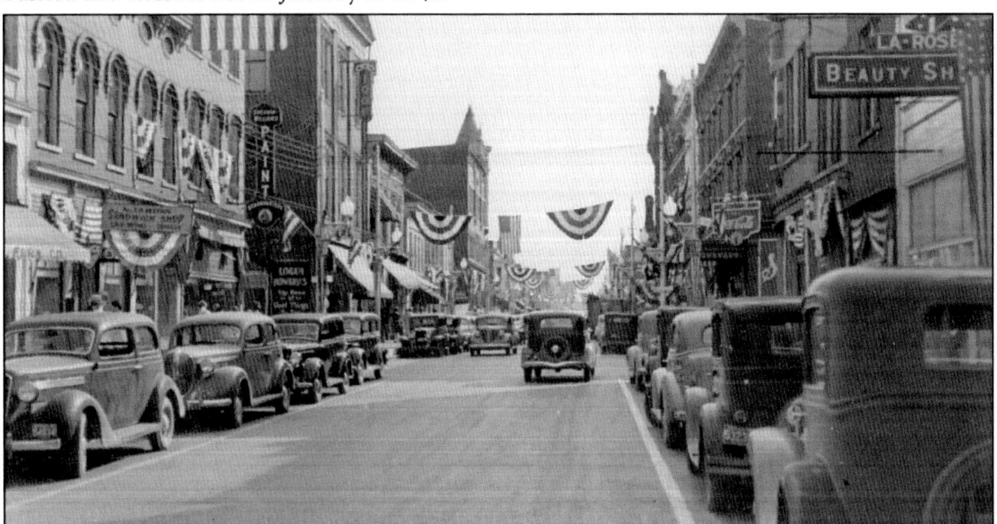

Main Street in Red, White, and Blue. The nation may have been just getting out of the Great Depression, but patriotism was never out of style in Paris, as this scene from the late 1930s reveals.

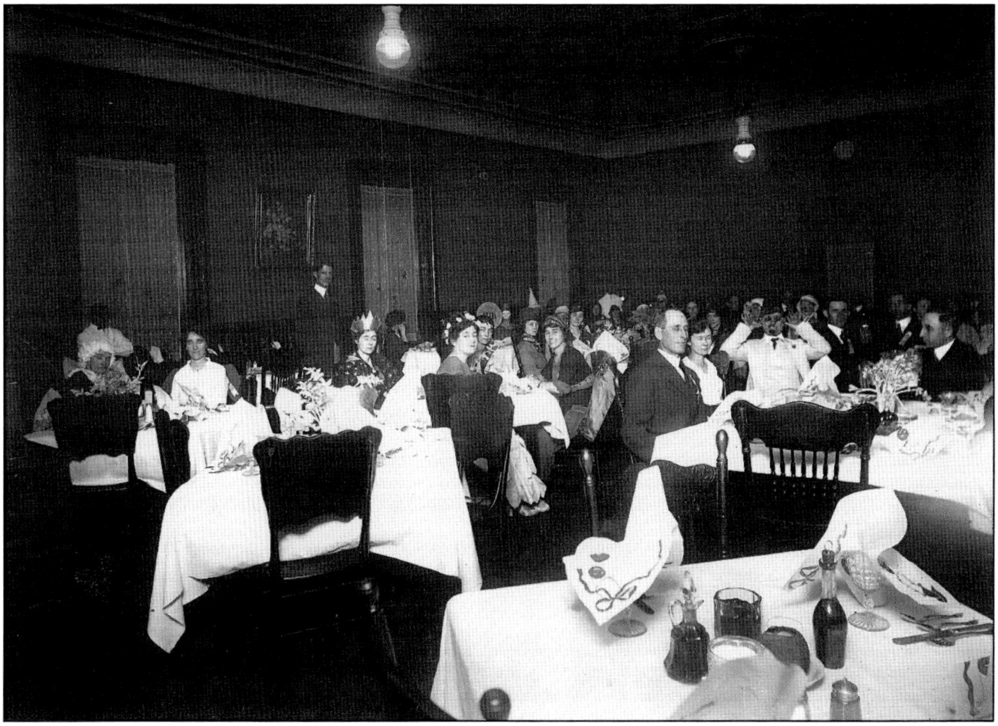

Fun down on Main Street. This festive party may have been held in the Windsor Hotel— it was known for its gala balls during the Bourbon County Fairs, but we are not sure. People at this gathering were having a good time at one of Main Street's hotels or banquet rooms. The party hats worn by some of the diners suggest it could have been New Year's Eve.

You are cordially invited to attend
a Dance given by
The Independent Dancing Club
at Varden's Hall, Paris, Ky.
Friday evening, March the eighteenth
nineteen twenty-one
Chaperones
Mr. and Mrs. W. B. Kiser, Mr. and Mrs. Roy Turner
Mr. and Mrs. Earl Ingles, Mr. and Mrs. Clyde Larkin
Hours nine till three A. M.
THIS CARD MUST BE PRESENTED AT DOOR

"You are Cordially Invited to Attend." This 1921 invitation to "The Independent Dancing Club's" party at the hall on the second story above Varden's Drugs, which was an annex of the Fordham Hotel next door, specifically listed the chaperones. It also promised fun until three a.m.! Now those were "the good old nights."

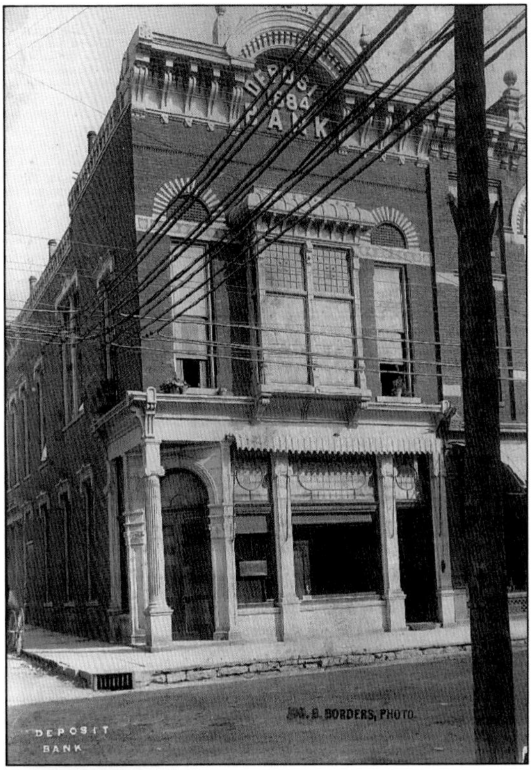

Deposit Bank. This building at the corner of Fourth and Main was constructed in 1884 at a cost of $20,000 for one of the first financial institutions in the city. The Deposit Bank was organized in 1851 and was housed in the present Memorial Building on Ardery Place until their move to Main Street. In 1914 they acquired the People's Bank and did business as the People's Deposit Bank until they were absorbed by Bourbon Agricultural Bank in 1984.

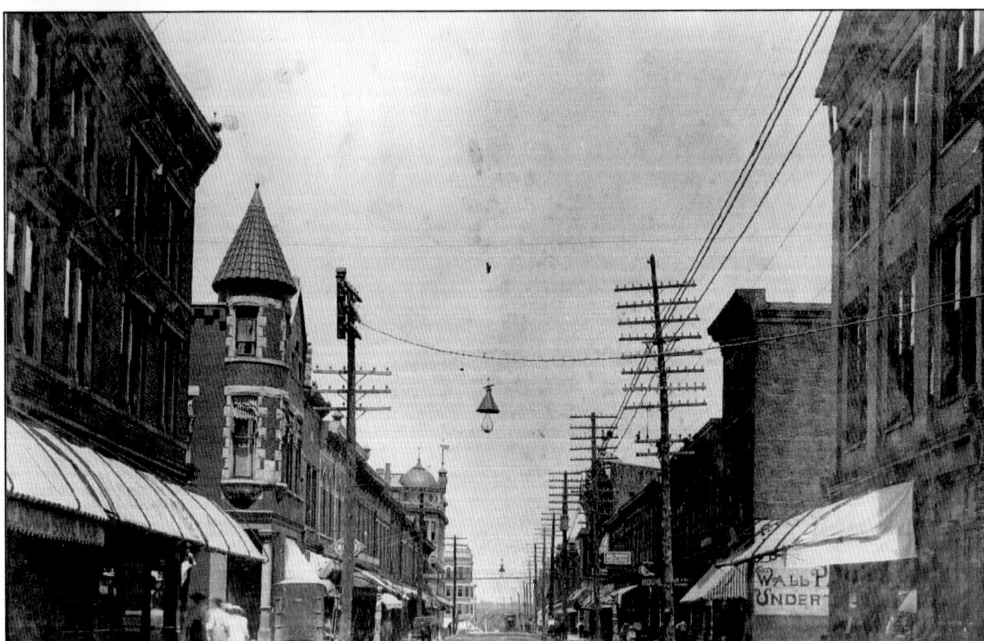

Main Street Changed Only a Little—But a Time Gone Forever. A number of architectural historians have said Paris's Main Street is one of the most intact Victorian streetscapes left in the region. But studying the images of daily life on the street before World War II reveals that the landscape of that era has surrendered to inevitable change.

Four

EDUCATION IN BLACK AND WHITE

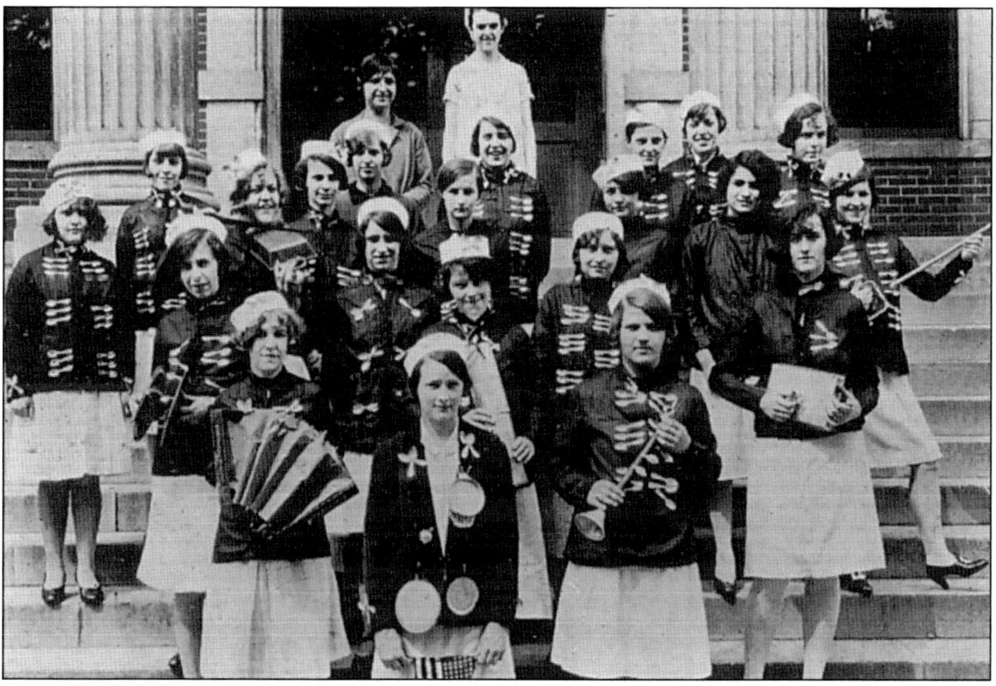

THIS 1927 BAND PLAYED MUSIC THAT "REALLY COOKED." It was during the Jazz Age when this group of students at Paris High School formed a "Kitchen Cabinet Orchestra" using instruments made from cooking utensils. Notice the spoons used to decorate their uniforms. This was also the first year that students occupied the new Paris Senior High School building. Prior to that, all the city school students shared the same building.

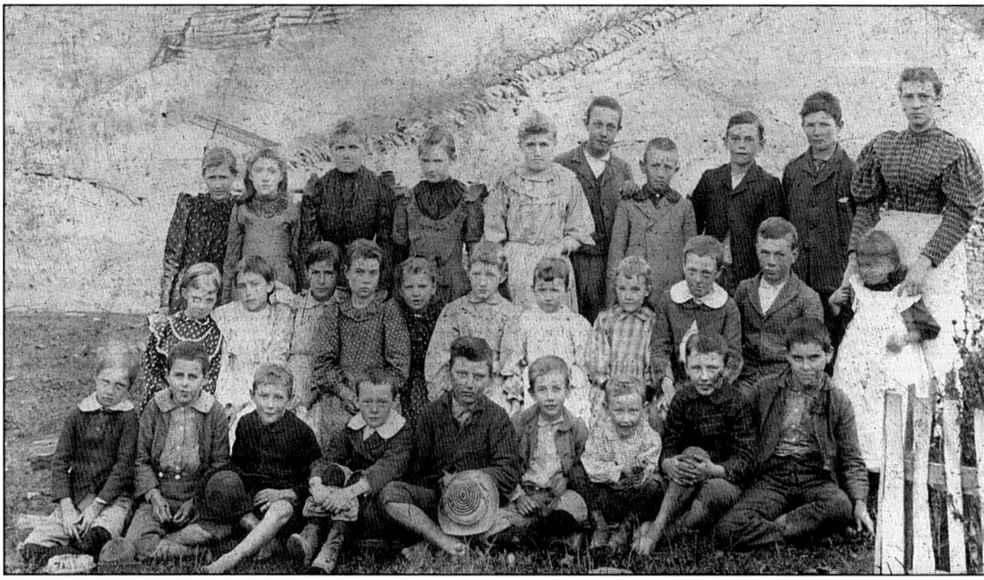

Burris School #1 c. 1894. This is representative of the more than 35 one-room schools situated throughout Bourbon County during the late 1800s and the early 1900s. This school was located on the Burris Road and it was in use from about 1882 to 1900, when it was replaced by Burris School #2. The teacher shown here is Miss Nellie Herrick.

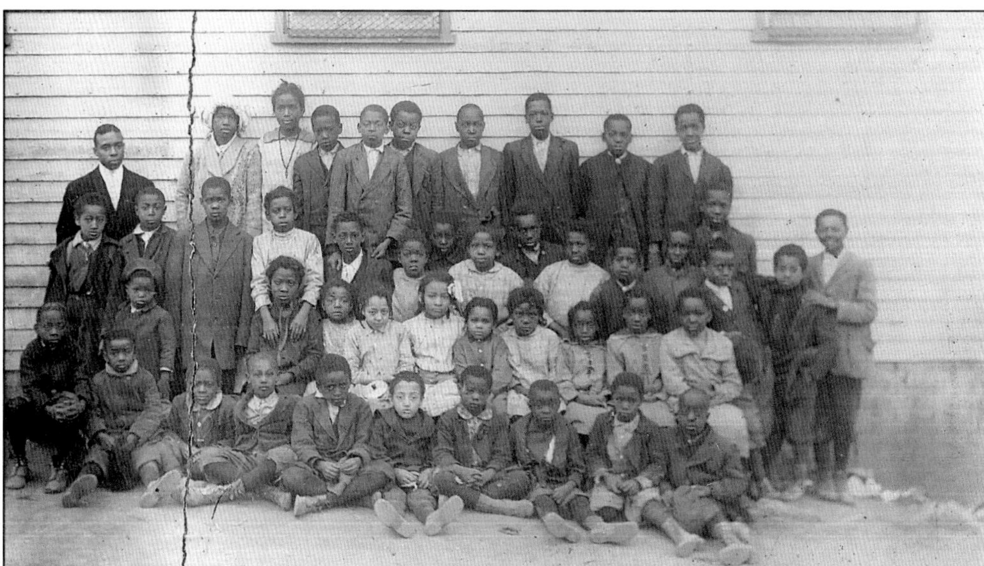

North Middletown One-Room School. This photograph of the students and teacher at a one-room school for black children in North Middletown was taken on March 30, 1915. No information exists about the names of the students or the teacher. At that time, there were 12 one-room schools for Bourbon County black children who lived outside the city limits. The schools were spread out so that each school served about the same number of children.

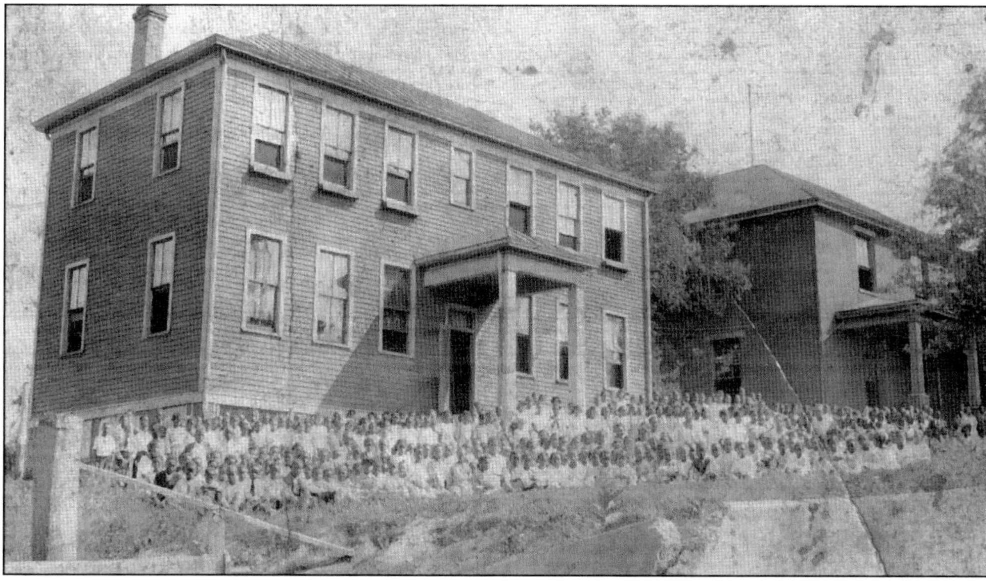

EARLY PHOTO OF PARIS'S WESTERN SCHOOL. Western School opened in the late 1800s as a school for African-American children living in Paris. In 1880, there were more than 1,000 "colored" students (as African-American children were called in that era) at Western. It looks like about that number turned out to have their picture taken.

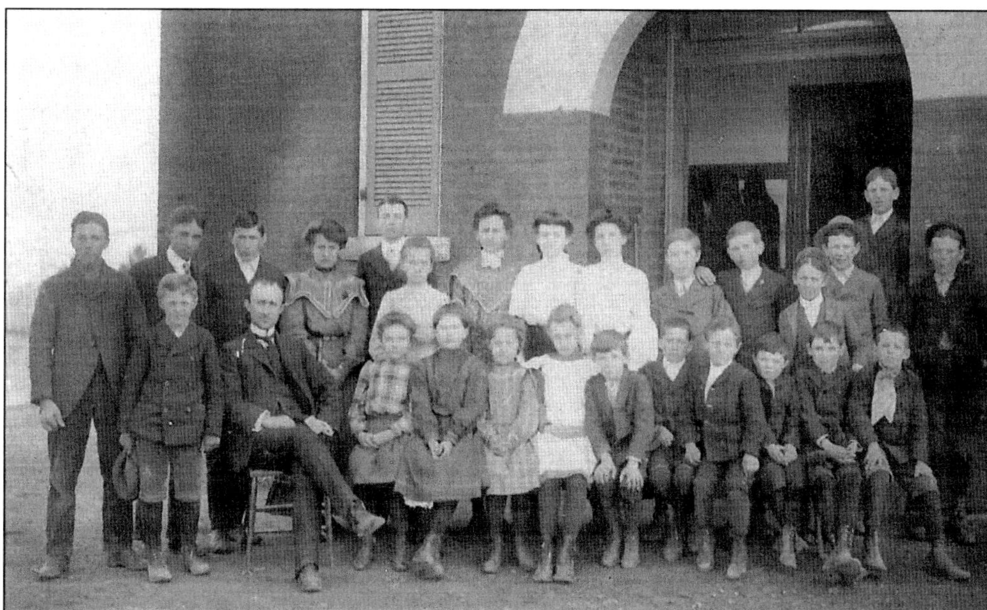

CLINTONVILLE COMMON GRADED SCHOOL. This 1903 photograph shows the substantial brick Clintonville two-room school. Shown from left to right are (front row) G.C. Thompson, Mr. Jesse C. Berry (teacher), Grace Haskins, Mary Elizabeth Beasley, Ella Ray Nichols, Katherine Weathers, Jimmie Bounds, Fisher Collins, Lapsley Haskins, Dewey Beasley, Ernest Darnaby, and Allen Lary; (second row) Lucien Terrell, Carl Howell, Tom Haley, Mattie Lou Stipp, Curtis Lary, Sallie Collins, Roberta Gorham, Evelyn McDonald, Mary Gorham, Jim Stephenson, Robert Thompson, John Stipp, I.C. Haley, Tom Kennedy, and Jerome Parrish.

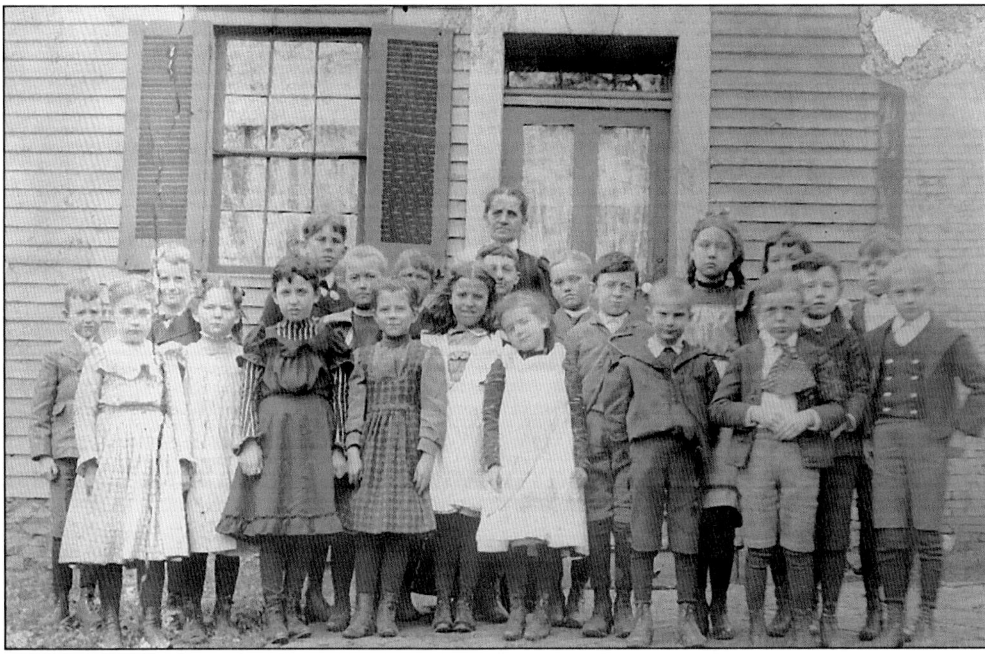

Miss Lizzie Walker's School. This was one of several small, private schools in the county before about 1930. Those pictured in 1900 include (not in order) William Kenney Ferguson, William Woodford, Jason Redmon, Barton Rogers, Brooks Woodford, Stokley Rion, Garrett Turner, Charlton Clay, Oscar Hinton, Hugh Ferguson, Oscar Locknane, Harold Harris, Henrietta Goff, Helen Hutchcraft, Virginia Smith, William Mapples, Elizabeth Bayless, Katherine Davis, Myra Booth, Nannie Clay, and Louise Wyatt.

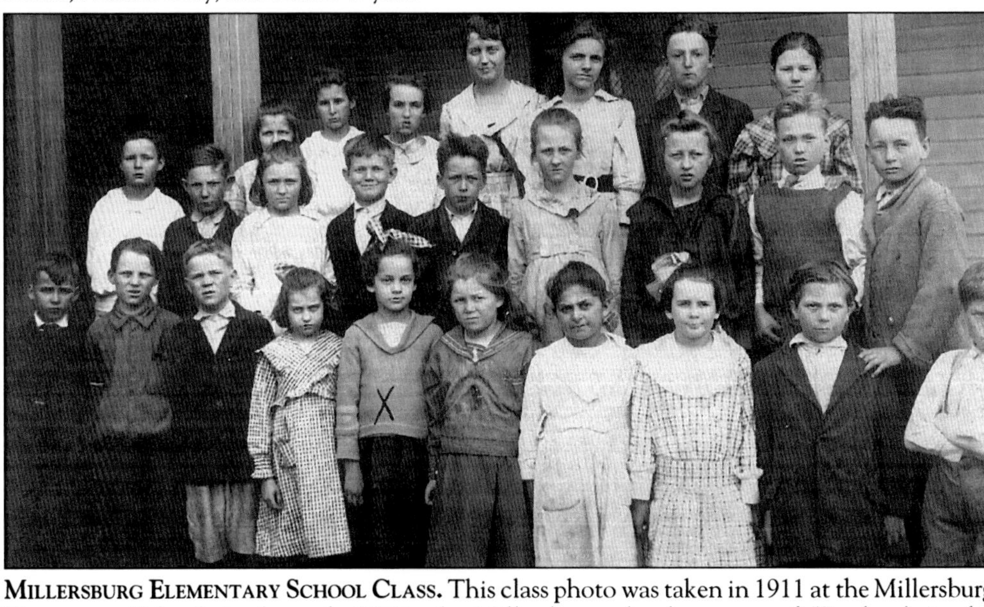

Millersburg Elementary School Class. This class photo was taken in 1911 at the Millersburg Elementary School. In the early 1900s, the Millersburg school was one of 57 schools in the Bourbon County system including 35 schools for white children and 22 schools for black children. The next decades would see the number of schools in the county shrink dramatically as many were consolidated into larger schools built in the 1920s.

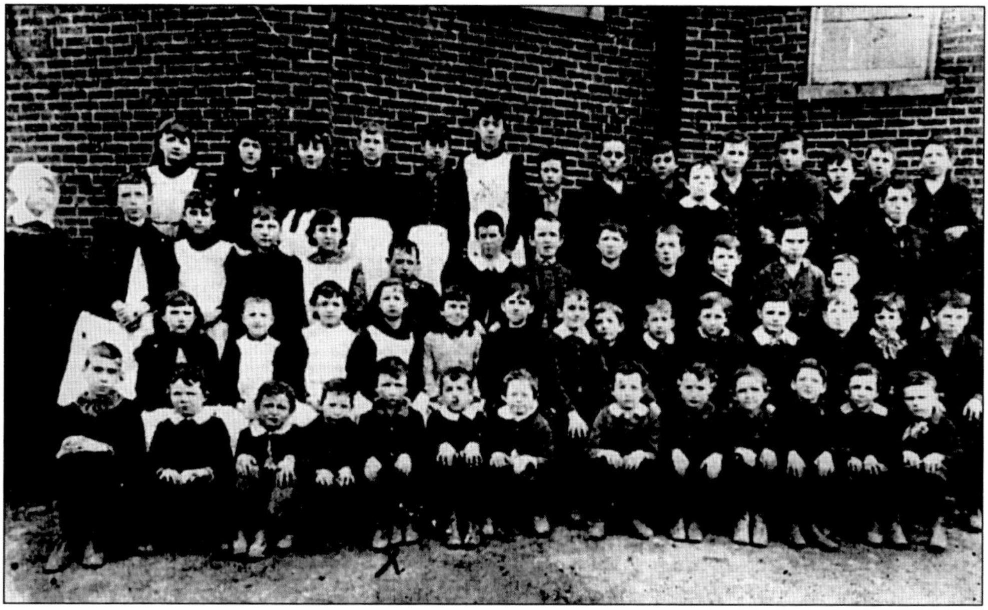

CATHOLIC SCHOOL CLASS, 1890. A two-story building with electric lighting held Catholic parochial school classes at that time in a frame building on High Street, which was replaced in 1895. In 1913, the second story of that school building burned. The school re-opened in September of that year in the building on Main Street that is still in use as a parochial school.

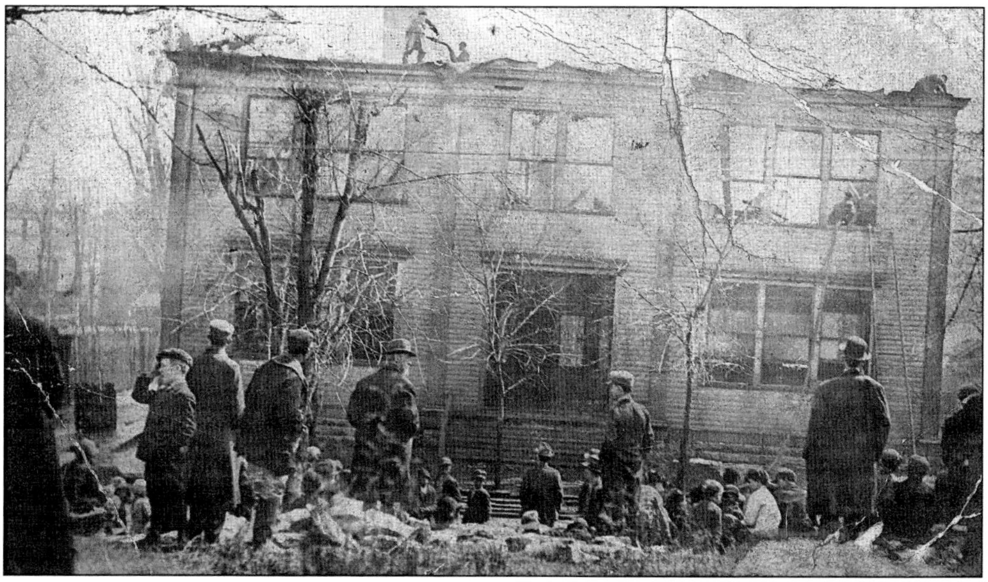

FIRE! CATHOLIC SCHOOL ON HIGH STREET IN FLAMES. Firefighters can be seen on the roof and in the second-floor windows as they try valiantly to extinguish the burning Catholic school building on High Street in 1913. Their efforts were at least partly successful since only the second story was destroyed and the shorter building is still in use as the parish hall.

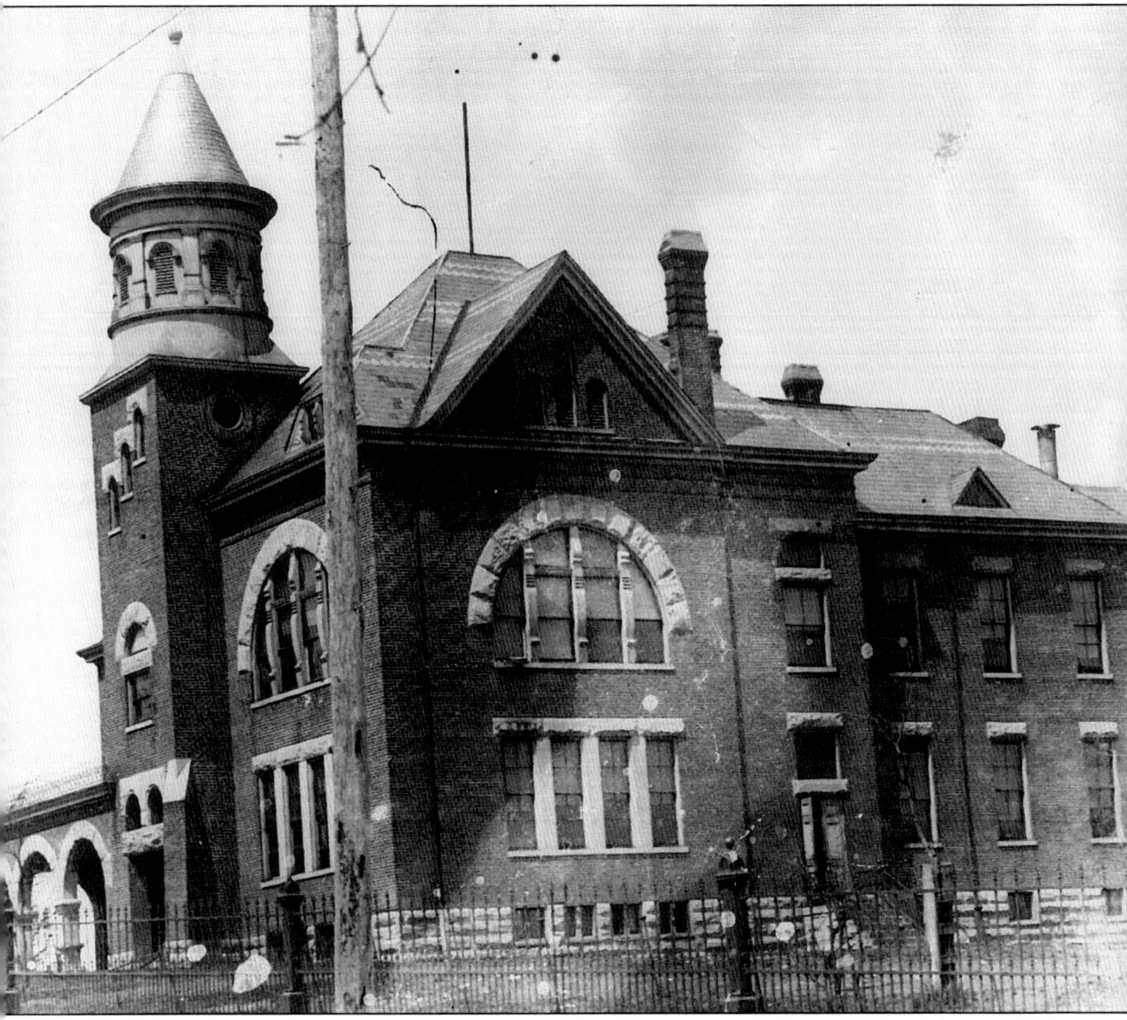

Paris Seventh Street School. This imposing structure was built in 1857 on the site of the current Paris High School and Middle School. After beginning with only a principal and three teachers, enrollment had increased enough by 1875 to require six teachers, a music instructor, and a building addition. The building burned in 1907.

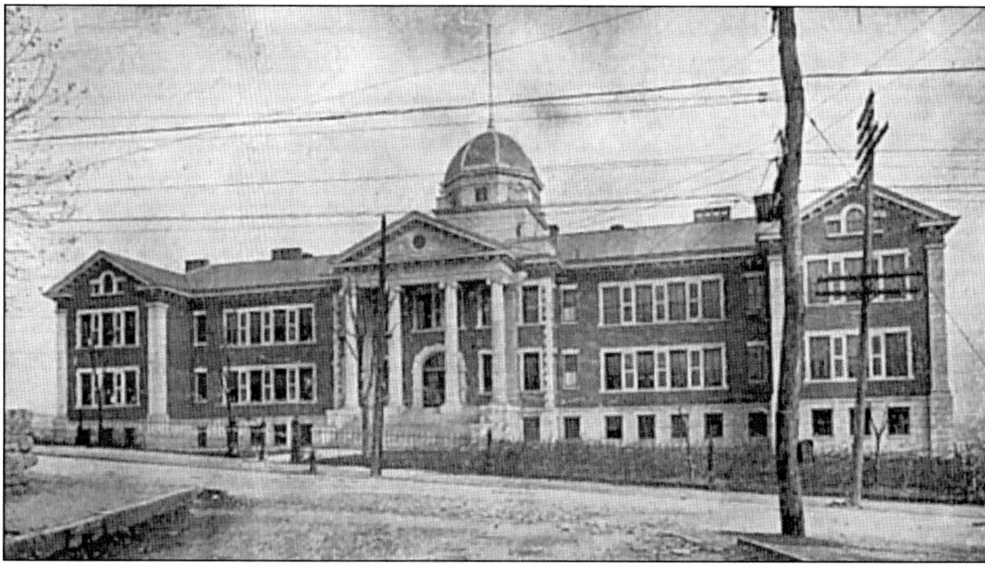

New Paris City School. This school opened in 1908 on Seventh Street; it had a dome and white columns and replaced the older school building which burned. According to the *1910 Report of Paris City Schools*, the building was "equipped with all the sanitary devices known as to modern science." The building was demolished in 1966.

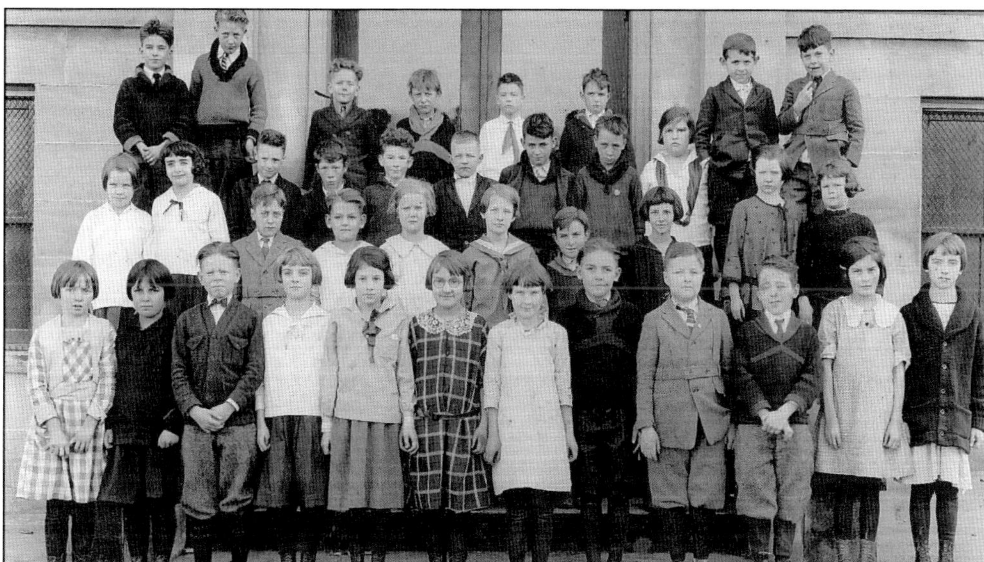

Miss Clara Brannon's 1923–1924 Fourth Grade Class at Paris City School. Shown from left to right are (front row) Catherine Bowman, unidentified, Norman Violett, unidentified, Ann Baldwin, Carolyn Bush, unidentified, Robert Rankin, John Craig, Sam Milner, unidentified, unidentified; (second row) Esther Briggs, Blanche Friedman, unidentified, unidentified, Mary Elizabeth Clay, Mildred Snell, unidentified, unidentified, Sarah Whaley, Bell Brent Woodford. In the third row, Joe Prather is second, Buck Hinkle is third and Jack Shout is sixth. In the top row, Claude Harding and Guthrie Bell are second and third and Steve Bacon is at the end.

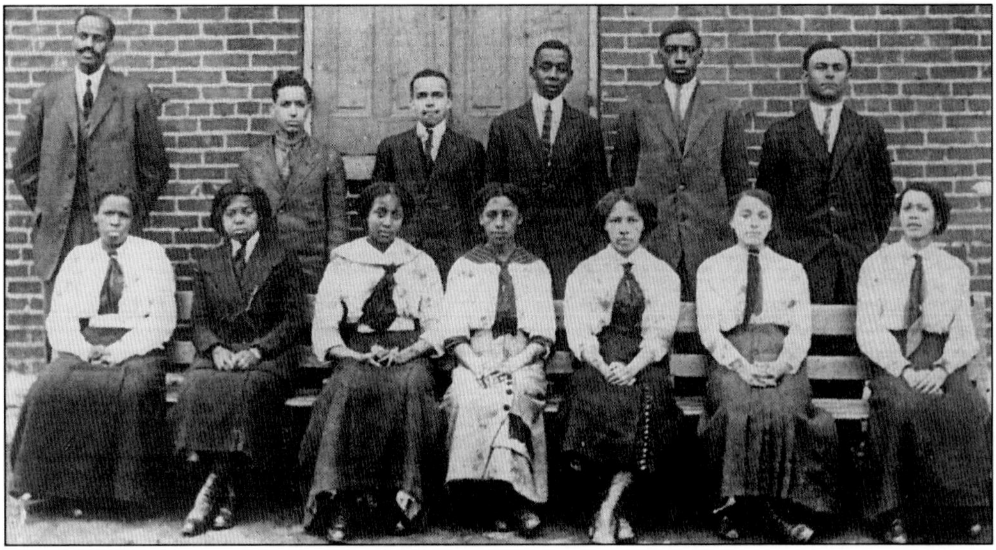

WESTERN SCHOOL. Built around 1888, Western School was located on Seventh Street. A part of the city school system, Western educated generations of African Americans in Bourbon County. The school served students up to eighth grade until 1904, when three upper grades were added. F.M. Wood took over as principal in 1911 and expanded Western High to a four-year program. Professor Wood was principal of Western until 1923 when he took over as president of Kentucky State University.

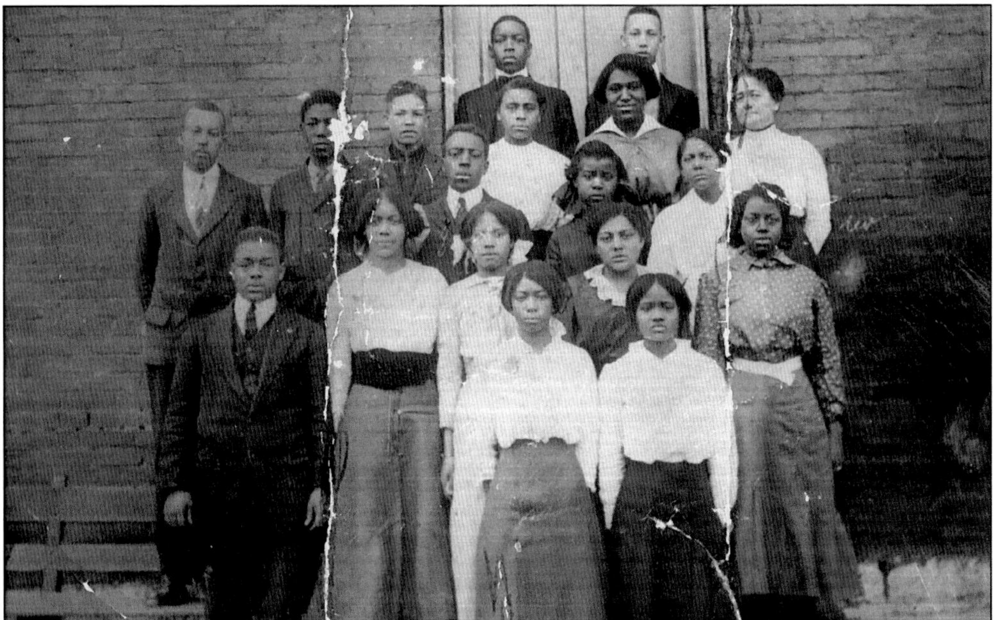

FRESHMAN CLASS OF 1914 AT WESTERN HIGH SCHOOL. Shown from left to right are (first row) Mamie Brown, Louise Patterson; (second row) Jerome Haners, Gladys Hays, Maggie Marie Samuels, Ova Bedinger, and Evelyn Mack; (third row) William Doyle, Elizabeth Parker Thomas, and Ada Hughes; (fourth row) James Mack, Lawrence Kellis, Kelly Gainer, Carry Marshall, Carrie Whaley, and the Latin teacher, Mrs. Mary Graves; (fifth row) Robert Jackson, Maceo Bishop.

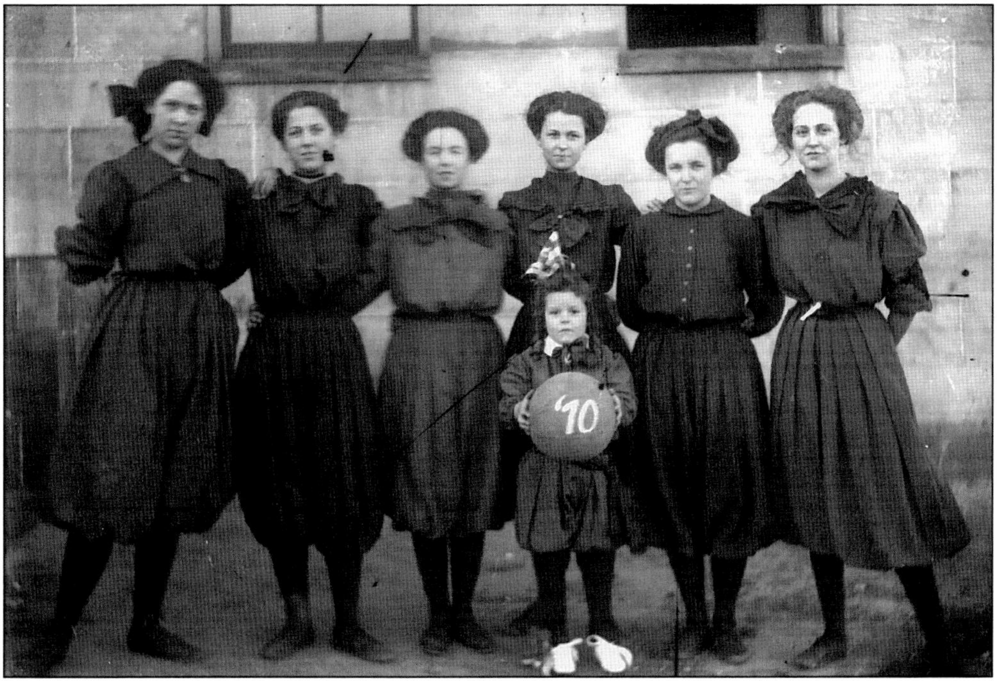

1910 Paris High School Girl's Basketball Team Went 8-4. Actually, the team was 7-1 against other high school teams, but went 1-3 against college teams including Weslyan College, State University, and Transylvania. Shown from left to right are Nellie Rumman, Freida Heller (captain), Ethel McGinley, Elsie Heller, Olive Taul, and Mary Lou Rice. Mascot Elizabeth Johnson is in front holding the ball.

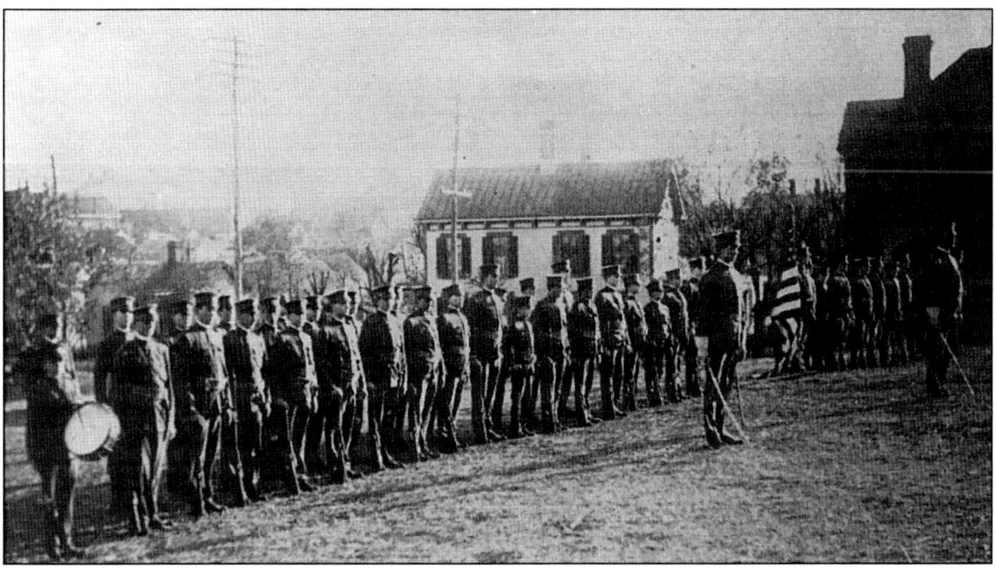

1912 Paris High School Cadets Allowed to "Bear Arms" by Governor. Even though, at first glance, it might look like this photo was taken at MMI or another military school in the area, it was actually taken at the Paris City Schools. According to the *1912 Report of Paris Public Schools*, the Governor "has authorized the issue of rifles and equipment for the High School boys, and given his permission for them to bear arms."

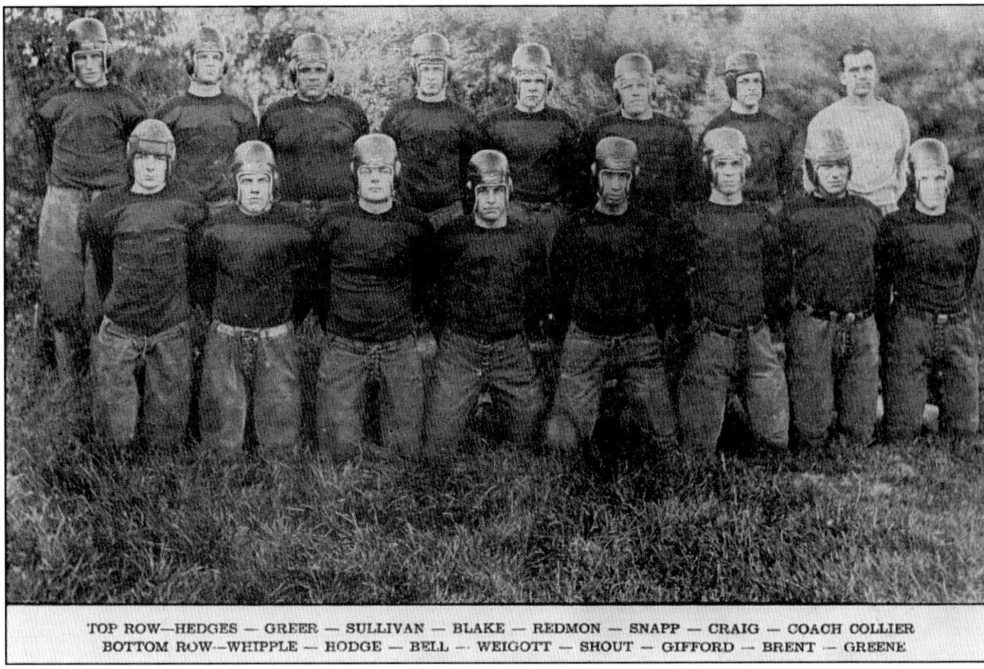

1932 PARIS HIGH FOOTBALL TEAM COACHED BY BLANTON COLLIER. Collier, a Paris High School graduate, went on to coach at the University of Kentucky and the NFL's Cleveland Browns. Shown from left to right are (front row) Dodge Whipple, Walter Hodge, Guthrie Bell, Robert Weigott (captain), Jack Shout, Clarence Gifford, Hugh Brent, and Charles Green; (back row) Joe Hedges, George "Pup" Greer, George Sullivan, Billy Blake, Hiram Redmon, Emmett "Bull" Snapp, John Craig, and Coach Collier.

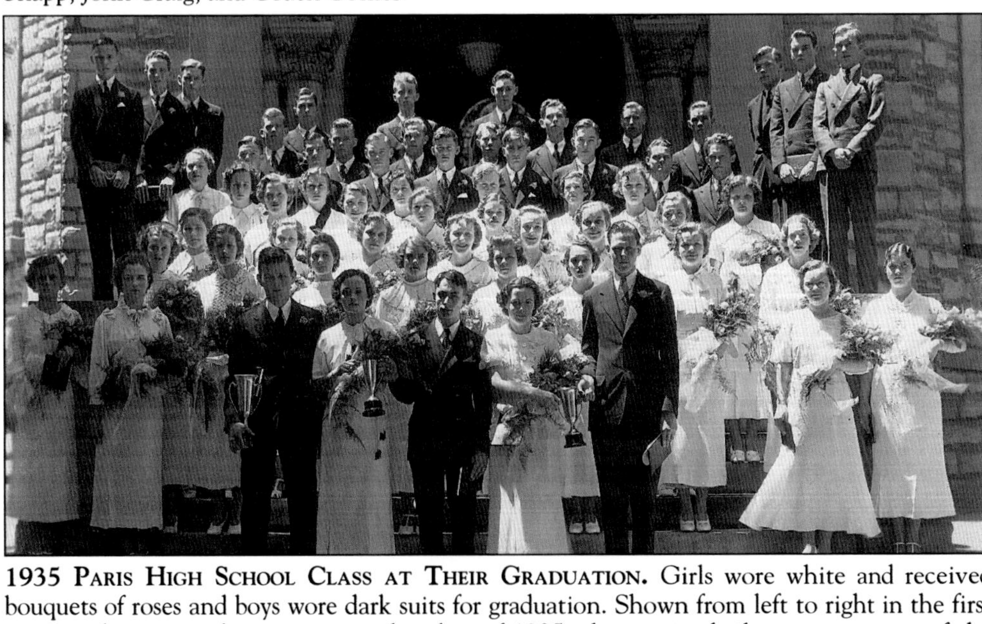

1935 PARIS HIGH SCHOOL CLASS AT THEIR GRADUATION. Girls wore white and received bouquets of roses and boys wore dark suits for graduation. Shown from left to right in the first row are the outstanding seniors in the class of 1935 who received silver cups as part of the graduation ceremonies: Rodes Shackleford Parrish, Anne Catherine Young, Elies Elvove, Sarah Gaitskill (class vice-president), and Sam Clay II (class president).

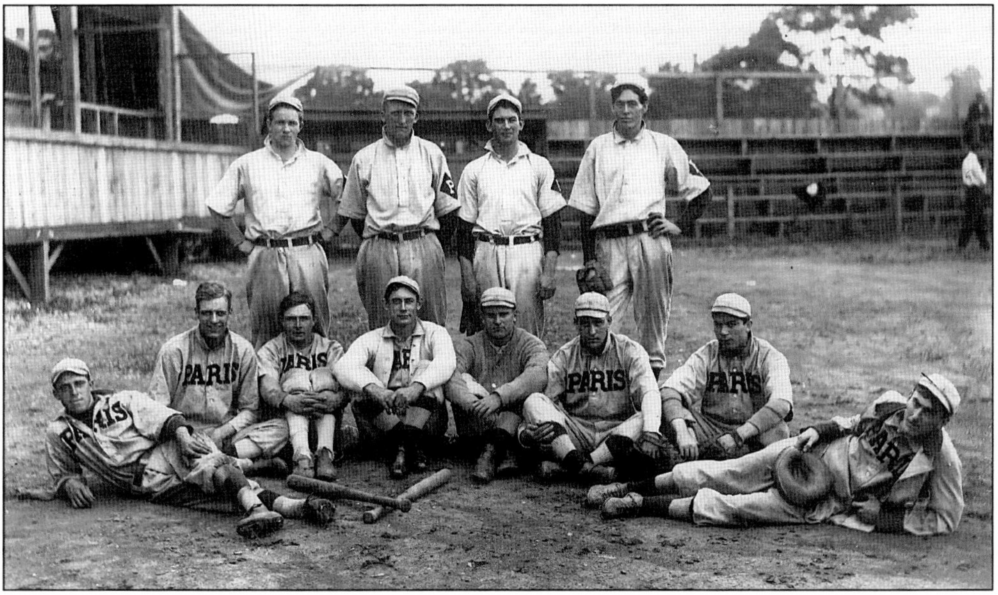

BASEBALL IN PARIS. This Paris High School baseball team is unidentified, but is representative of the school teams that played at Hancock Field, which can be seen in the background. Hancock Field was named for Mr. A.B. Hancock Sr., who donated the land for the ball field, which was located on the Winchester Road. Local semi-pro baseball teams also used the field.

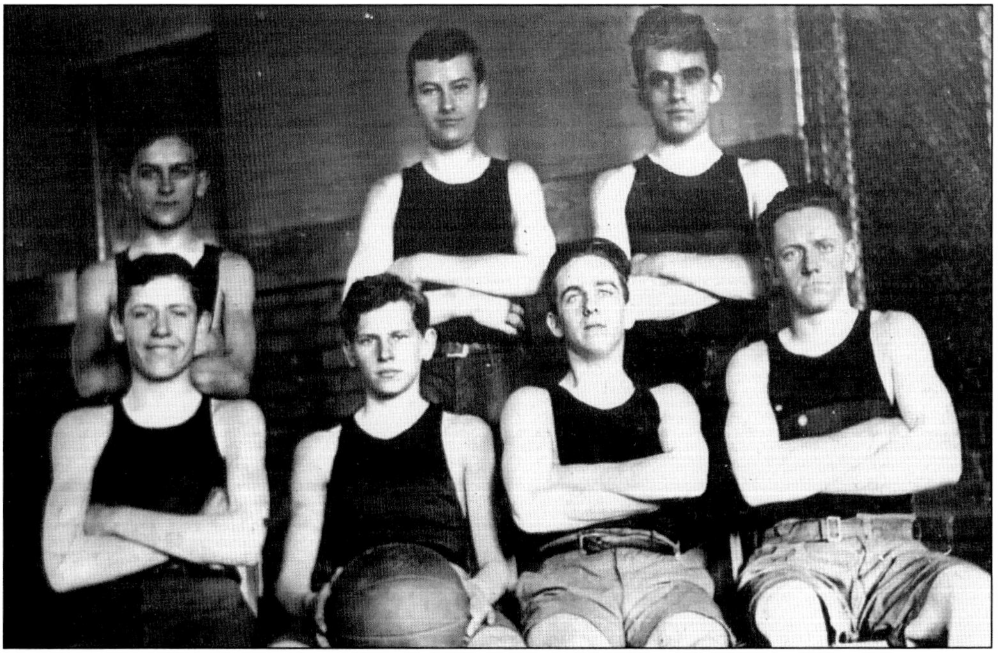

FUTURE ALL-AMERICAN ON 1915 PARIS HIGH TEAM. Basil Hayden, the young man holding the basketball, played on the Paris High School team in 1915. In 1918 he would be named the first All-American from what would become the famous University of Kentucky basketball program. In this picture taken at the Paris YMCA are, from left to right, (standing) Russell Roberts, unidentified, and Albert Lavin; (seated) Bob Burnett, Basil Hayden, Bobby Lavin, and Hiram Adair.

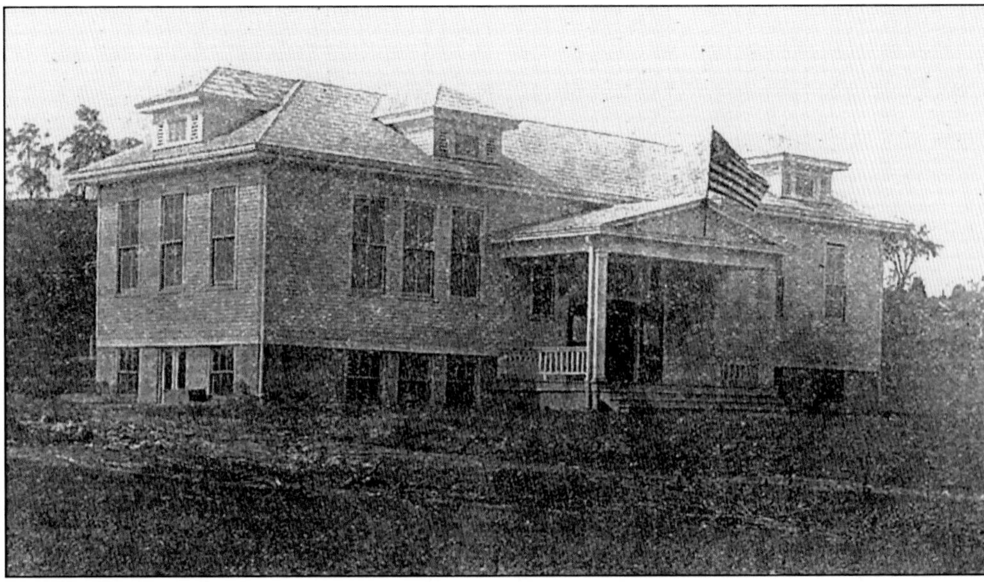

LITTLE ROCK INDEPENDENT GRADED SCHOOL, 1911. Built using tax money raised in Little Rock, this frame building was constructed in 1911 and served students from all grade levels, including high school. In 1925, the citizens of Little Rock voted themselves back into the county system. The building was torn down in 1929 and replaced by a brick school building.

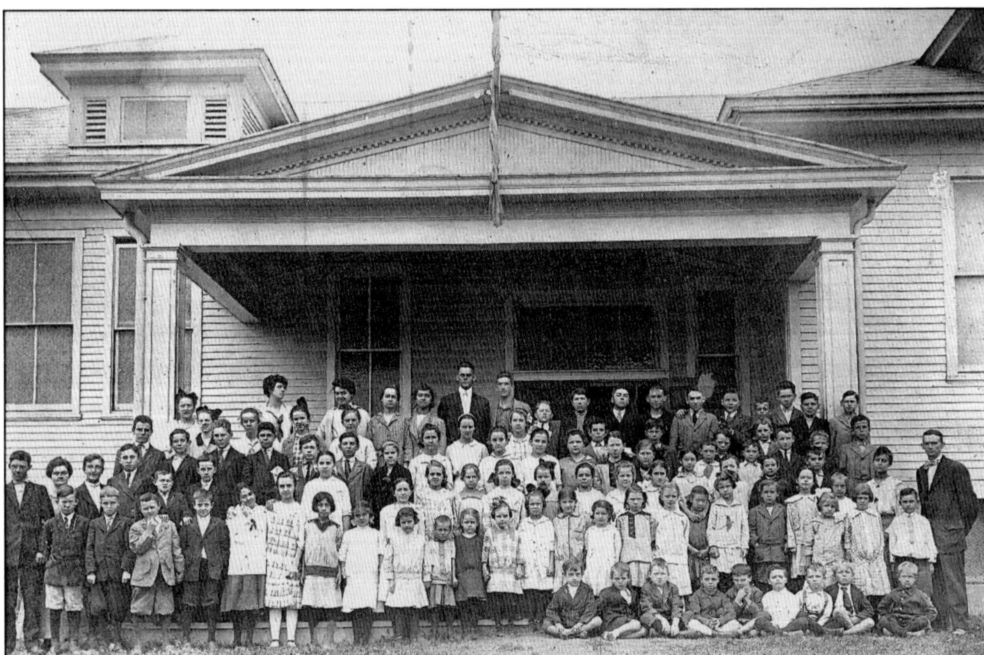

LITTLE ROCK SCHOOL STUDENTS AND STAFF AROUND 1917. The staff included Professor Byron M. Roberts, principal and high school teacher, who can be seen to the far right on the front row. Near him is teacher, Christine Thomasine. By 1927, the school had graduated 47 students "who have entered the following businesses and professions: 15 teachers, 1 doctor, 12 farmers, 10 businessmen and several mechanics," according to a booklet published that year.

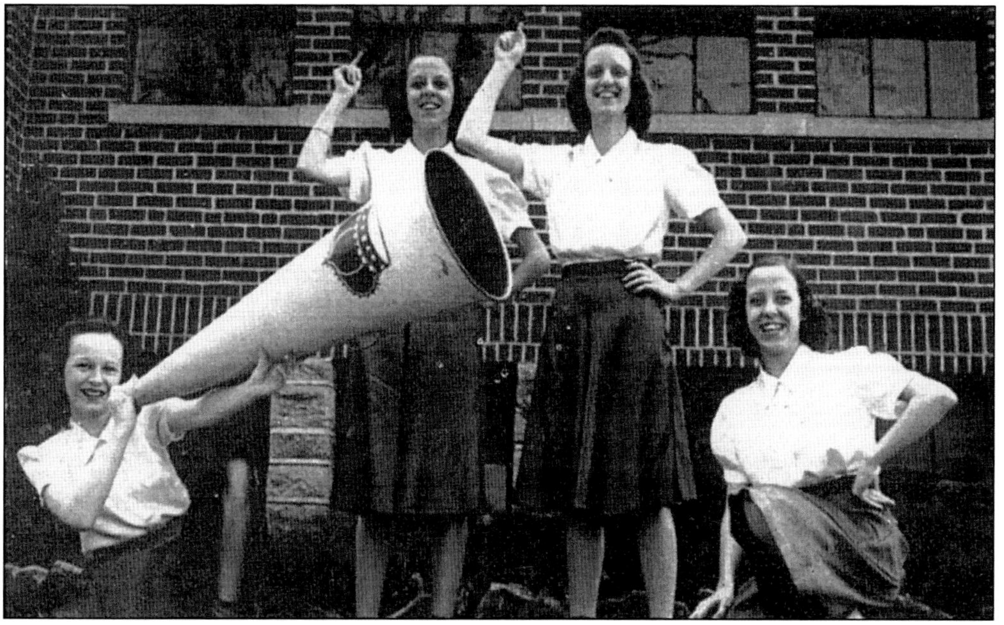

North Middletown High School Cheerleaders, 1939. These girls were ready to root on the Bourbon Kings to victory. Shown from left to right are Jane Dick, Emily Jones, Billye J. Jones, and Marie Jones. The team was named for the famous Saddlebred horse. The North Middletown school became one of the county system's six consolidated schools in 1926.

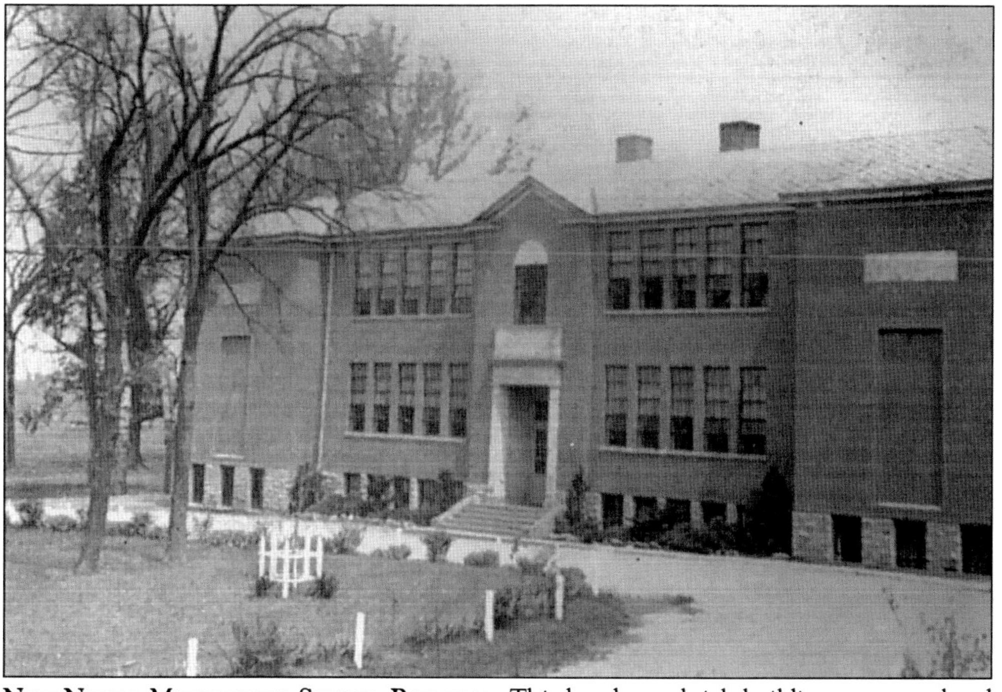

New North Middletown School Building. This handsome brick building was completed in 1927 at a cost of about $50,000. That year, the faculty consisted of R.H. Ellett (principal) and teachers Lucille Caywood, Sam Denny, Mamie McDaniel, Ruth Herd, Mary Ellett, Delia Tinder, and Mrs. H.T. Richart.

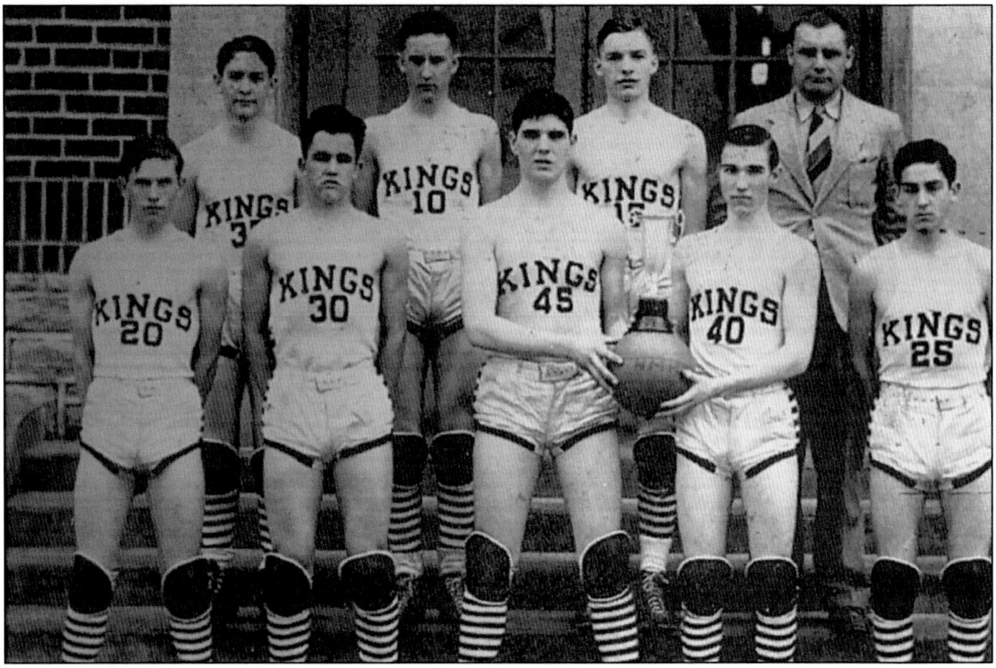

NORTH MIDDLETOWN BASKETBALL TEAM, 1939–1940. The team beat out a veteran Little Rock team 20-15 in the Bourbon County championship game. Shown with the trophy are, from left to right, (front row) Lionel King, John H. Thomas, Phil Jones, Bill Bryan (captain), and Charley Meng; (second row) Edwin Burris, Eugene Harney, Raymer Jones, and Coach John Teeney Gentry. The team lost to MMI in the finals of the district tournament.

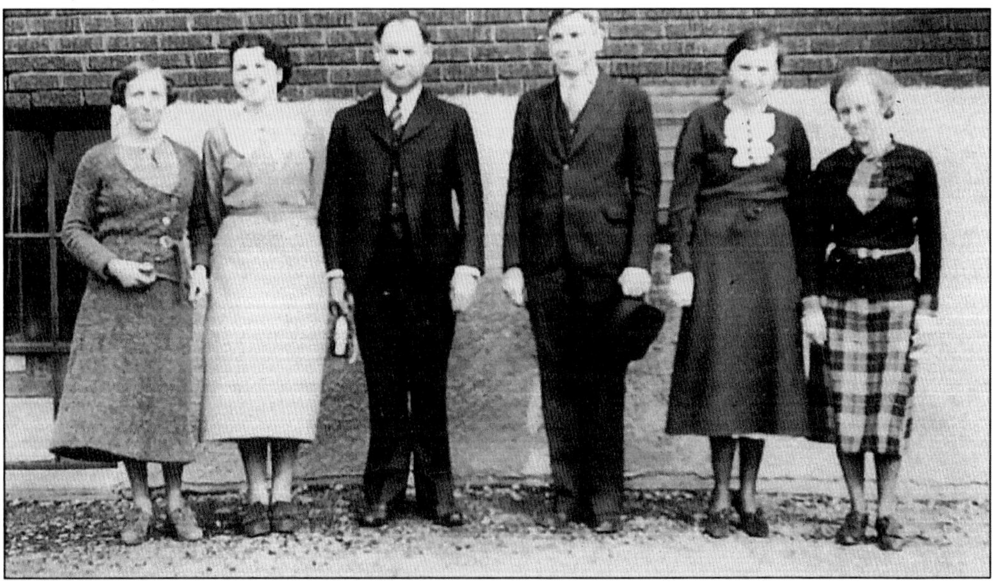

FACULTY AT CLINTONVILLE CONSOLIDATED SCHOOL, 1930s. Shown are (from left to right) Elizabeth (Biz) Weathers, Frances Dudley Kenton, F.M. Stoker, Ernest Daranaby (principal), Natalie Kash Haskins, and Lorraine Weathers Little. Darnaby served two stints as principal of the Clintonville School: 1925–27 and 1933–37. He was named superintendent of the Bourbon County school system in 1939.

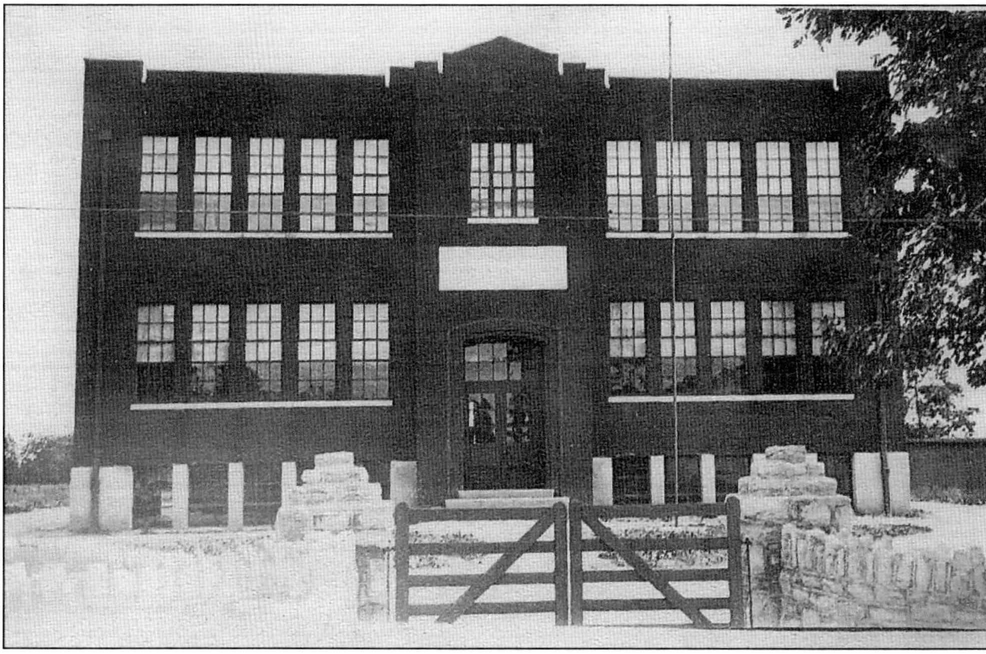

CLINTONVILLE CONSOLIDATED SCHOOL. Built in 1925 during the county school building boom, the new Clintonville School building was the third brick structure to stand on approximately the same site. In 1936, a gymnasium, indoor plumbing, and a lunchroom were added. The first year, there were three teachers: Mrs. Loraine Little, Bertha Tabor, and Elizabeth Crouch. The school offered one year of high school in 1925 and there were two freshmen that year, Marietta Brown and Julian Moore.

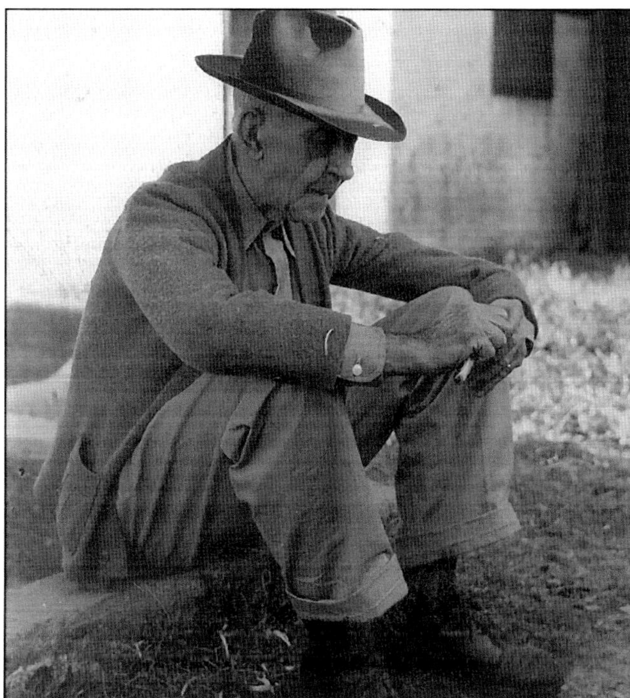

MR. JIMMIE MCDONALD, CUSTODIAN AT THE CLINTONVILLE SCHOOL. He represents all the hard-working support personnel that have kept schools going through the years and continue to do so today. McDonald was a custodian with the school for more than 16 years.

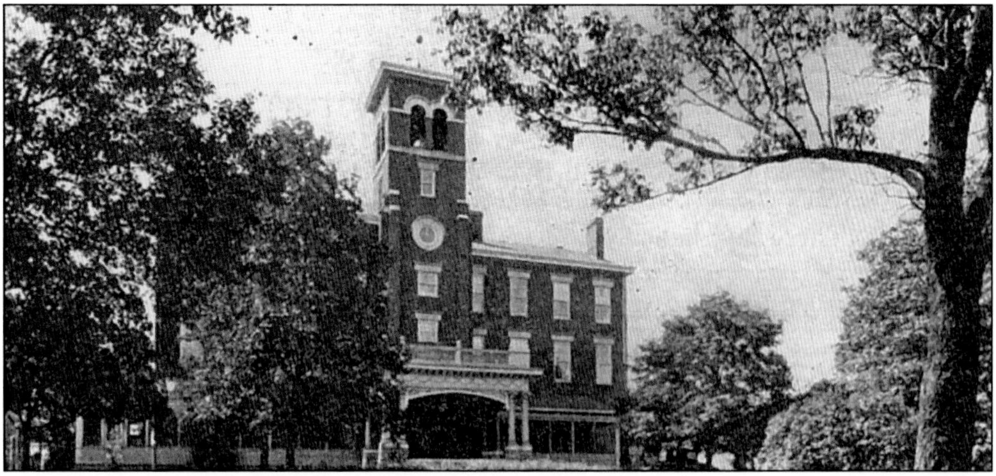

Bourbon County High School at Millersburg. Before the new Bourbon County Vocational High School opened in 1948, the school in Millersburg was known as Bourbon County High School. It was established in 1920 utilizing the 1858 building shown here, which was the first site of Kentucky Wesleyan College. The building was purchased in 1893 by Col. C.M. Best to serve as the location for MMI. He sold the building to the Bourbon County Board of Education in 1920.

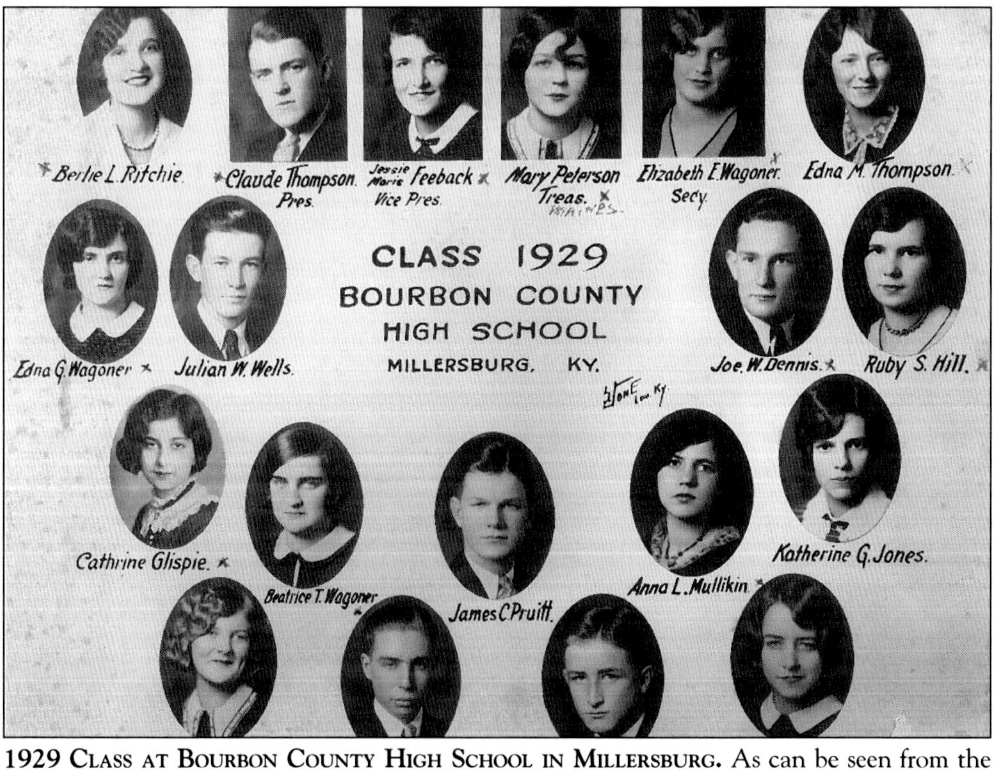

1929 Class at Bourbon County High School in Millersburg. As can be seen from the photo, boys in 1929 wore their hair slicked-back. Girls had more choices—they could have their hair treated with steam vapor, marcelled, or given a permanent wave. Centered under the class information is a photo of James C. Pruitt, who turned 90 in 2001 and is one of the last surviving members of this class.

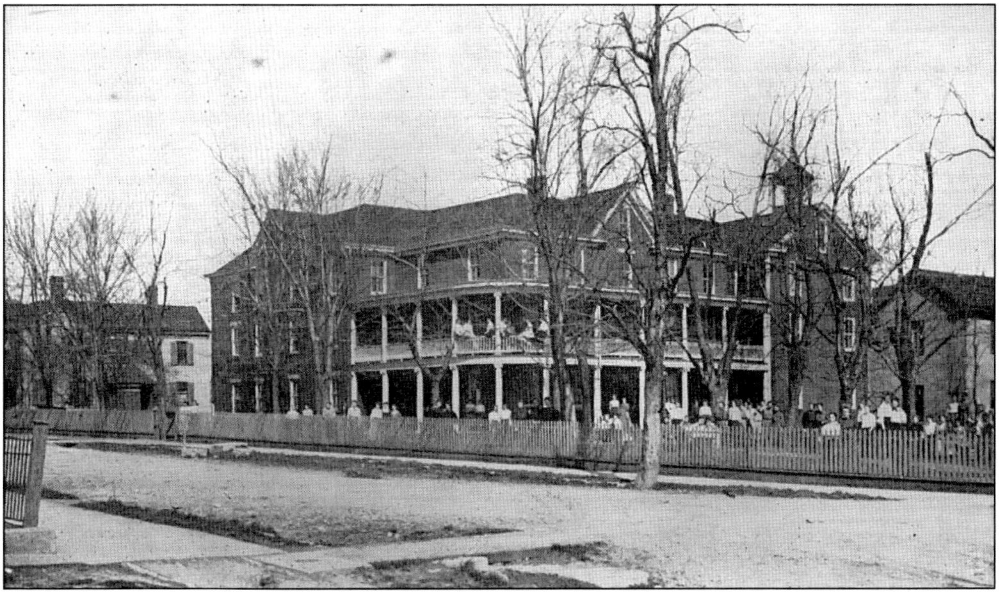

MILLERSBURG FEMALE COLLEGE. The large number of girls that can be seen in this photo from the 1906 MFC yearbook is a testament to the fact that the school attracted a lot of students. In 1911, there were more than 85 girls in the collegiate department. Millersburg Female College held its 75th annual commencement in 1925.

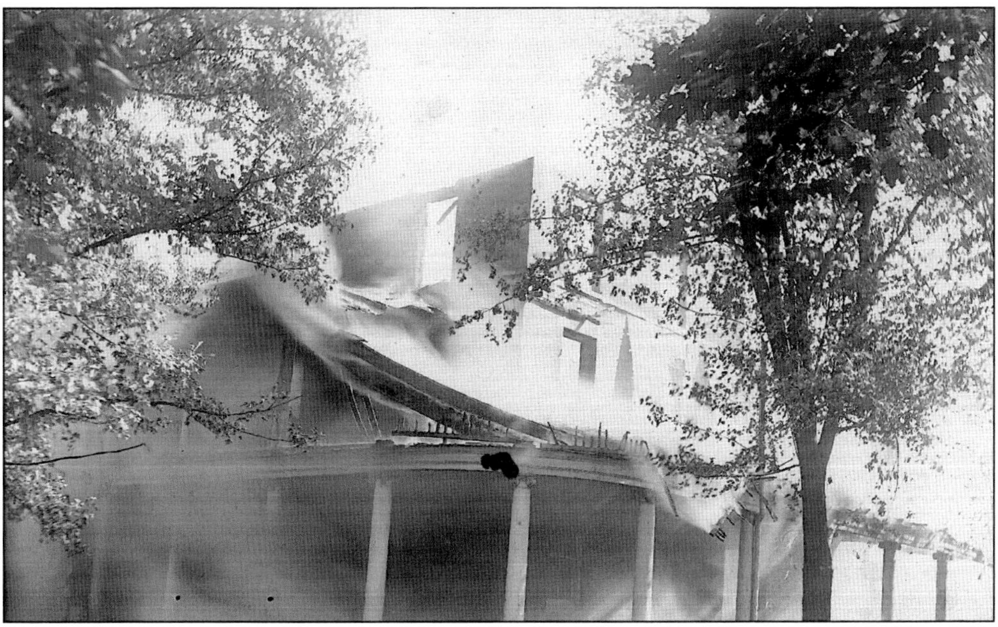

MILLERSBURG FEMALE COLLEGE FIRE IN 1907. Fire brought down another school in 1907 as the Millersburg Female College was destroyed in the same year that the Seventh Street School in Paris burned. The community of Millersburg rallied to help the school rebuild and a commodious new building was constructed. In a booklet published in 1927, an advertisement for the school's 77th session read, "The first two years of college work are given, thoroughness is especially stressed."

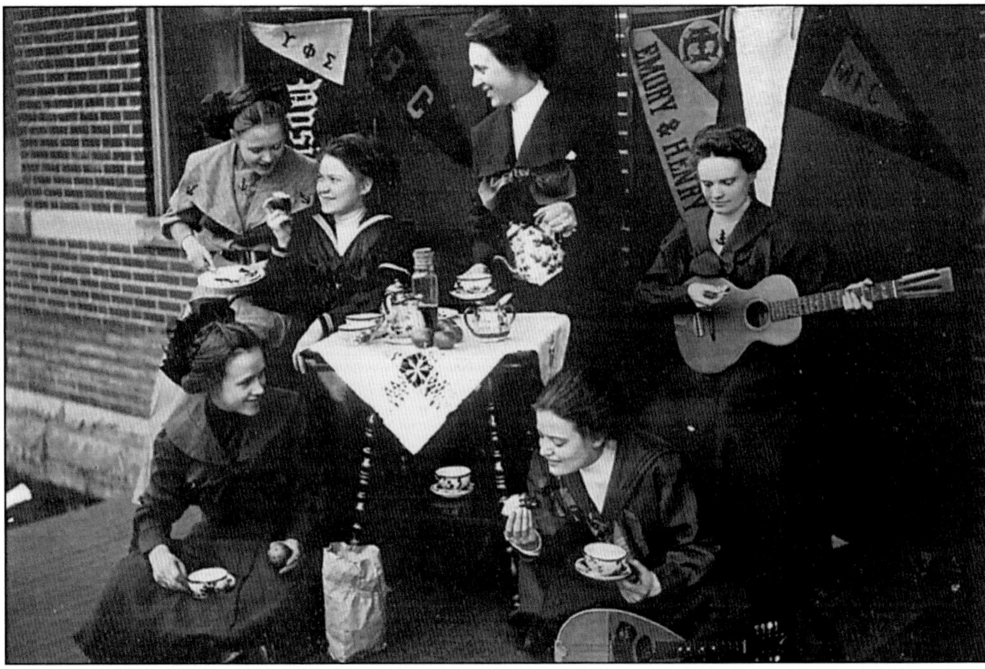

Eta Bita Pie, 1911. The Group's Motto at MFC was "I Will Either Find a Pie or Make One." Their flower was the pie plant and their song was listed as "Who stole that pie" in the 1911 MFC yearbook. The six girls in the group all had humorous titles listed after their name including "Imperial Distributor of the Flaky Product" and "Perpetual Masticator."

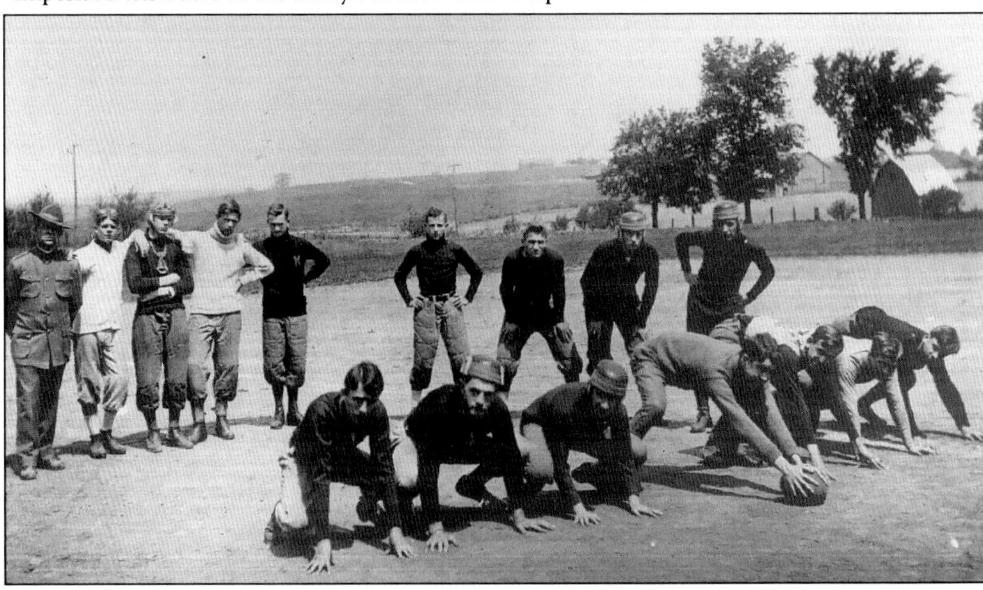

MMI Football Team, 1911. Team members and their hometowns are listed on this old photo: left end, Wiglesworth F., Cynthiana; left tackle, Gentry, Lexington; left guard, Blackburn, Georgetown; center, Land, Lexington; right guard, Freas, Boston, Mass.; right tackle, Harris; right end, Curry, Myers, Ky.; quarterback, Miller, Lexington; left half-back, Wiglesworth E., Cynthiana; full back, Jacoby, Lexington; right half back, Barton, Millersburg; subs: Snow, Tampa, Flaorida; Davis, Maysville; McClure and Cash, Winchester.

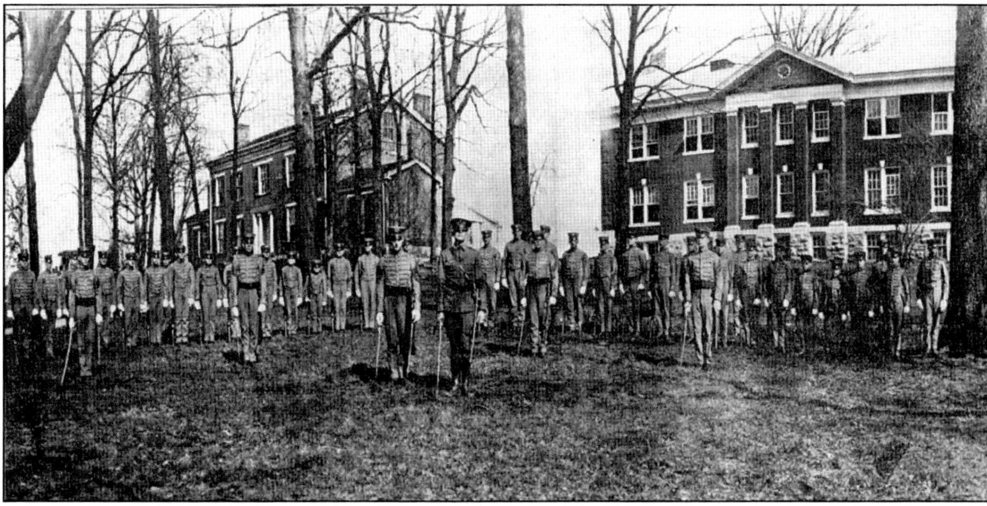

MILLERSBURG MILITARY INSTITUTE. Cadets are shown standing at attention in front of their school in 1927. MMI school authorities purchased the Allen homestead in 1921 after the former MMI campus was sold by Colonel Best to the Bourbon County school system. By 1927, there were "four modern buildings, athletic grounds, and equipment to accommodate 75 boarding pupils," according to a contemporary article.

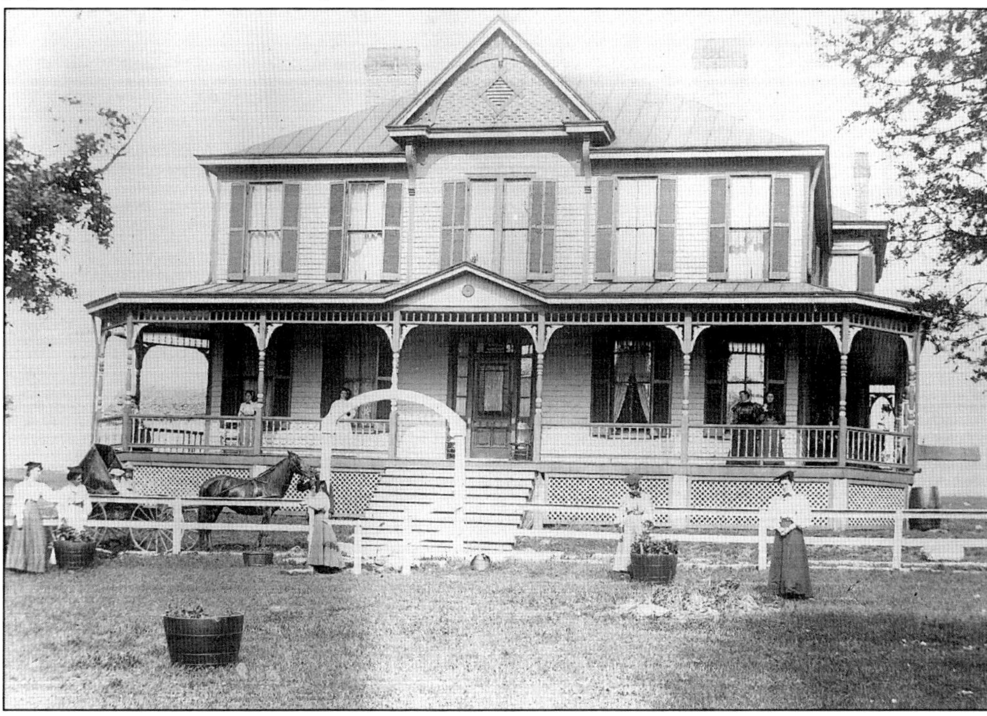

NEW KENTUCKY CLASSICAL BUSINESS COLLEGE BUILDING. Constructed in 1890, this building replaced the original Kentucky Classical Business College which burned in 1889. Located in North Middletown, KCBC was the only co-educational, upper level school in the county and continued in operation until 1920, when it was converted to an independent graded school. In 1926 it was deeded to the county and in 1927 it was used as a teacherage. It was demolished in 1967 due to its rundown condition.

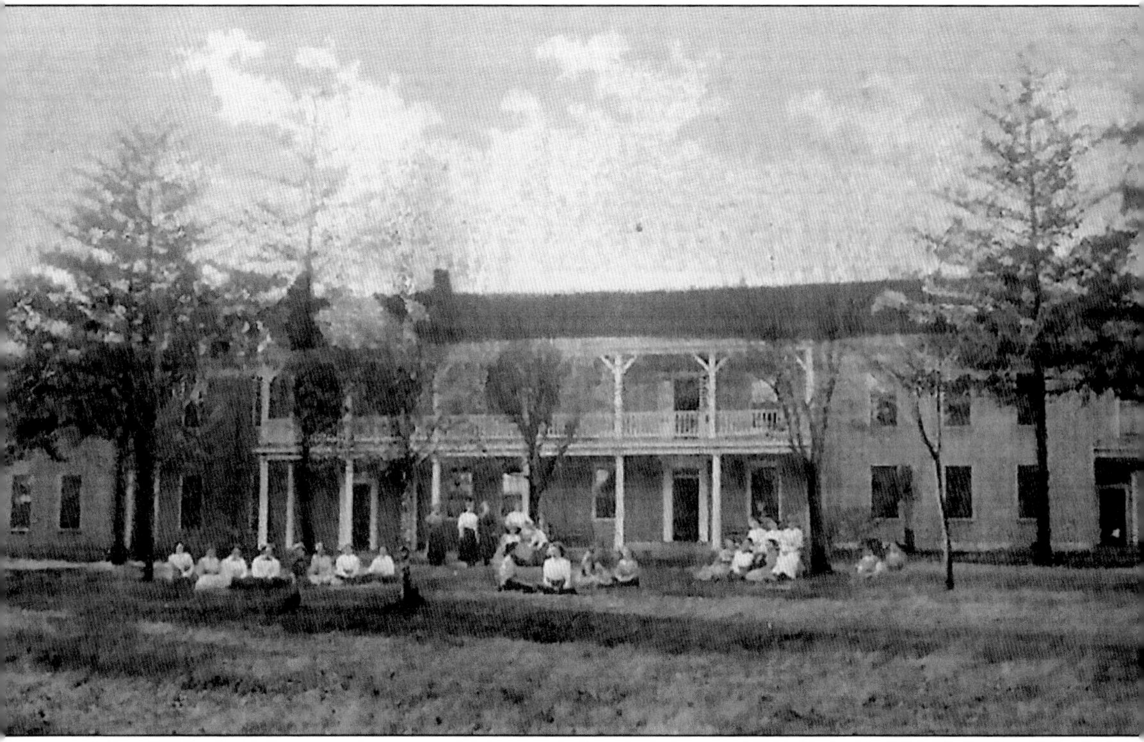

Bourbon Female College. The school was located in a building originally used as a house, then as a convent school. Around the turn of the century, Professor and Mrs. M.G. Thompson purchased this rambling structure on a large piece of wooded ground and opened the Bourbon Female College. The school was very successful, attracting up to 90 young women per term. After Professor Thompson died in 1914, his widow merged the school with Hamilton College in Lexington.

Five

Paris City Scenes

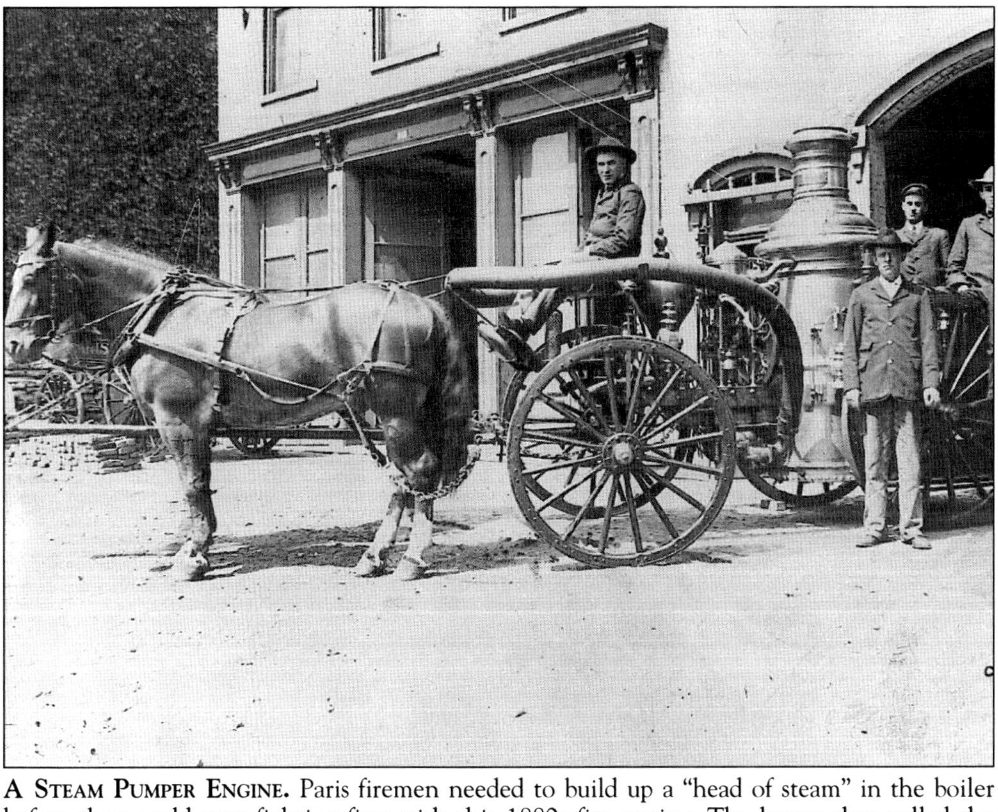

A Steam Pumper Engine. Paris firemen needed to build up a "head of steam" in the boiler before they could start fighting fires with this 1880s fire engine. The horses that pulled the equipment were stabled in the basement of the fire station on Courthouse Square, but two horses were always kept upstairs to be ready quickly. Paris had early fire fighting equipment by 1810 but the first formally trained fire company was not formed until 1874 after the disastrous courthouse fire.

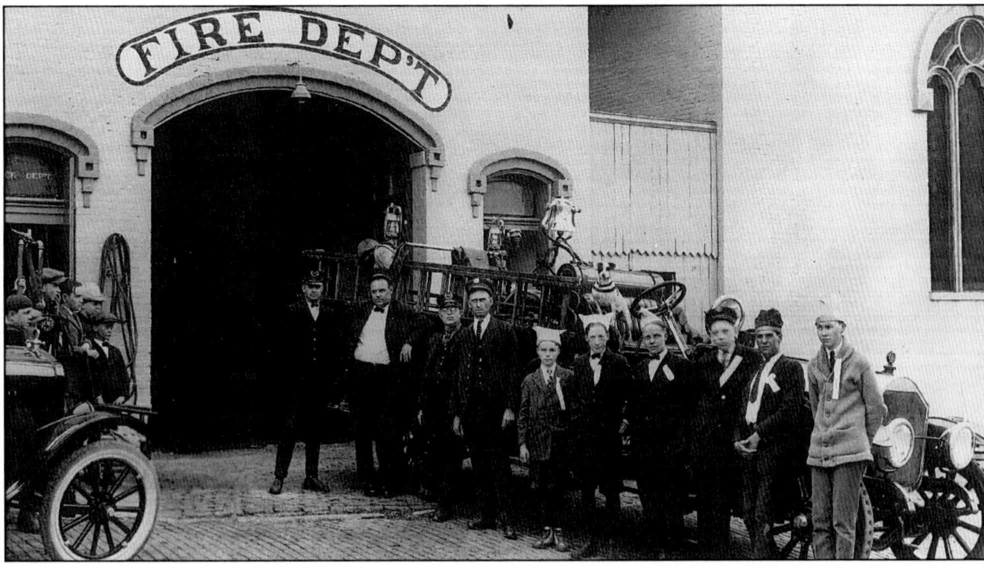

Birthday Party With One of Paris's First "Horseless" Fire Engines. The Paris Fire Department became motorized in 1915 with the purchase of a Gran-Berstine pumper truck and this American LaFrance hose and chemical truck. The dog in the driver's seat is a traditional mascot, but the department also about this time had a South American monkey, given to them by John Lair. From the looks of the boys' hats, the firehouse was a good place for a birthday party.

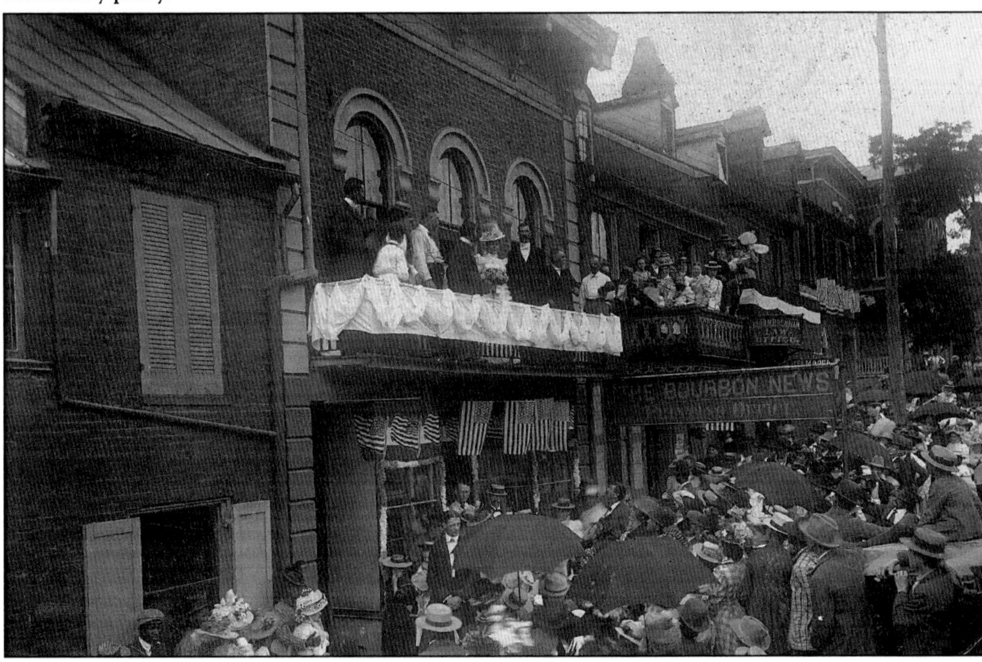

Public Wedding on Ardery Place. The public wedding promised in the banner in the opening picture of Chapter One was held on the wrought iron balcony of the *Bourbon News* in August of 1899. Weddings were considered highly entertaining in those days when "womanless weddings" and nuptials on vaudeville stages were not uncommon. One hopes that all the spectators brought the happy couple appropriate gifts.

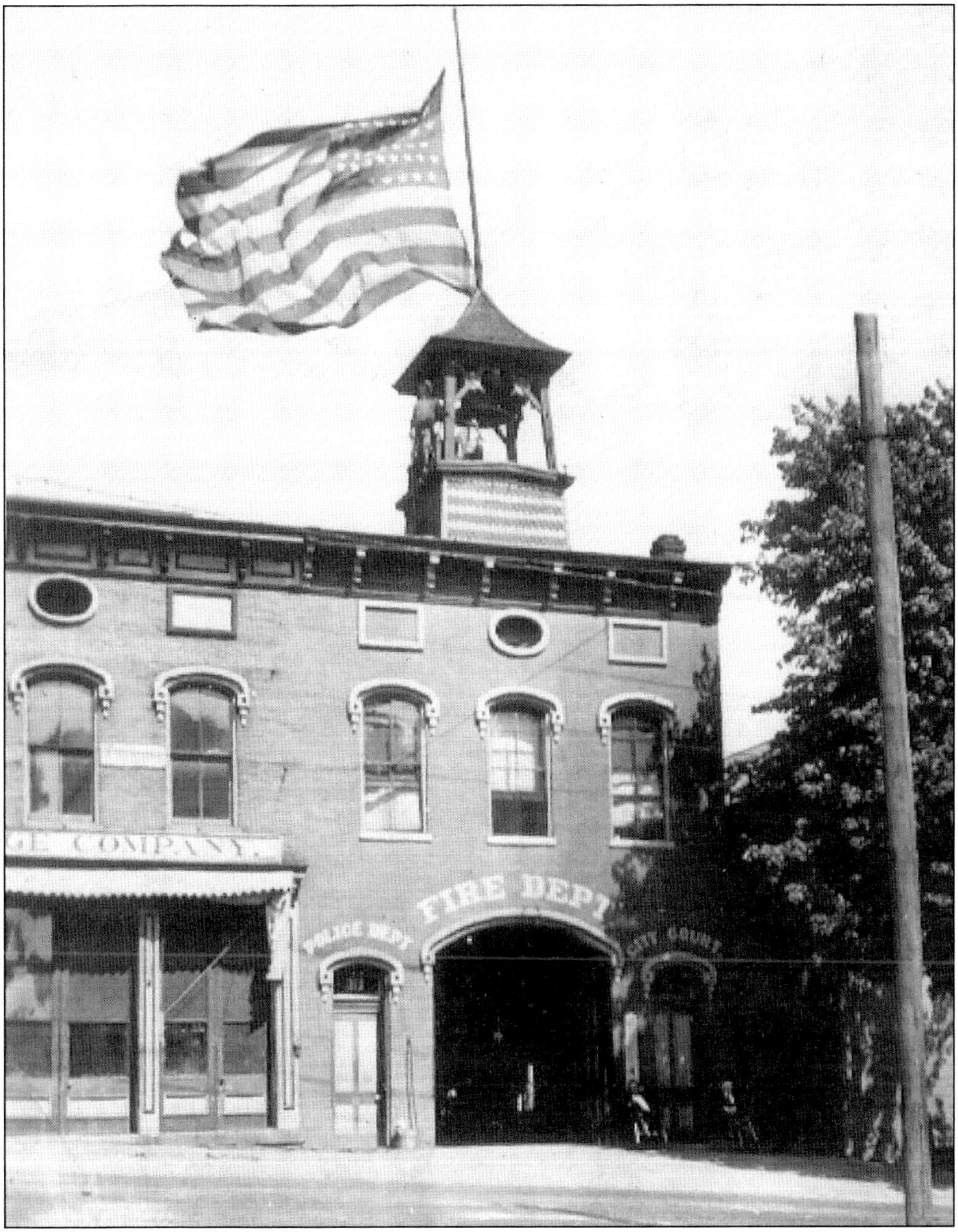

Fire Department Waves "Old Glory." A fire engine of some type has been housed in this building since it was built in 1875, making it one of the oldest fire stations in continuous use in the state. Originally known as the Rescue Fire Company, an all-volunteer group organized on March 16, 1874, the Paris Fire Department was later established in 1889. City Hall and the police department were still housed on the second floor when this photo was taken in the 1890s. The building adjoining it on the left was built as the Holliday & Huddleston Carriage Factory and served as that and an automobile dealership until a fire in 1927 when it was rebuilt as an extension of the fire station. The giant 45-star flag flying from the fire bell tower is estimated to be at least 16 feet by 30 feet in size.

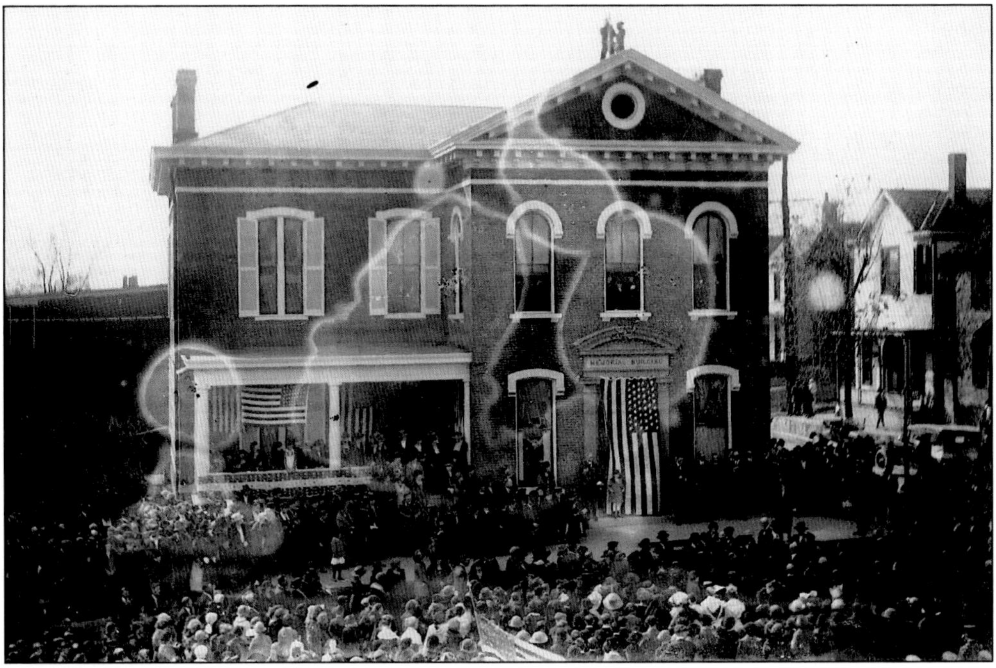

Memorial Building Dedication. Despite the damage to the glass negative that holds this image, one can see that many local residents turned out to see the dedication of the Memorial Building in 1922 to the memory of the Bourbon Countians who died in World War I. The building was built in 1854 to house the Deposit Bank. After the bank moved to the corner of Fourth and Main in 1884, the building became a private residence.

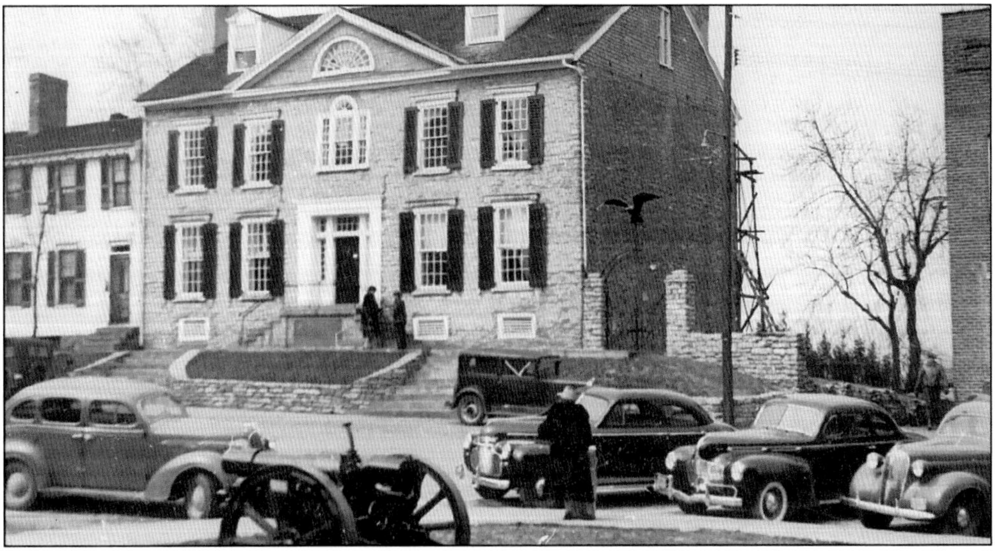

Duncan Tavern Renewed. By 1940 Duncan Tavern, which was built in 1788, had been renovated by the Daughters of the American Revolution (DAR) and its fine limestone facade had been renewed. The adjoining home of Major Duncan's widow had not yet acquired its stone facing when this photo was taken. When the World War I cannon seen in this photo disappeared from the courthouse lawn is not clear, but it could have been a victim of a World War II scrap metal drive.

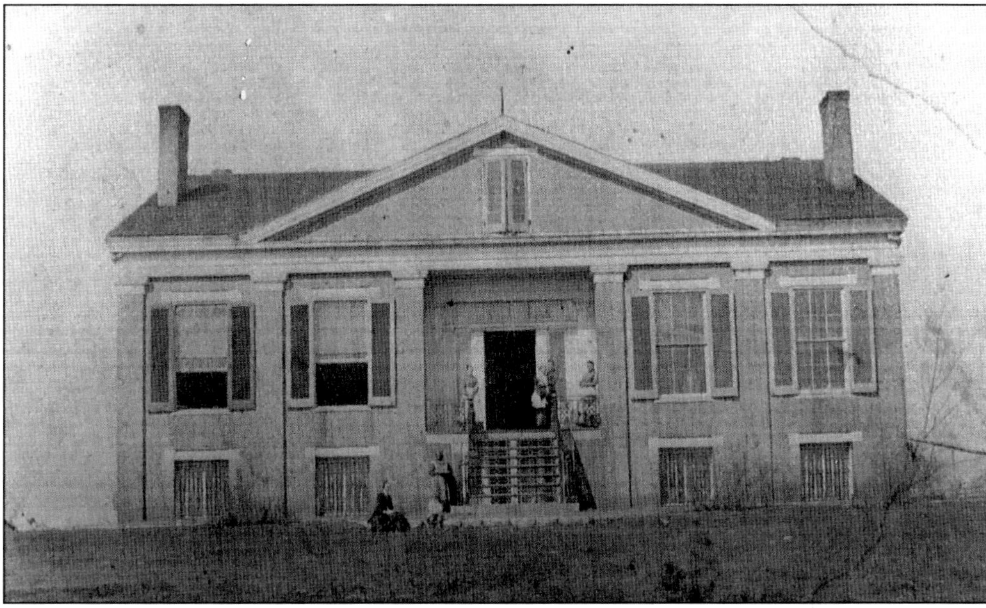

BLEAK HOUSE. The Benedict Beau Marsh home, called "Bleak House," was built about 1845, making this image one of the oldest in this book. Marsh was a successful jeweler and silversmith who was born in 1804. Instead of having two full stories above a basement, this dwelling had a single tall story and attic rooms over a raised "English basement." It was located where the old TB hospital still stands.

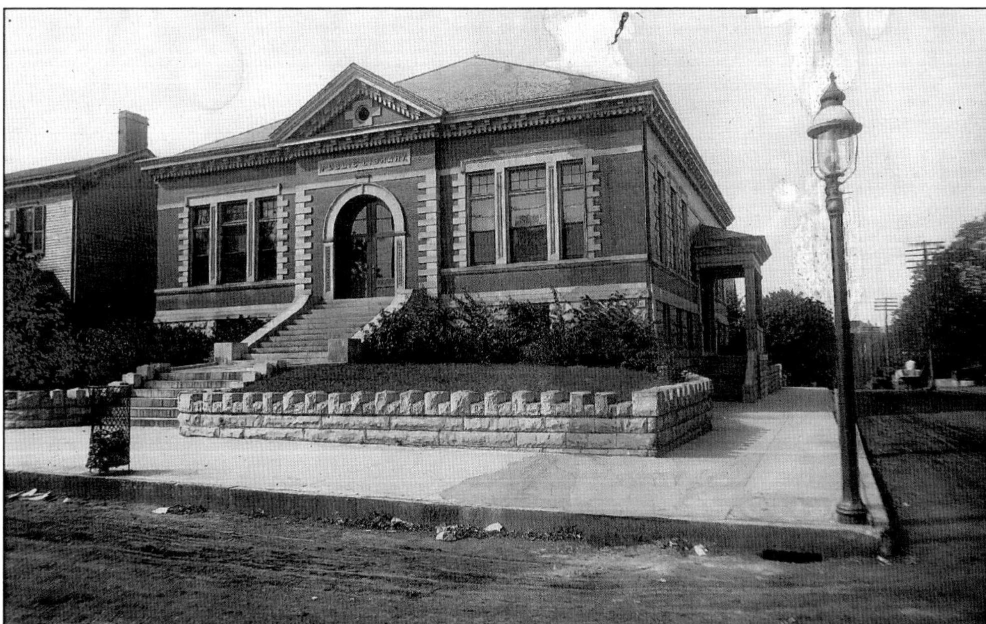

PARIS PUBLIC LIBRARY. Built in 1904, the library at the corner of Seventh and High Streets was partly financed with a $12,000 grant from philanthropist Andrew Carnegie. The first major work in Bourbon County of Paris architect Edwin Stammer, the library was completed at a cost of $23,000. This photo, like several others in this book, was taken to be used to produce a handcolored and retouched post card for Clarke & Co. Pharmacists.

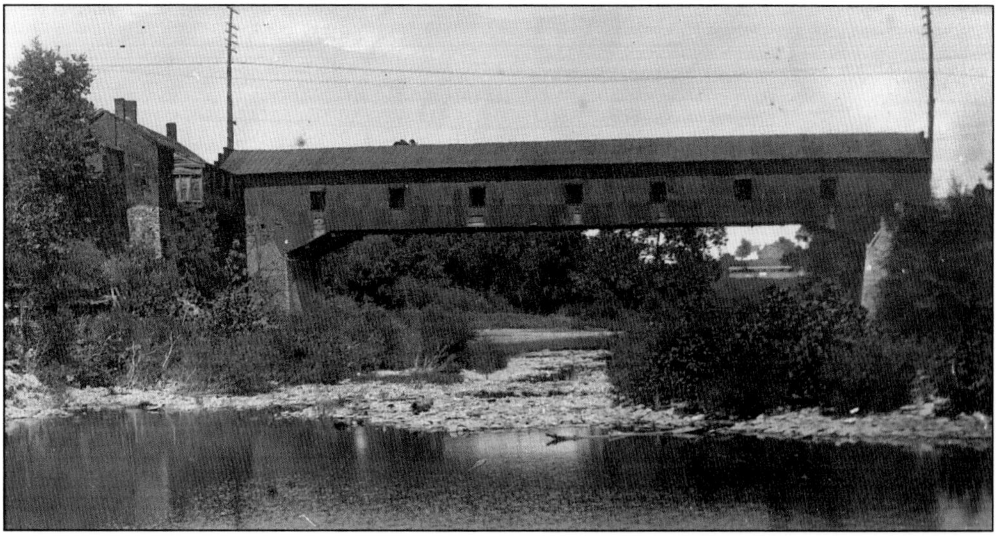

OLD COTTONTOWN BRIDGE. This is another view of the covered bridge that appears on page four of this book. Taken from upstream on Stoner Creek this photo shows the "double-barreled" Cottontown Bridge in the early part of the 20th century. Built in 1833, it served Bourbon Countians for 100 years until it was torn down in 1933 to make room for a concrete bridge better able to handle modern cars and trucks.

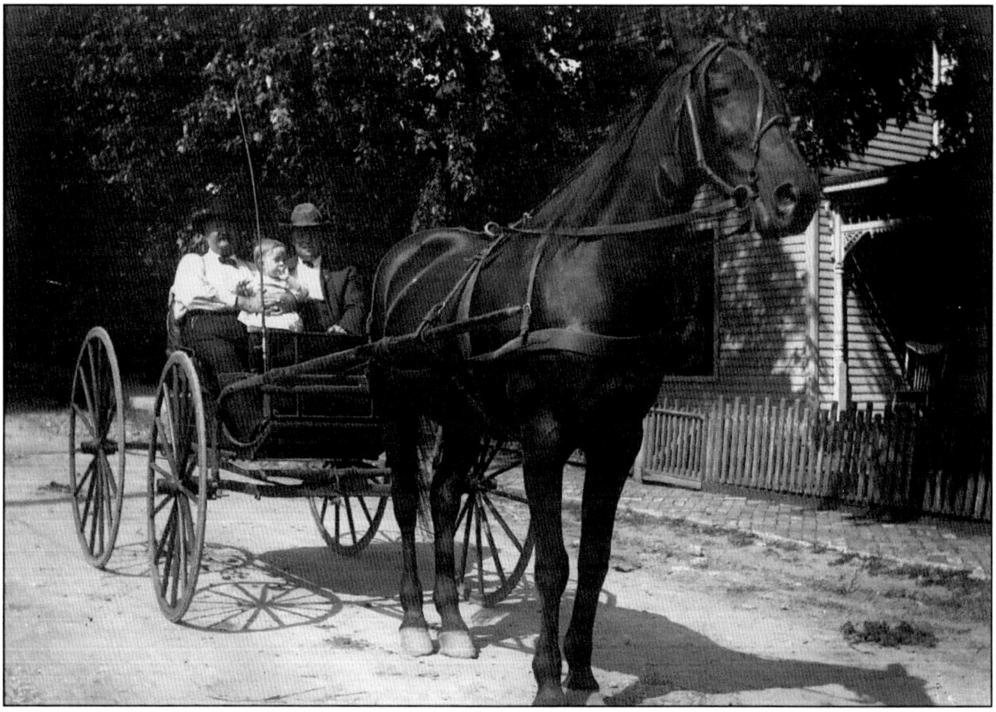

THREE GENERATIONS OF COUNTY CLERKS. This photo, taken in 1905 on Mt. Airy Avenue, shows three generations of the Paton family. The trio held the elected position of Bourbon County Clerk for a total of 66 years. Ed D. Patton (in black hat on left) served from 1895 to 1906; Pearce Paton (on right) served 1906 to 1942; and little Ed Drane Paton (in his grandfather's lap) would serve from 1948 to 1967. The horse is identified as "Queen."

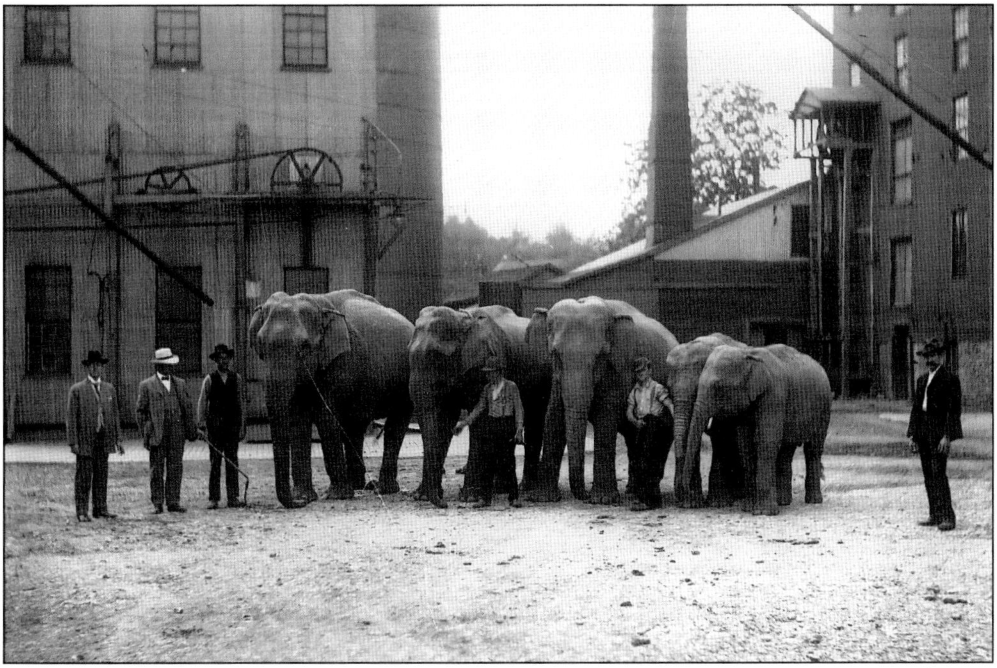

CIRCUS IN TOWN? We can't tell too much about this photo other than that it was taken at the turn of the century at a local mill. One would imagine that the circus was in town or that someone was trying to develop a string of Bourbon County racing elephants. One local man recalled feeding elephants to get free tickets to a circus and then being so sick from hay fever that he couldn't use them.

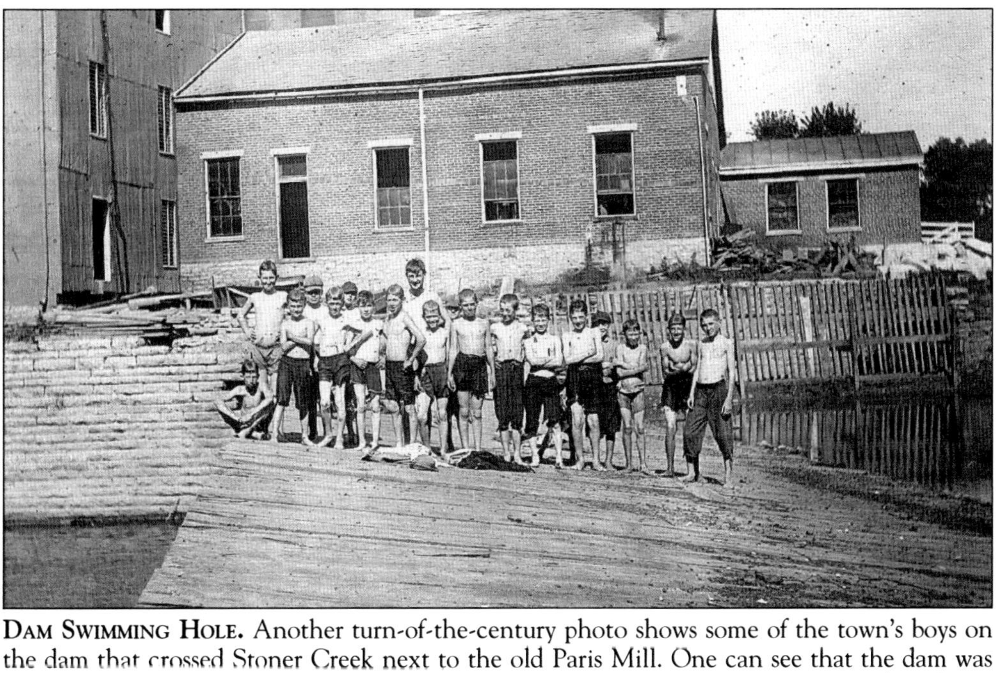

DAM SWIMMING HOLE. Another turn-of-the-century photo shows some of the town's boys on the dam that crossed Stoner Creek next to the old Paris Mill. One can see that the dam was topped with planks and was possibly used as another way of crossing the creek. Another photo, probably taken moments after this one, shows the boys fearlessly leaping into the water.

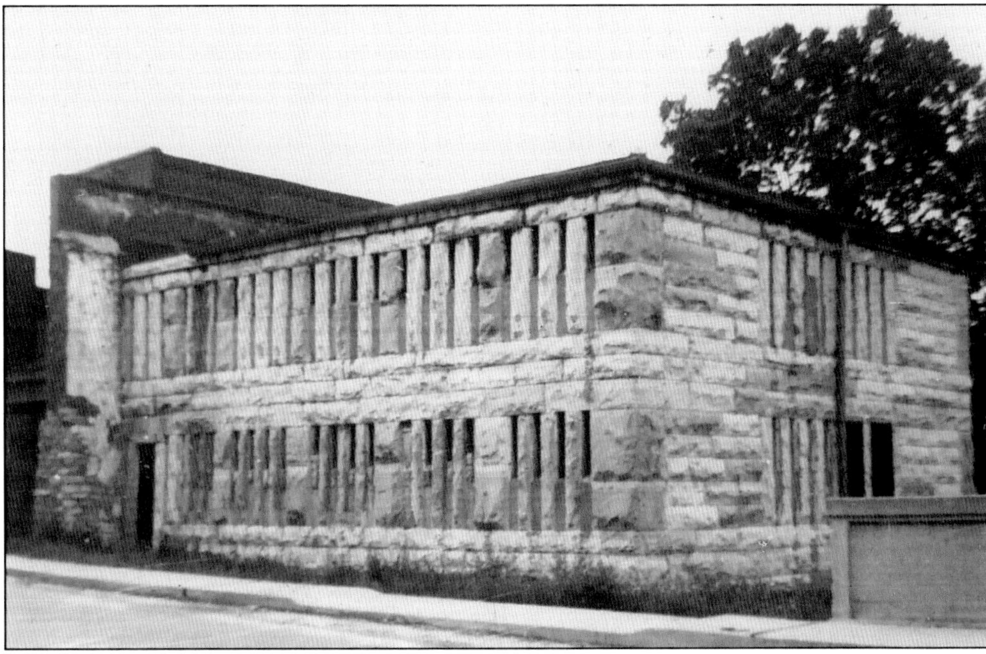

Old Jail was Real Punishment. In 1878, Bourbon County built this jail on the courthouse side of Stoner Creek by the Cottontown Bridge at a cost of $15,000. Constructed of stone with most of the cells on the lower levels—there is another floor below the grade seen here—it was described as "a real dungeon of a place." It was used until 1939 when it was replaced by a new jail on Courthouse Square.

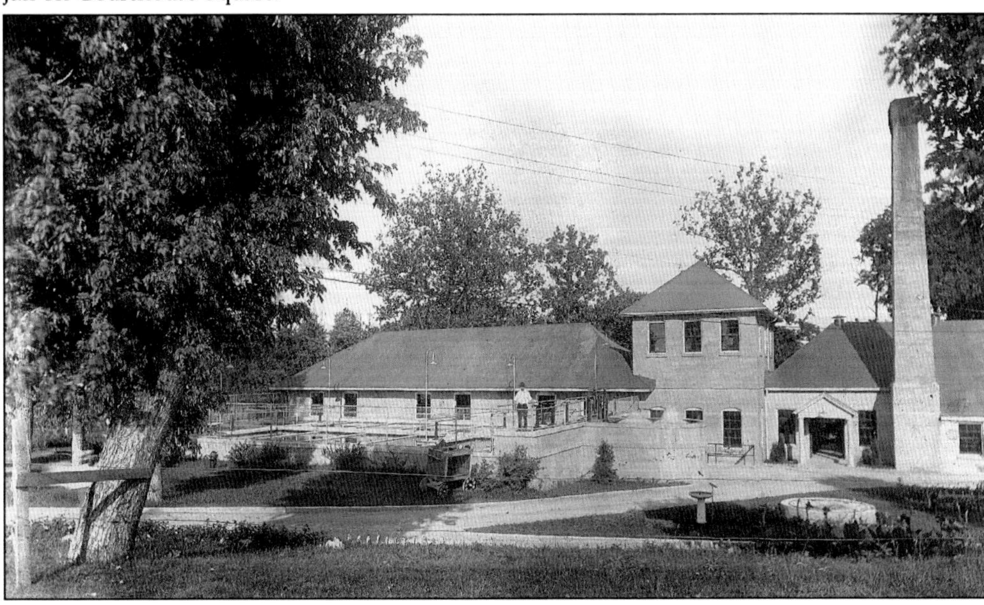

Municipal Light & Water Plant in 1930s. Up until 1931, the Paris Water Company was a private concern. That year the city bought the company for $168,000 and renovated and updated the buildings and equipment. The oldest buildings at that location were built in 1890. In 1933 the city built the Light Plant facility next to the water works. Pictured is Robert "Bob" Watson, who was in charge of the water plant.

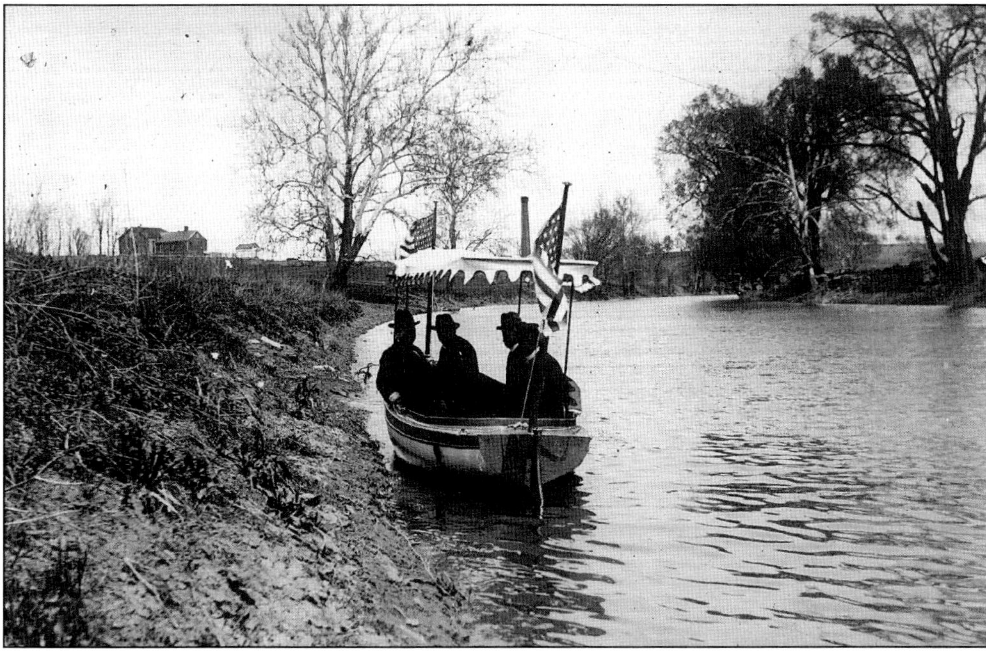

THE PARIS NAVY ON STONER CREEK? The four men in the boat are identified on the back of the picture as "Elmer Foote, Mr. Fothergill, 'Scrub' Webb, Bob Porter." Why is the boat decked out with flags, fore, and aft? Why are the men so dressed up in suits and hats? Your guess is as good as ours.

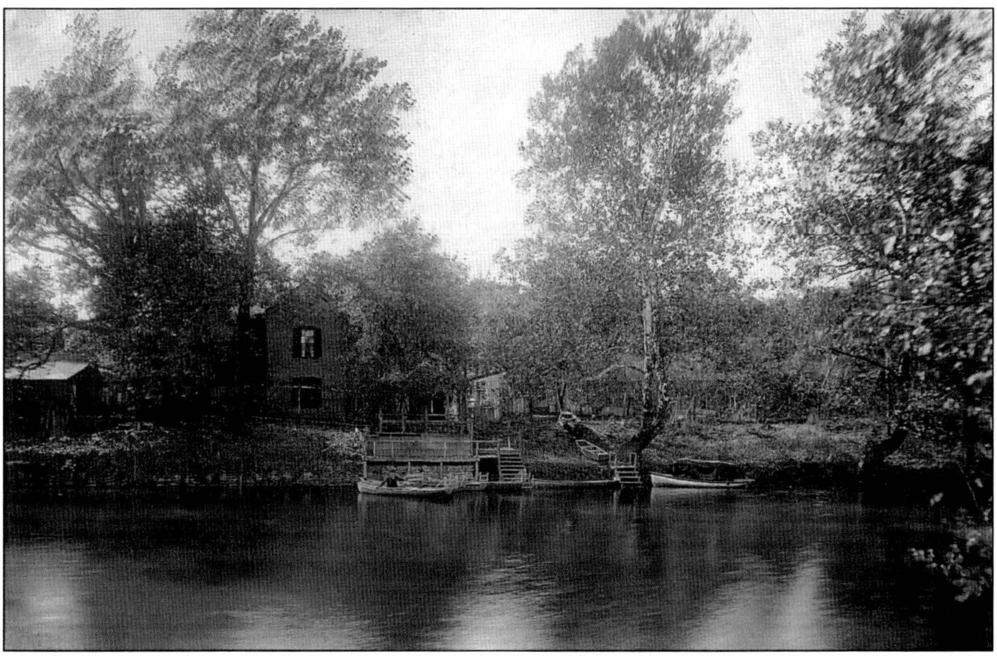

FOOTE'S LANDING ON STONER CREEK. The importance of Stoner Creek as the county's major watercourse and source of plentiful fresh water for the city of Paris cannot be over stated. It remains an almost "hidden corner" of our area and the people, who have homes along it or enjoy the bountiful fishing on it, probably don't mind that at all.

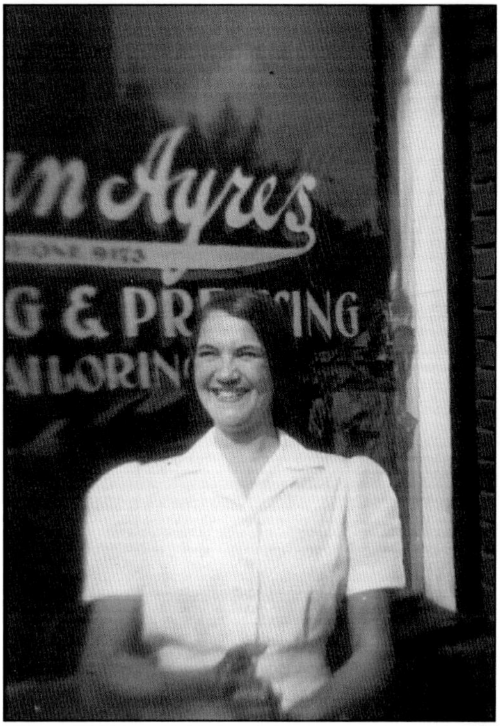

SUCCESSFUL LAUNDRY AND TAILORING BUSINESS ON EIGHTH STREET. Logan Ayres and his wife Laura Ayres (seen here in the late 1930s) ran one of the successful African-American businesses found on Eighth Street at this time. Another popular business nearby was Webster's Restaurant, reportedly a favorite breakfast spot for both blacks and whites.

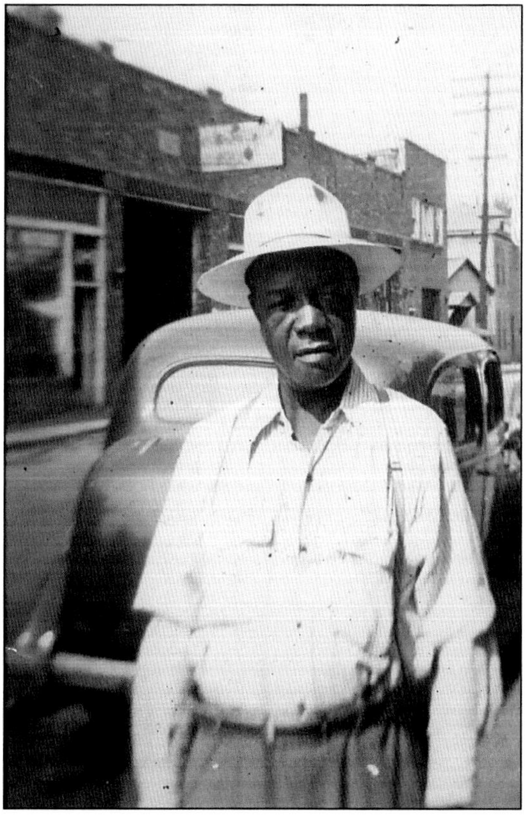

WELL-KNOWN PARIS BARBER. Bill Brown was a popular barber who worked at a number of shops around town, including Hitch's Barber Shop located on the east side of the 700 block of Main Street in the 1930s.

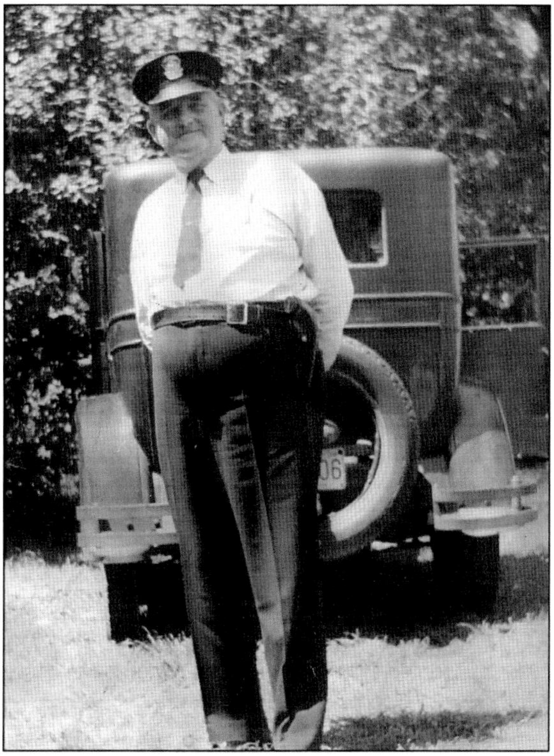

NIGHT POLICE CHIEF. Officer John Patrick Maher served as Paris "Night Police Chief" from the 1930s until 1947 when he died. A life-long Paris resident, he was born to Irish immigrant parents in 1876. He was a familiar figure in the evenings on Main Street, checking locks and directing traffic when the theaters let out.

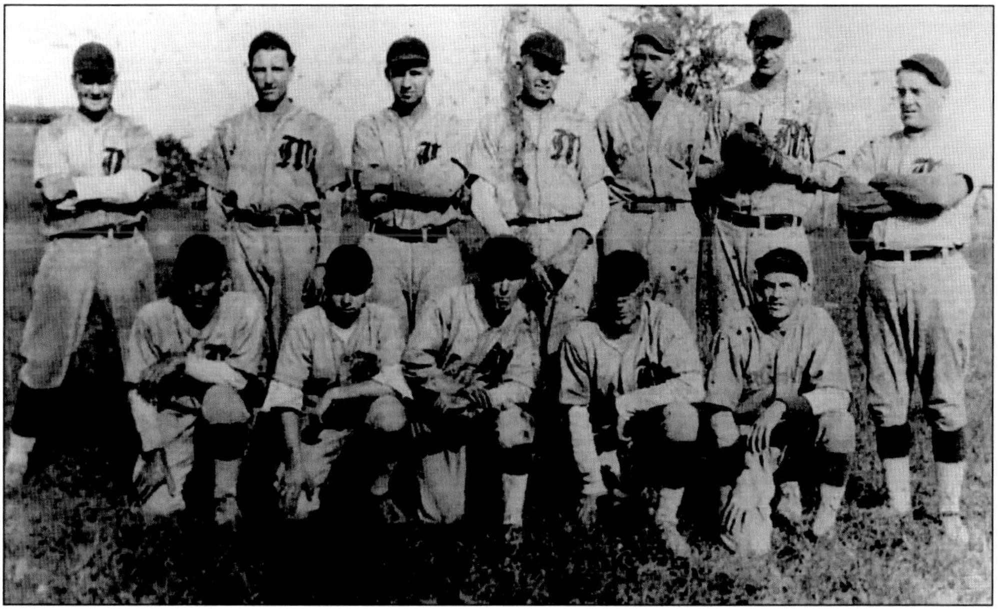

PARIS MERCHANTS BASEBALL TEAM. Baseball was an important summer pastime in Bourbon County between 1920 and 1935. This Paris semi-pro team was called the Merchants and they played their home games at Hancock Field on the Winchester Road. Shown from left to right are (front row) Russell Horton, Shirel Wills, "Frosty" Carrick, Earl Lawhorn, and William Lytle; (back row) Coach "Chan" Thompson, Theodore Butler, Harry Lancaster, "Stiffy" Burnett, Jack Shout, John Williams, and Coach "Bud" Lancaster.

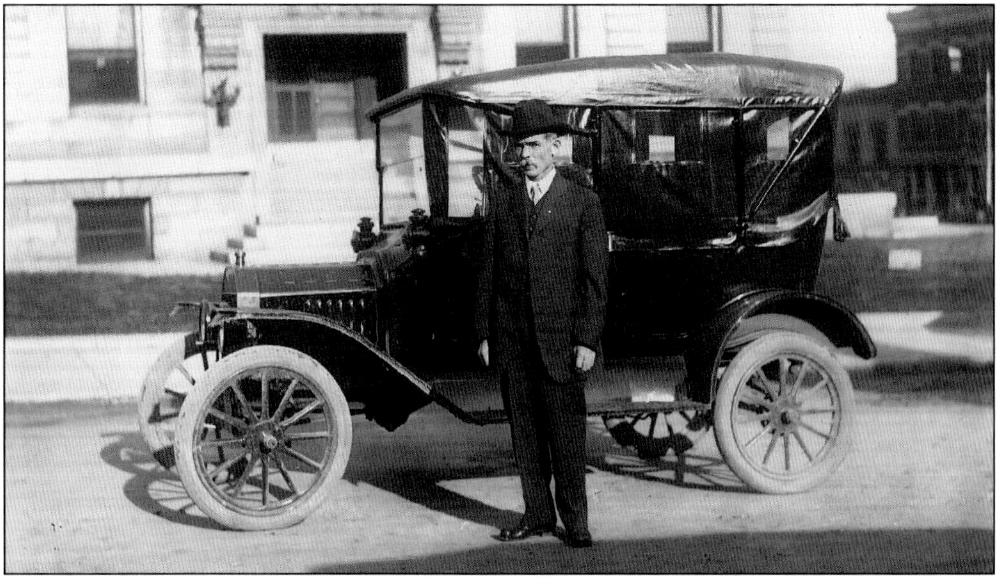

MANUFACTURER OF THE FAMOUS "STONER" CIGAR. Thomas Haynie, owner of the Thos. Haynie Cigar Manufactory, is shown with his new Model T Ford in front of the side entrance to the courthouse. The Stoner cigar was described in a contemporary newspaper supplement as "one of the best five-cent cigars on the market." The cigar manufacturing facility was located on Main Street across from the courthouse.

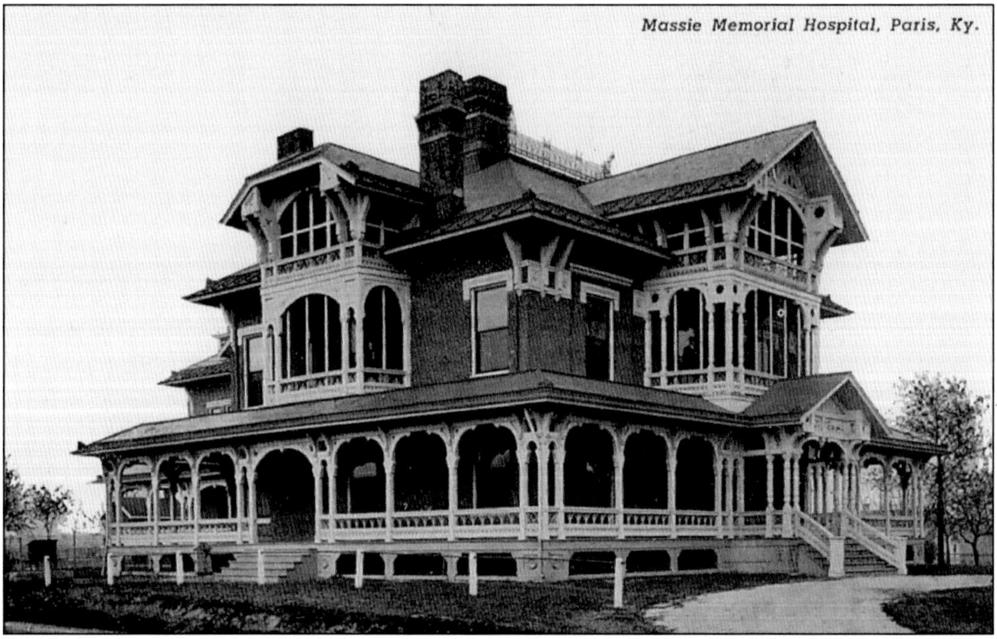

MASSIE MEMORIAL HOSPITAL. Opened in 1913, this hospital served the people of Bourbon County until a new hospital on High Street opened in 1952. Named in memory of Mrs. W. Massie who willed the money to buy the home of Mrs. George White, the rambling 1880s home on Fithian Avenue near Garrard Park that was converted into the hospital. The hospital was demolished shortly after it was closed; a separate building that was used as nurses' home is still standing.

PARIS LINEMAN ON FOURTH STREET. This photograph, like others in this book, is from a glass negative made at the turn of the century. It shows a lineman at the top of a newly installed pole, possibly installing the wires connecting a fire alarm system which was supposed to alert the populace and the fire department to the densely built town's most dreaded occurrence. We think it gives a good "side street view" of the time.

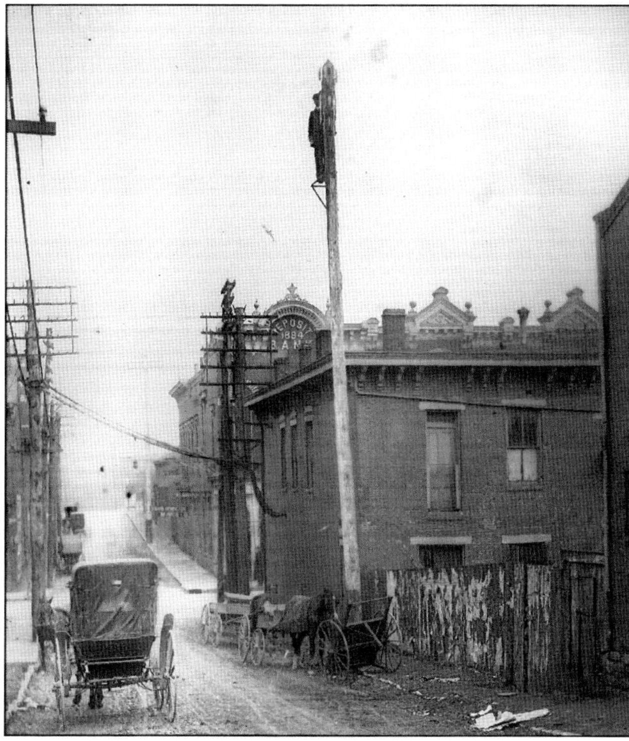

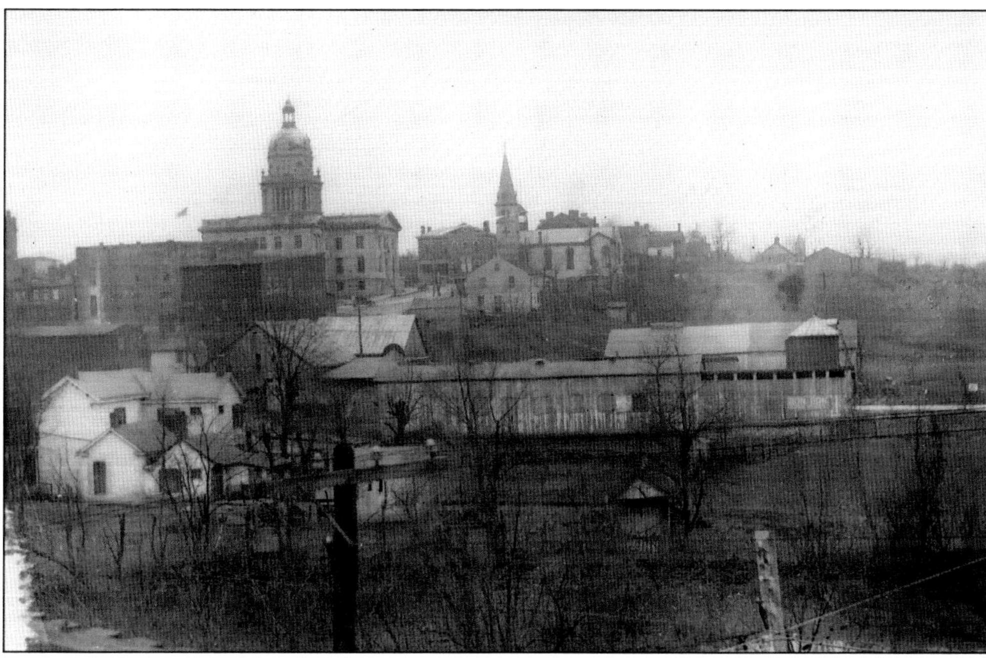

PARIS SCENE VIEWED FROM RAILROAD TRESTLE. The photographer set up his large bulky camera on the L&N Railroad trestle (as it crosses Houston Creek north of downtown) about 1905 to get this picture. Besides the familiar form of the new courthouse and the spire of St. Peter's Church, we can see the large livery and lumber sheds on Second Street and Sandy Bottom where Hopewell Springs is located.

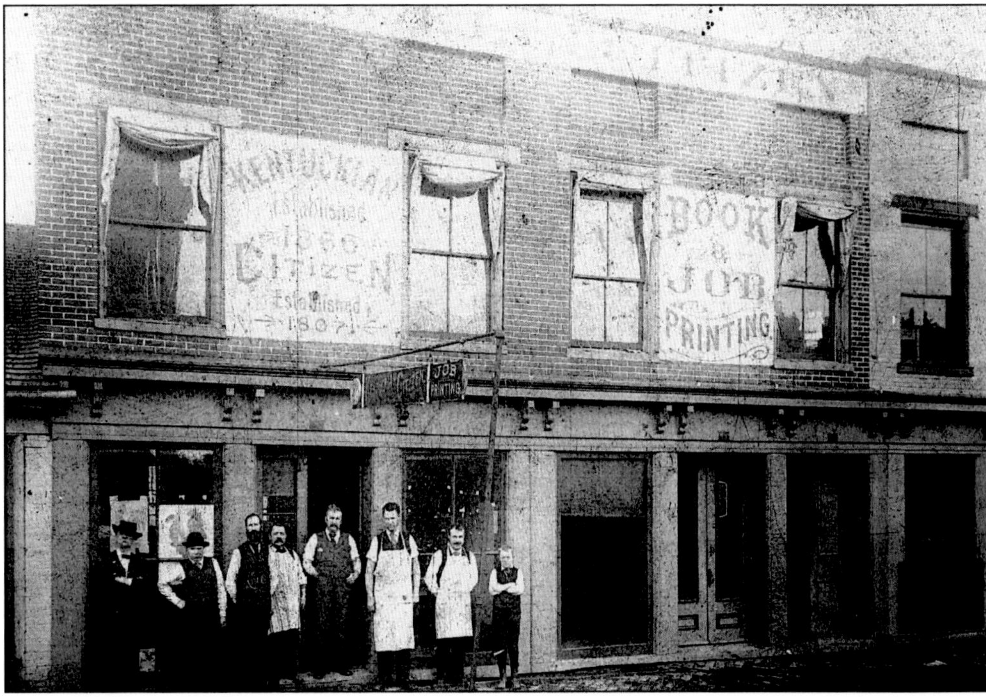

PARIS *CITIZEN*—"OLDEST CONTINUALLY PUBLISHED NEWSPAPER IN AMERICA." The first paper published in Paris was the *Kentucky Herald*, established in a log cabin on High Street in 1797 by Daniel Bradford. The *Herald* closed after a little more than a year and Paris was without a newspaper until 1807 when Joel R. Lyle opened the *Western Citizen*. This picture shows the staff of the *Kentuckian-Citizen* in front of the Bank Row office some time in the 1890s.

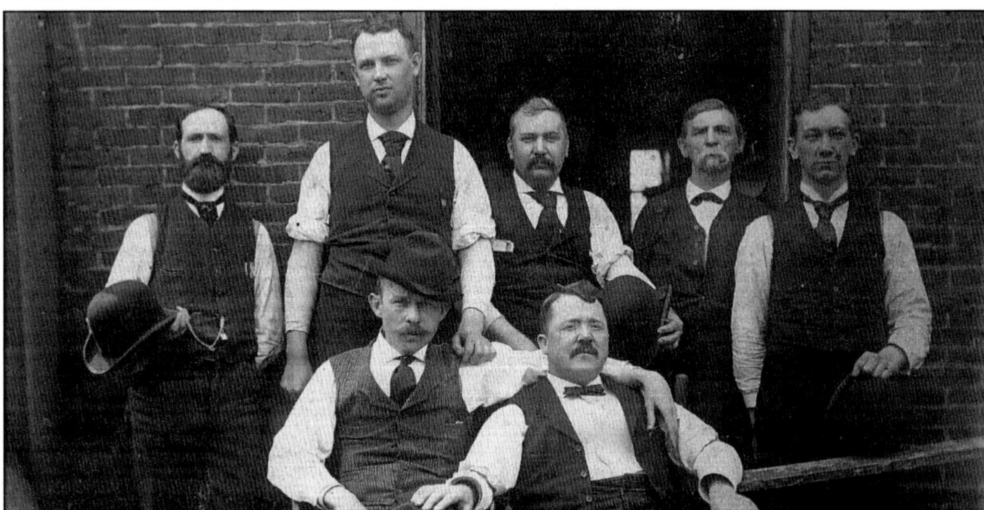

PARIS NEWSPAPERMEN AT THE *KENTUCKIAN-CITIZEN*. Paris was long a "hot bed" of newspaper activity. At one time during the 19th century, there were four newspapers being published in town. This picture from about 1890 identifies seven of the *Kentuckian Citizen's* journalists, some of whom would later work at other papers. Standing from left to right are Charles W. Fothergill; Hopson Lowry; William Remington, editor; J.W. Hile; Frank Remington; (seated) Ed Hill and Charles W. "Scrub" Webb.

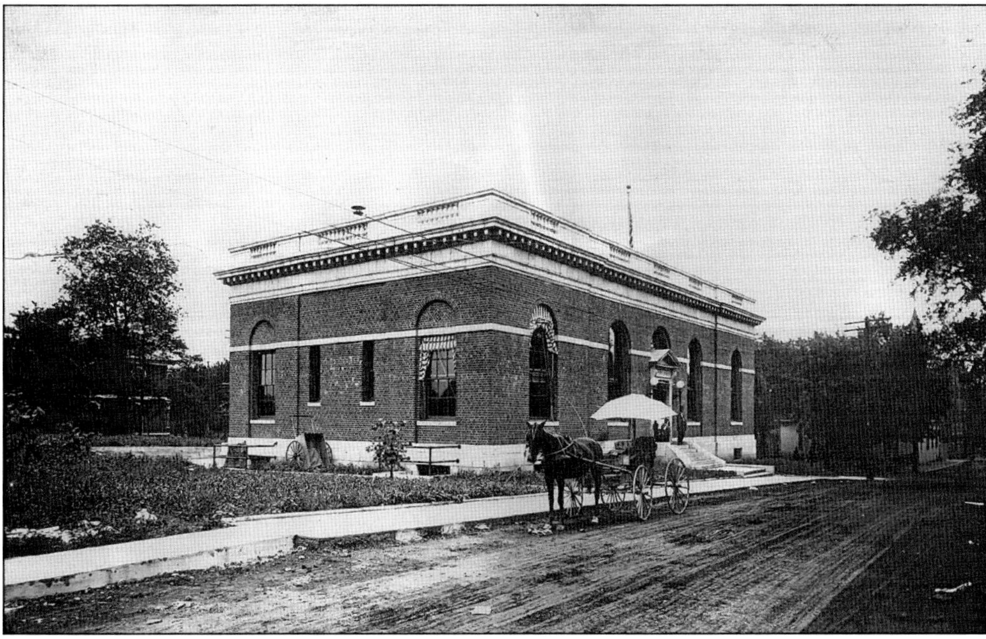

POST OFFICE/CITY HALL/HOPEWELL MUSEUM. This handsome Beaux-arts style post office building at 800 Pleasant Street is seen in a 1910 photo taken shortly after the building was completed. The photo was taken from the Eighth Street side of the building. The building served as the town's post office until 1967 when the City of Paris bought it to use as the Municipal Building. In 1996 the city gave the property to the Hopewell Museum.

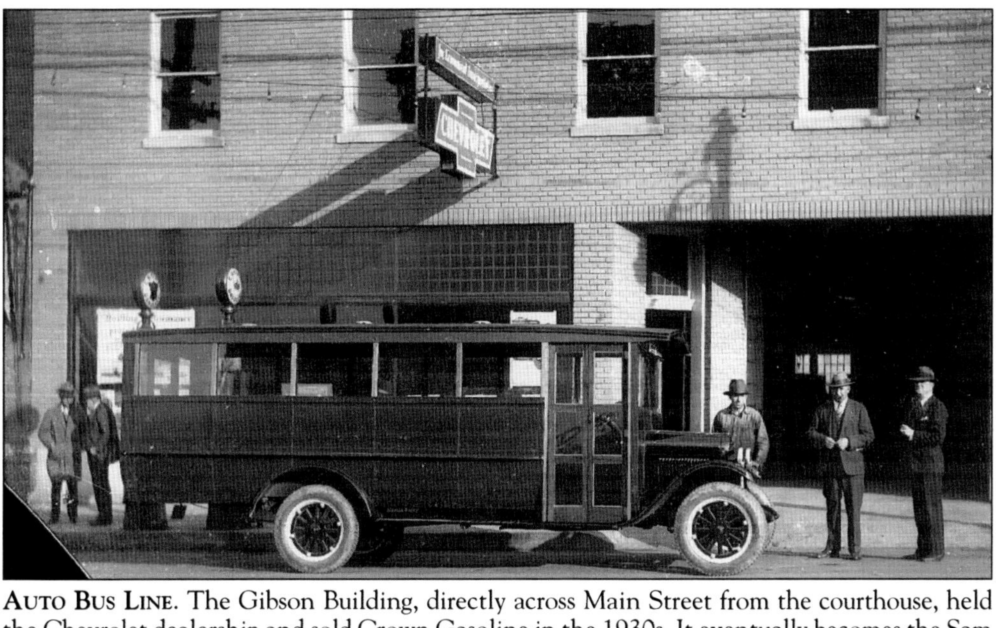

AUTO BUS LINE. The Gibson Building, directly across Main Street from the courthouse, held the Chevrolet dealership and sold Crown Gasoline in the 1930s. It eventually becomes the Sam Cummins garage selling all types of General Motors automobiles until 2000 when it was torn down to make room for the new courthouse annex. In the 1930s, it was also a stop for the Auto Bus Line that ran between Millersburg and Paris.

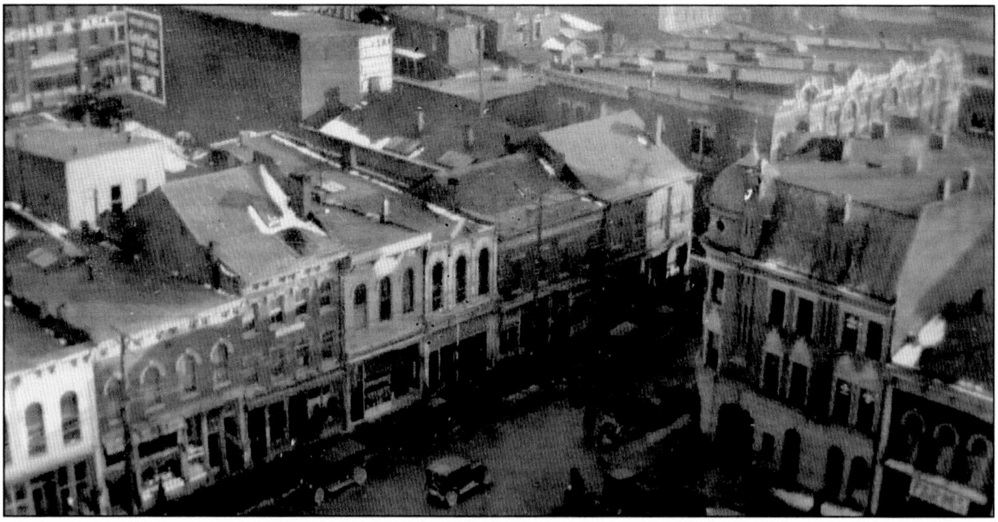

View from Courthouse Dome. The photographer who took this picture of downtown Paris one cold, wintry day in the 1920s saw many more buildings and much more activity than one would see today. The image isn't very sharp, but we felt it important to show how dense the downtown area was back then. The intersection at the bottom of the picture is of Main Street and Ardery Place, the site of so many of the images in this book.

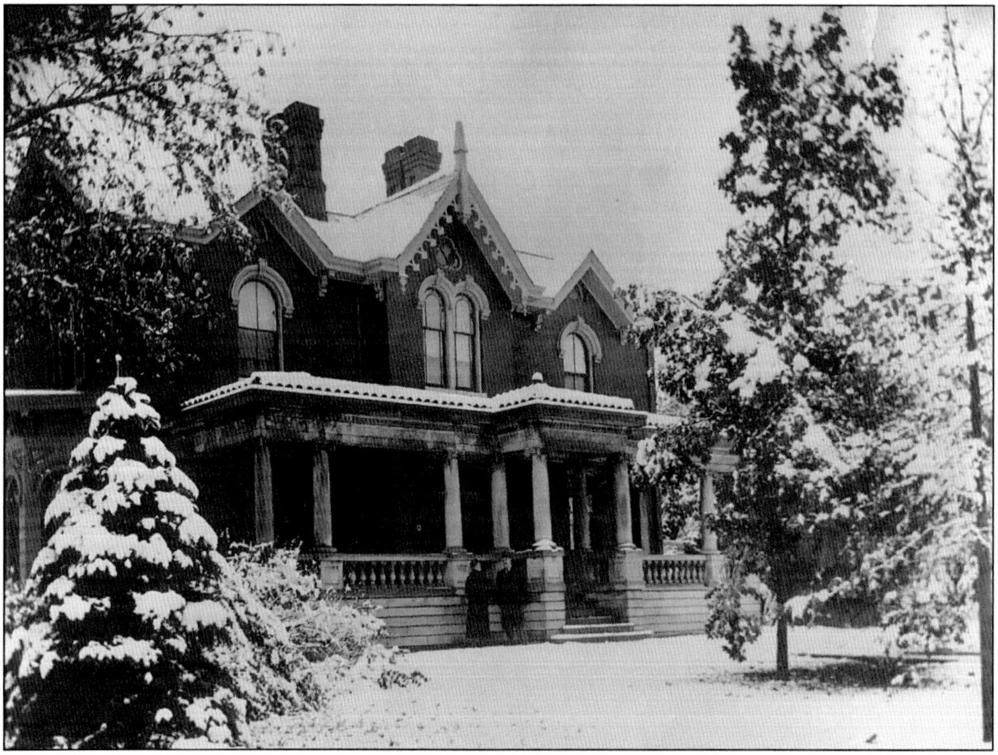

Bell Home Site of New Hospital. Mr. and Mrs. Duncan Bell are seen outside their lovely High Street home with the stone porch in this winter scene in 1939. This home, which sat on a large plot of land between Fifth and Sixth Streets, was torn down when the Bells donated the property as a site for the new Bourbon General Hospital in 1947.

Six

CHURCHES AND RELIGION

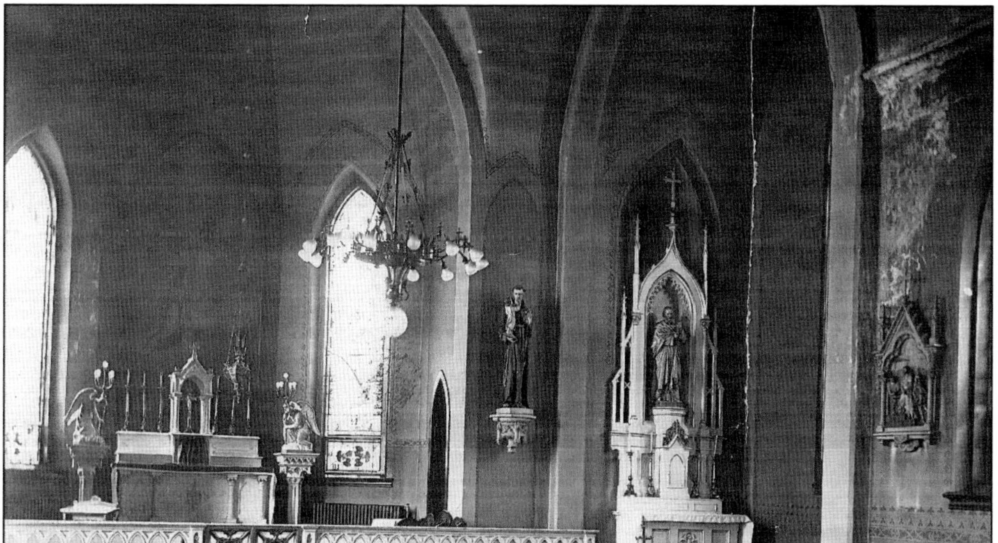

CATHOLIC CHURCH OF THE ANNUNCIATION, DEDICATED 1861. The Roman Catholic Church in Paris traces its roots to before 1855 when the land for the present church on South Main Street was deeded to the diocese. This picture of the interior is probably from 1930 or so after the marble altar was installed in 1925. Catholic education has its beginning in Paris as early as 1869 with the establishment of St. Charles Academy and continues today with St. Mary's School. Mount Olivet Catholic Cemetery, next to the Paris Cemetery, was established in 1864.

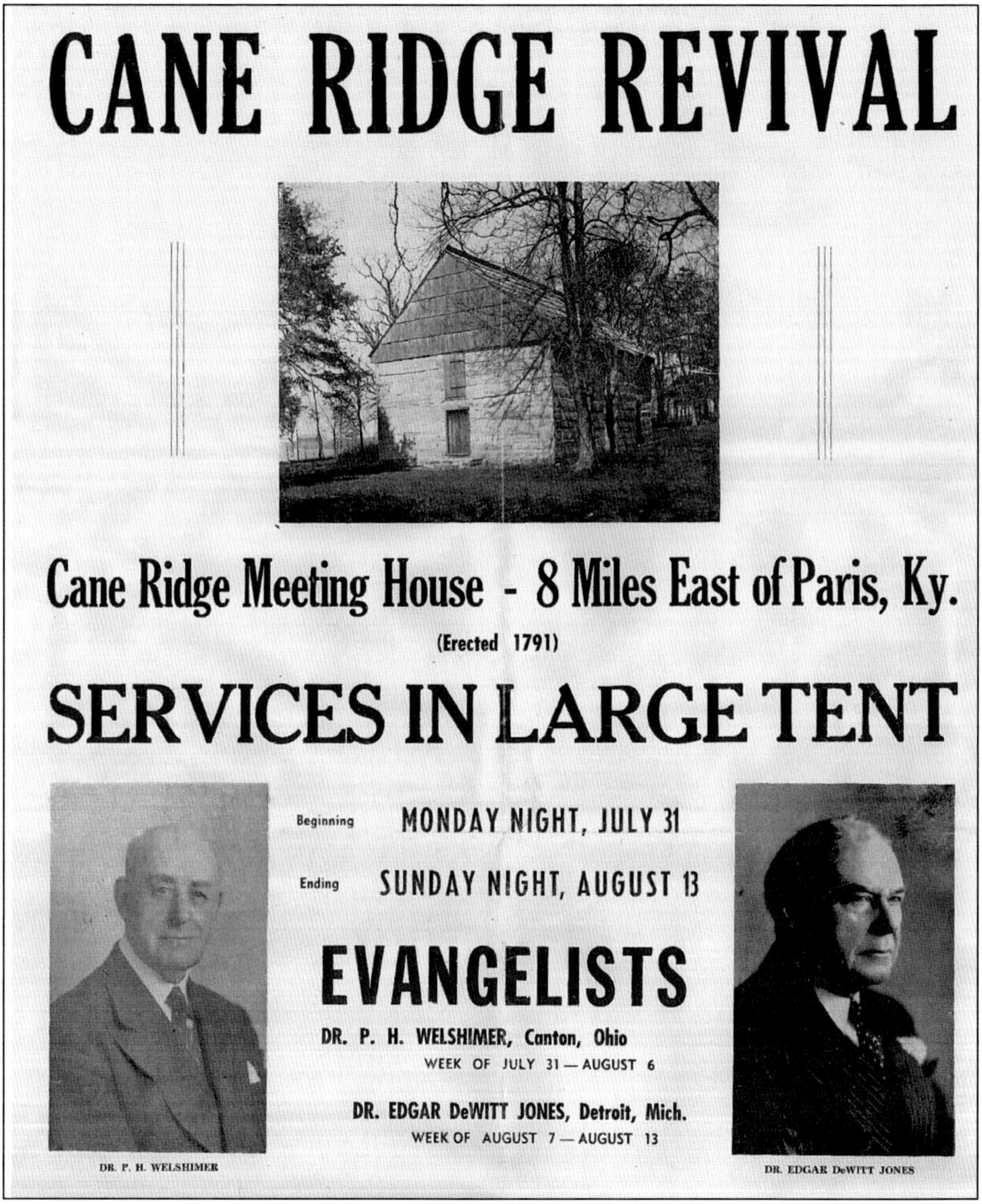

1930s Poster Promoting Revival at Cane Ridge. The two-week long revival featuring two nationally known evangelists was sponsored by the Laymen's League of the Christian Churches of Bourbon County. There were services each night, except Saturdays, beginning at 7:30 p.m. at the Cane Ridge Meetinghouse. Even if this revival attracted good crowds, the numbers would have paled in comparison to the 1801 Great Revival held on the grounds of the Meetinghouse, which attracted between 20,000 and 30,000 people.

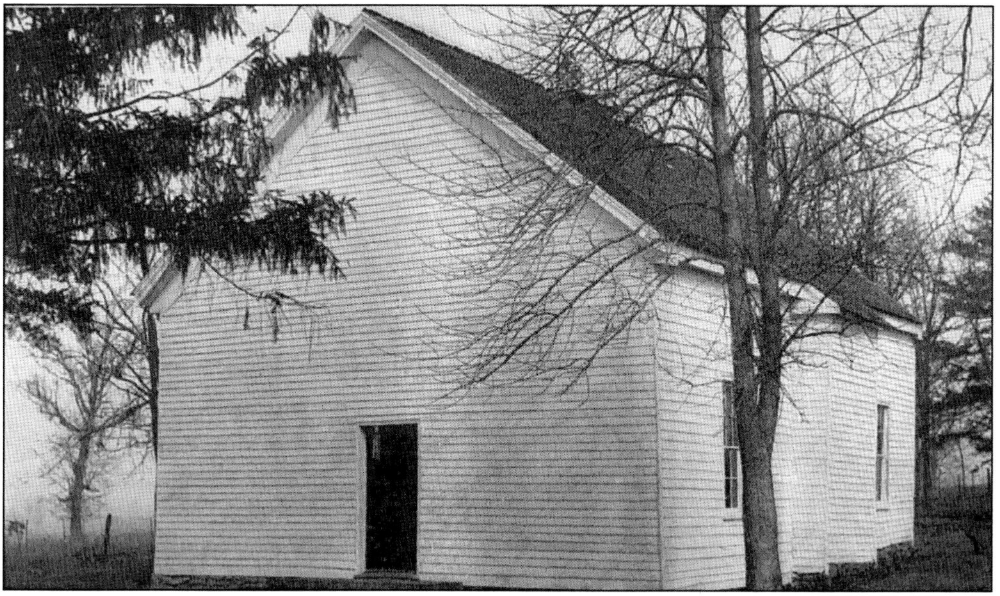

Cane Ridge Meetinghouse—the Birthplace of the Disciples of Christ. Bourbon County is one of the few places in the world where a religious movement led to the formation on a new denomination. In 1804, Barton Stone and three other ministers withdrew from the Presbyterian church and formed the Christian Church which later merged with another group who had led a similar movement to form the Disciples of Christ, which currently has more than two million members.

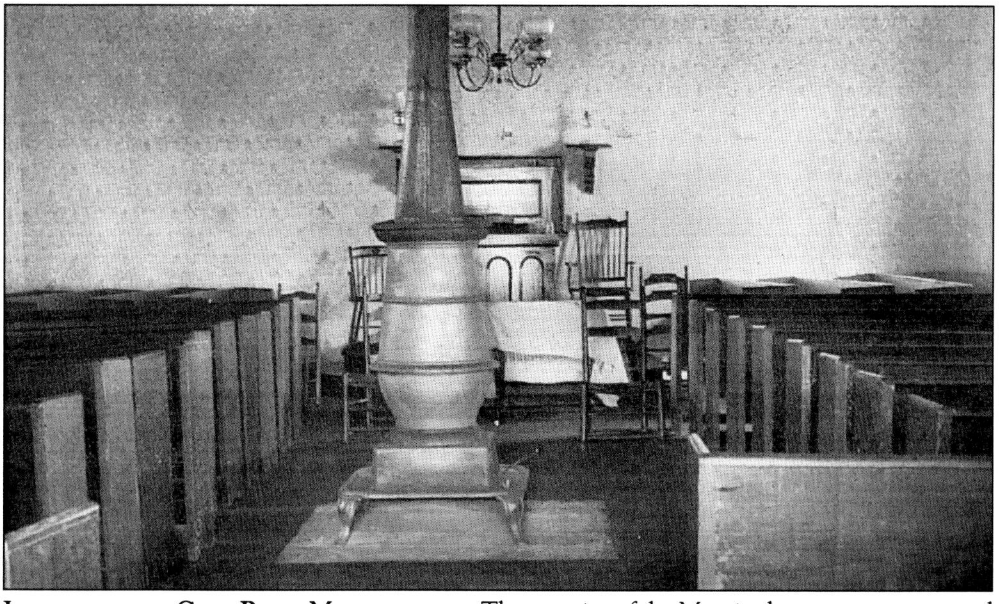

Interior of the Cane Ridge Meetinghouse. The exterior of the Meetinghouse was constructed about 1791 of blue-ash logs and is said to be the largest one-room log building still in existence today. The interior has undergone several modernization programs—this photo was taken after it was renovated in 1882. In an earlier renovation, the interior gallery originally used by slaves, which was reached through an outside door using a ladder, was removed.

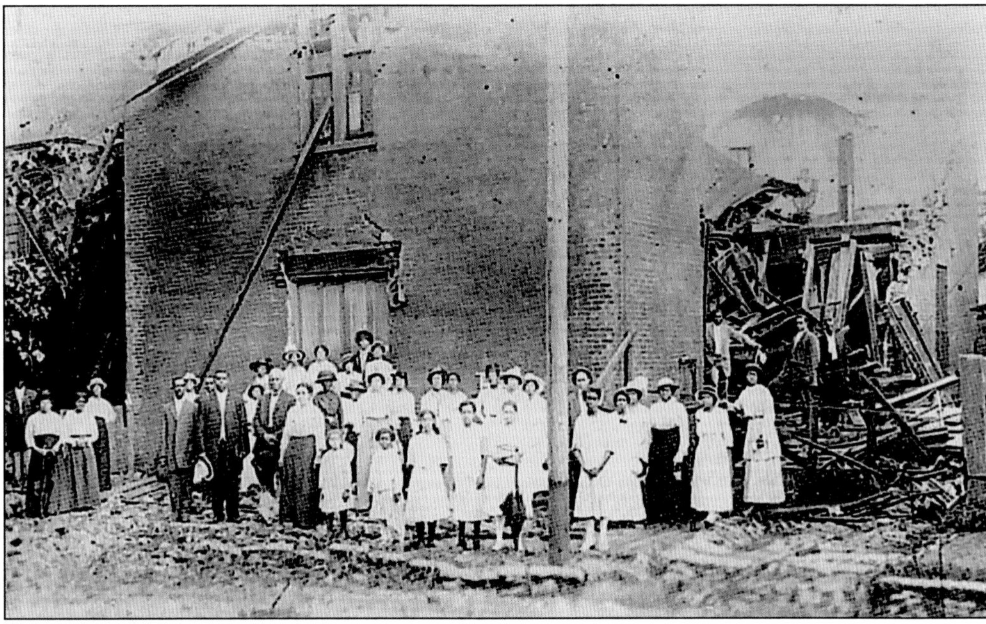

Tornado Destroyed Old Cottontown Methodist Church. With its beginnings reaching back to 1853, Paris's St. Paul United Methodist Church has a proud history of being the oldest black Methodist Church in Kentucky and the oldest black church in the county. As seen in the photo above, the congregation was meeting at what was known as the Cottontown Church in East Paris in 1865 when it was destroyed by a tornado.

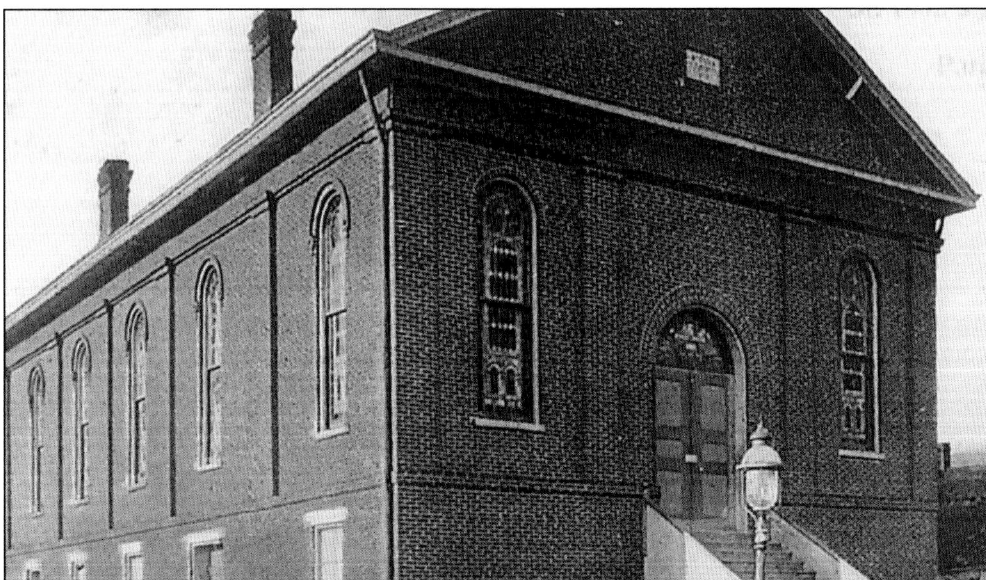

St. Paul United Methodist on High Street. After their first church was destroyed, members felt that God was directing them to build a larger facility and lots were purchased on High Street in Paris for a new church. Completed in 1870–1876, St. Paul's building has been a cornerstone of Paris's black community ever since. The church was one of the charter members of the Lexington conference that was formed in 1879 as a part of the Methodist Episcopal Church.

MILLERSBURG BAPTIST CHURCH. The Millersburg Baptist Church was established in 1818, a few months before the Presbyterian church. The first church building was located on Main Street and constructed around 1825. It was used until 1883 when it was converted into a private dwelling, which is still in use. This photo shows the building constructed on Main Street in 1883; it was taken in 1901.

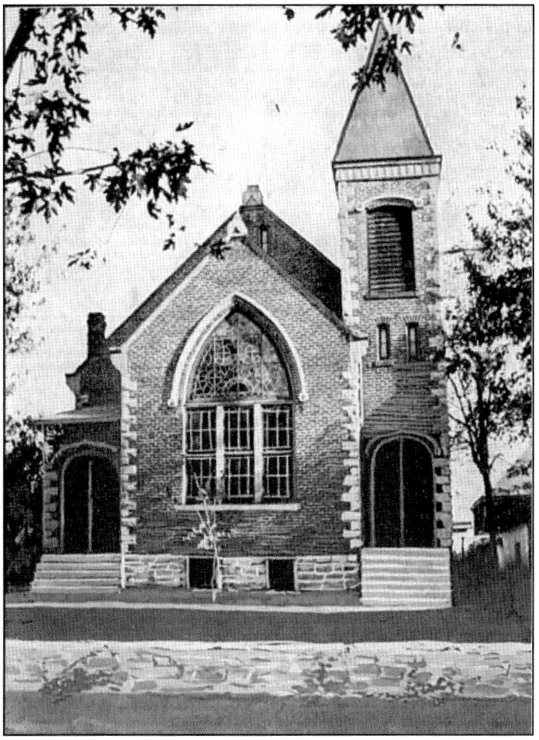

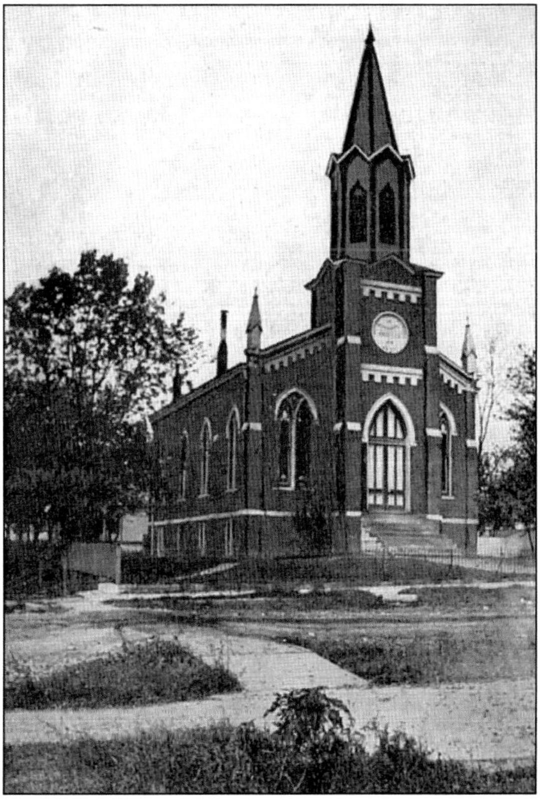

MILLERSBURG'S FIRST PRESBYTERIAN CHURCH—COMPLETED IN 1870. This church building on Millersburg's Main Street replaced a church that sat on the current town square. The Millersburg congregation had been served by visiting ministers from about 1797, but was not formally organized until 1818. This church building has been called "the best illustration of a Gothic Revival ecclesiastical structure in Bourbon County."

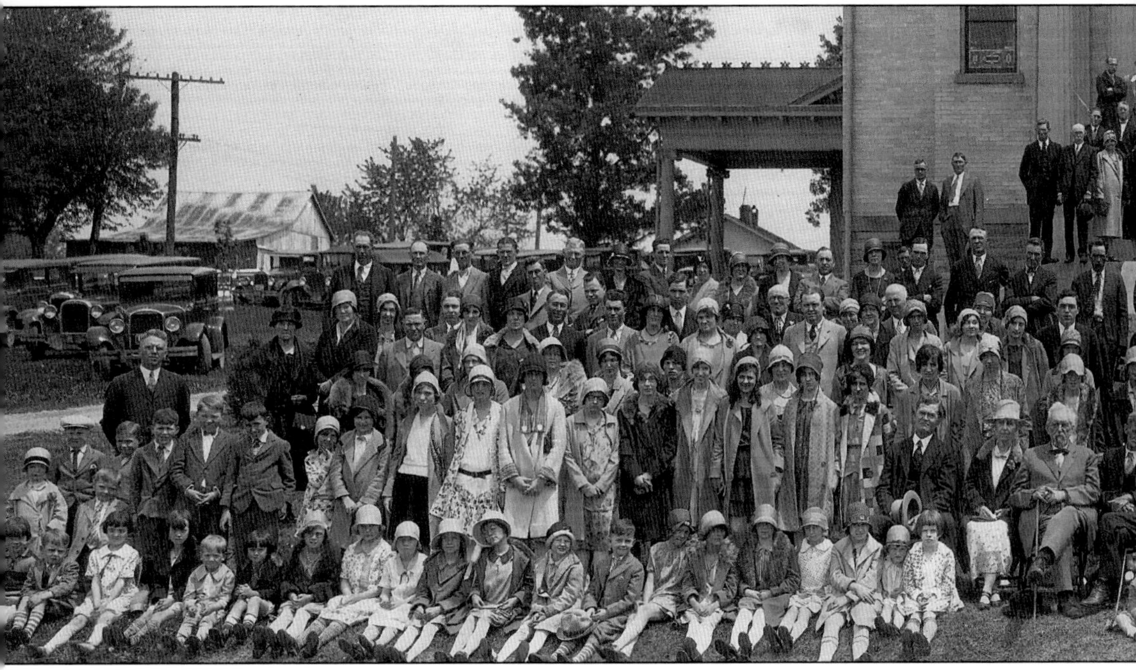

Good turnout at the North Middletown Christian Church. There are more than 200 people in this 1930 photo of what has been described as "the largest building in rural Kentucky." The church building seen here was dedicated on October 19, 1913. The

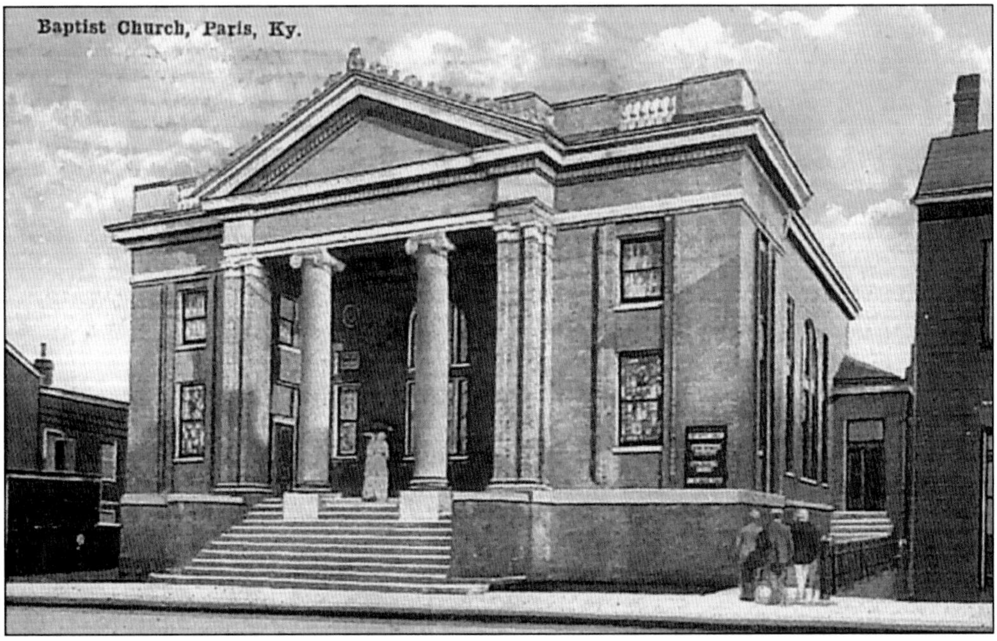

Paris's First Baptist Church. Construction was begun in 1907 on the church, located at Tenth and Main Streets. The new Baptist church was embellished with large stained glass windows. It was dedicated in December of 1910 with what was called "one of the most impressive ceremonies of that era." The speaker was Dr. E.Y. Mullins, president of the Baptist Seminary in Louisville and a well-known orator.

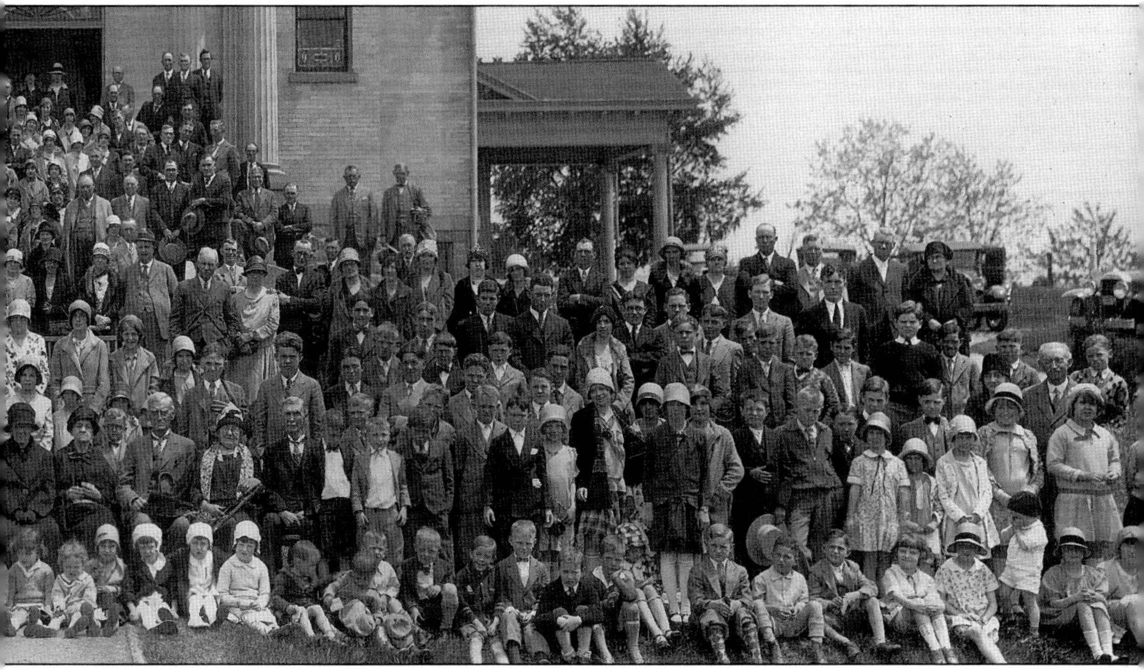

building was dedicated free of debt. That was unusual, as was the building's size—it has a seating capacity of 600. The church continues to be an important architectural and social element in this small community located in the northeast corner of Bourbon County.

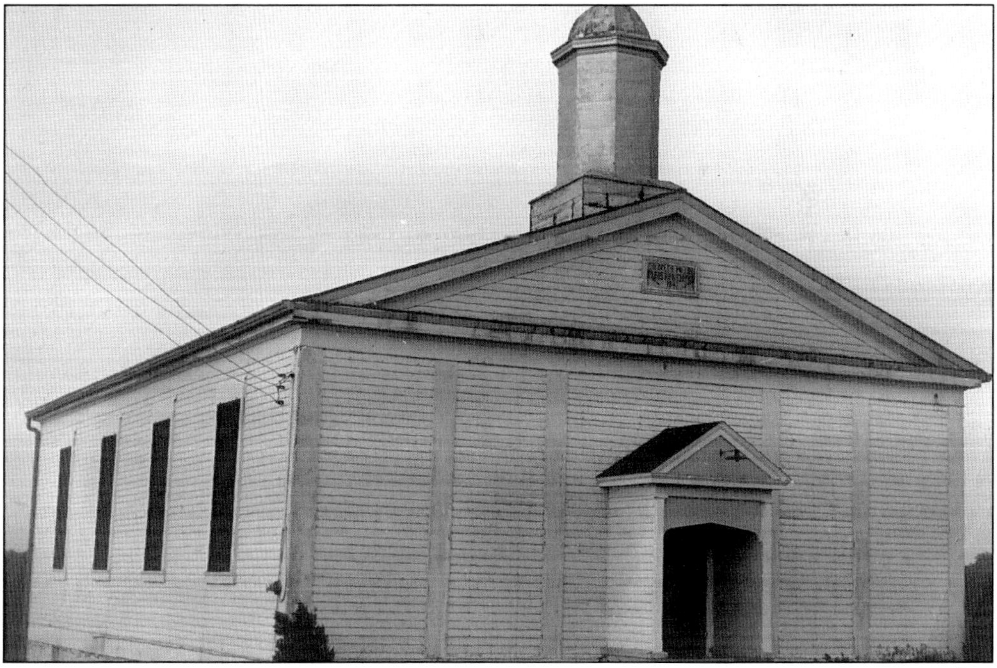

RUDDLES MILLS CHRISTIAN CHURCH. The church was organized in 1840 by John Gano, Allen Kendrick, John Rogers, and John Holton and this building was constructed in 1854. More than 250 people turned out for the church's centennial celebration in 1941, the same year that the Cane Ridge Meetinghouse celebrated its Sesquicentennial.

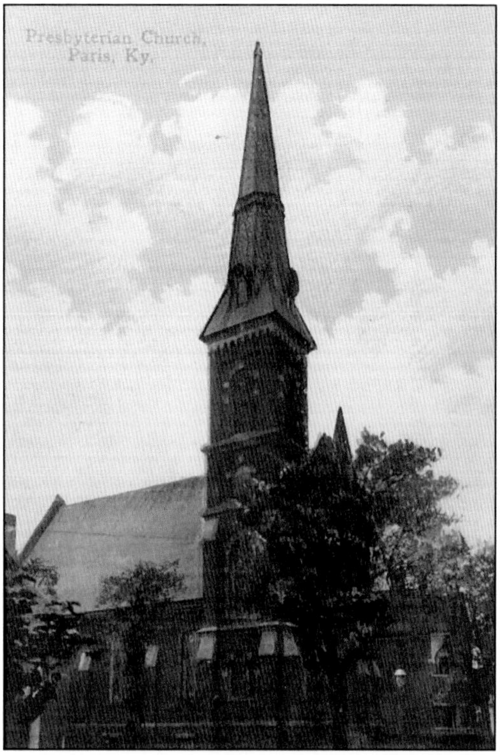

OLD FIRST PRESBYTERIAN CHURCH IN PARIS. This building at the corner of Sixth and Pleasant Streets was dedicated in 1870, but Presbyterians first organized in Paris in 1787. The towering steeple provided a well-known landmark until the church was torn down after a severe windstorm on March 26, 1916, destroyed the spire and damaged the church beyond repair.

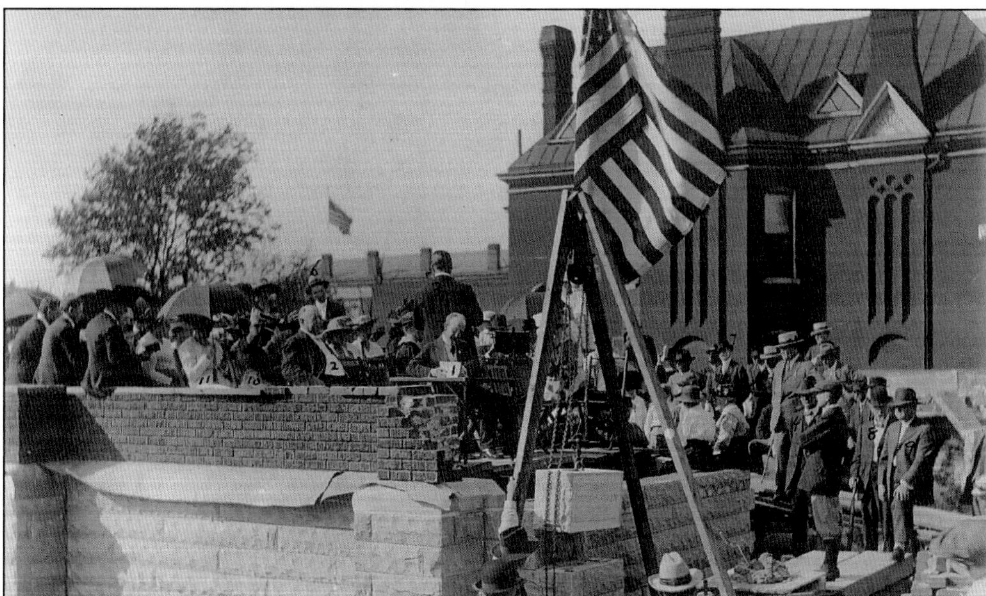

LAYING THE CORNERSTONE FOR THE NEW PRESBYTERIAN CHURCH. On May 20, 1917, just a few weeks after America's entry into World War I, the cornerstone for the new church was laid with much ceremony. Progress on the building was slow because of the scarcity of building materials during the war. During construction, the congregation worshiped at the courthouse. A severe epidemic of influenza in the fall of 1918 delayed the dedication of the new building until January 1919.

OLD METHODIST CHURCH—FORMALLY ORGANIZED IN 1807. The Paris Methodist congregation conducted services in private homes until 1820 when its first church building was completed. In 1860 that building was torn down and this larger brick church with a tall spire was erected just north of where the present church is now. The 1860 church had a seating capacity of 300 and reportedly had an impressive box pulpit with steps on both sides.

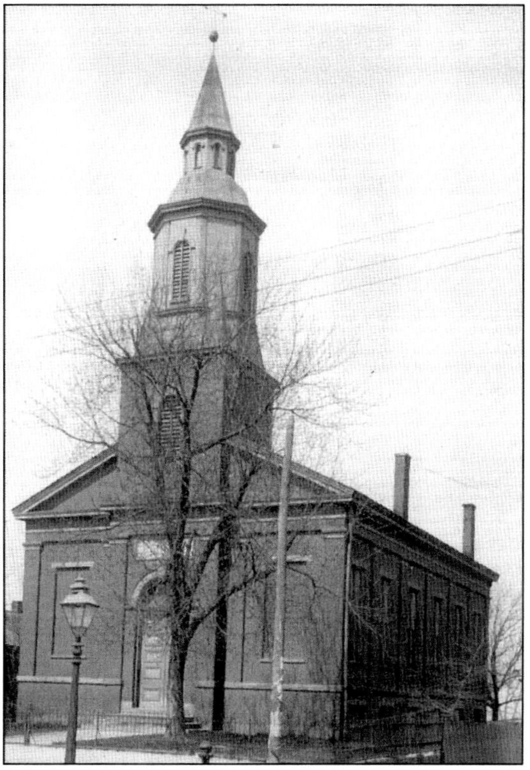

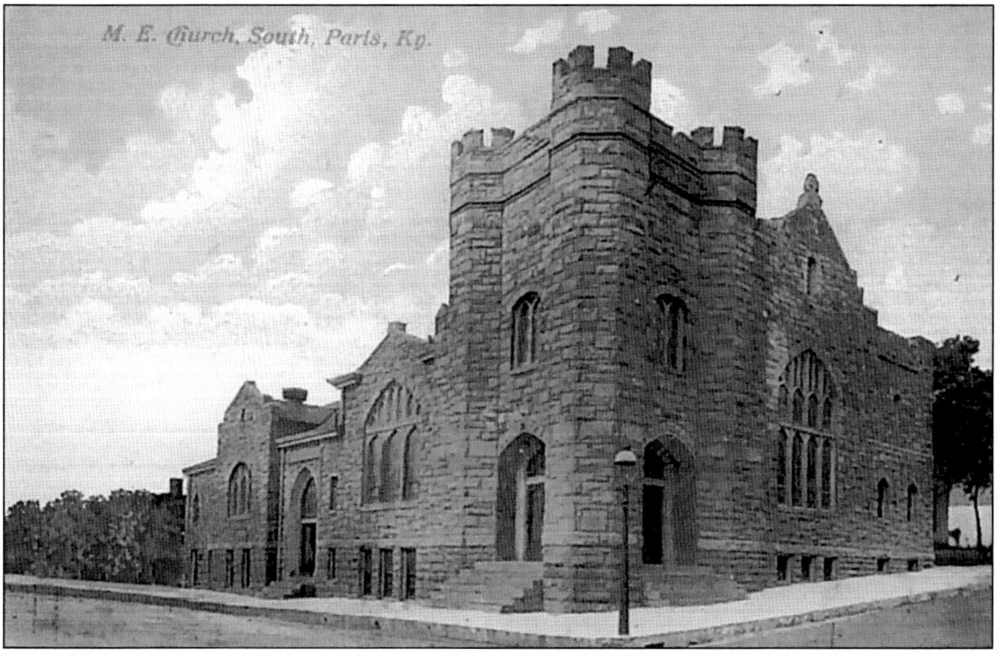

PARIS FIRST UNITED METHODIST CHURCH. In 1897 the Methodists built a church on the corner of Pleasant and Seventh Streets. On December 29, 1909, this building was ravaged by fire, but the solid gray stone walls remained and the congregation used them in rebuilding the church seen here, which still stands.

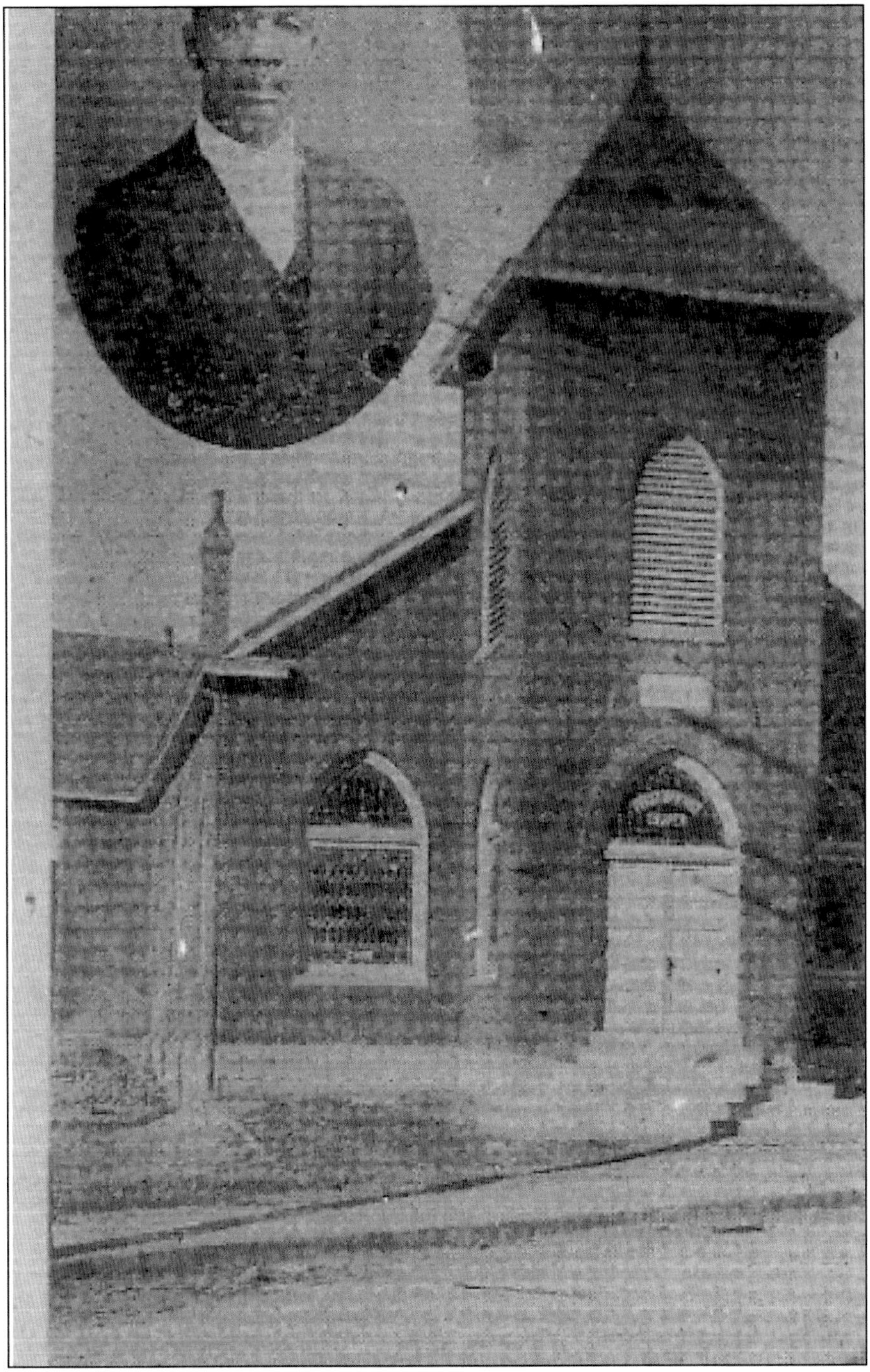

POSTCARD VIEW OF THE FIRST BAPTIST CHURCH ON EIGHTH STREET. This postcard of the First Baptist Church at 128 West Eighth Street shows the church that was built in 1858 and the pastor at the time the photograph was taken, the Reverend E.C. Cross. The interior of the church was damaged and the old stained-glass windows were destroyed in a 1940 fire, but the building was repaired.

Catholic Church of the Annunciation. The Catholic Diocese of Covington acquired the property where the Church of the Annunciation now stands in 1855. The cornerstone was laid in August 5, 1858, when the congregation numbered about 200. The first Mass was celebrated there on Christmas 1860. By 1869, the congregation had grown so much from the influx of Irish railroad workers that the church had to be enlarged.

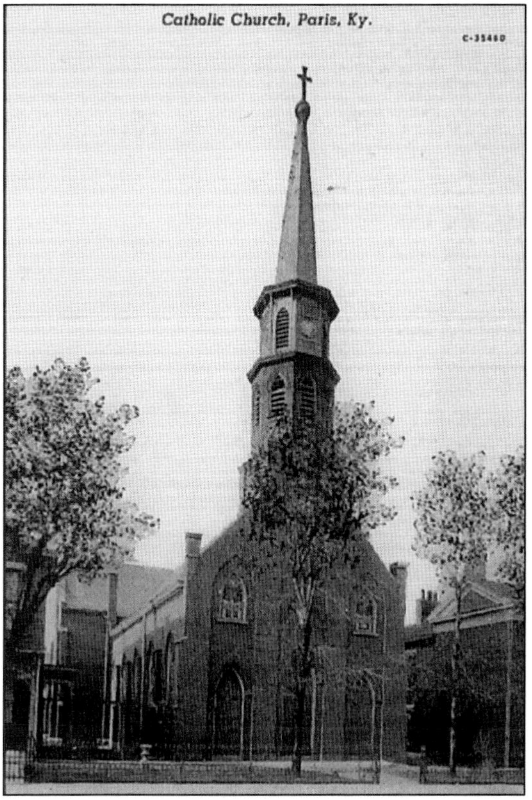

Paris First Christian Church. The largest church structure in Bourbon County was completed in 1902 on High Street. J.E. Desjardins, the famous Cincinnati architect, designed the $50,000 building. The massive stone church is topped by distinctive octagonal towers, one of which contains the 2,000-pound bell that was in the old church on Main Street. Paris Christian Church was organized in 1827 with just six charter members.

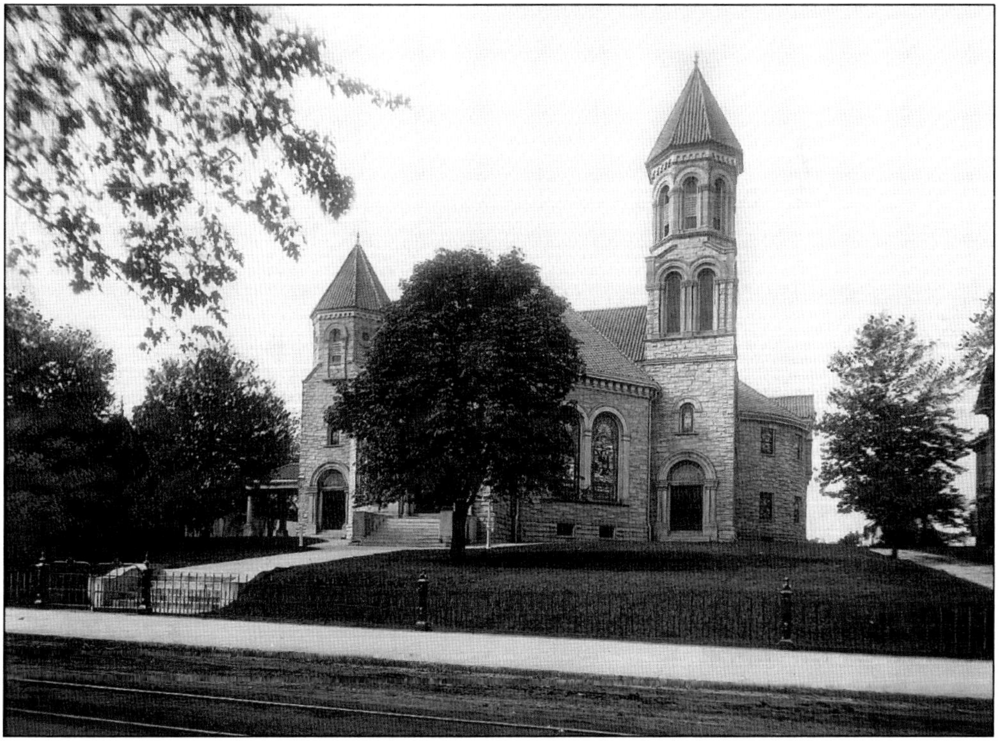

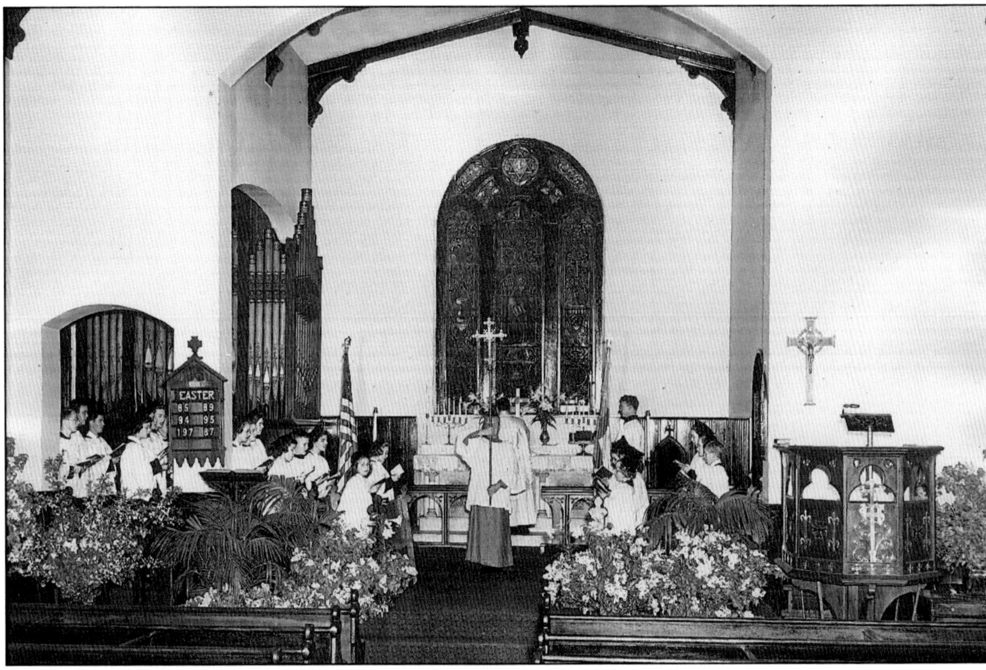

INTERIOR OF ST. PETER'S EPISCOPAL CHURCH AT EASTER. Consecrated in 1838 by the Rt. Rev. Benjamin Bosworth Smith, the first bishop of Kentucky, this building was extensively remodeled in 1870 and the interior has remained largely unchanged since that date. The first pipe organ was erected in 1880 and served the church until 1950 when it was replaced by a new organ that utilized the old organ case.

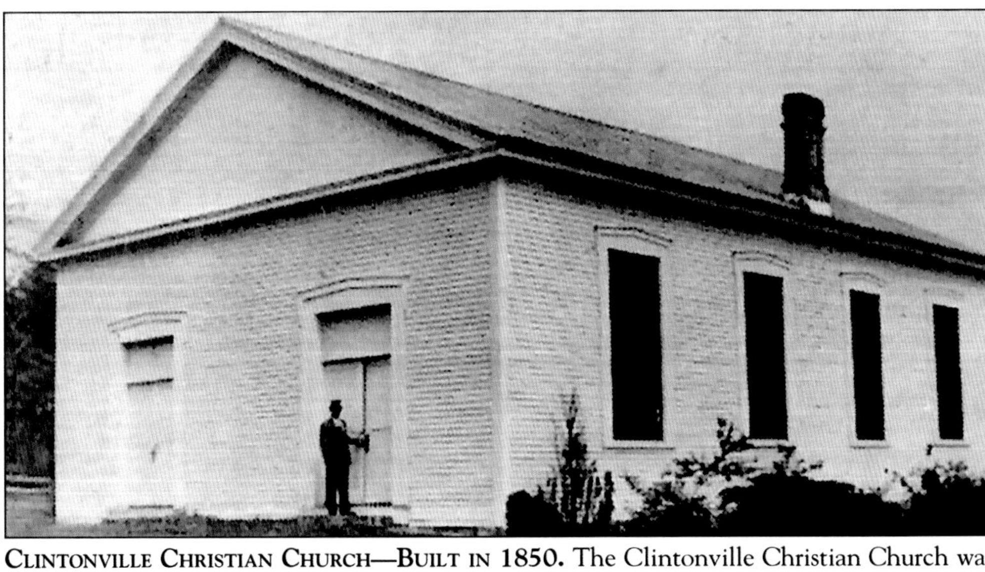

CLINTONVILLE CHRISTIAN CHURCH—BUILT IN 1850. The Clintonville Christian Church was organized in 1830 by the Rev. Thomas Miller Allen. The congregation met in a building shared by other denominations until 1850, when this building was constructed. Originally, the white congregation entered through the two front doors seen in the photo and slaves entered through a large double door in the rear. After the Civil War when the back door was removed.

Seven

Small Towns and Country Living

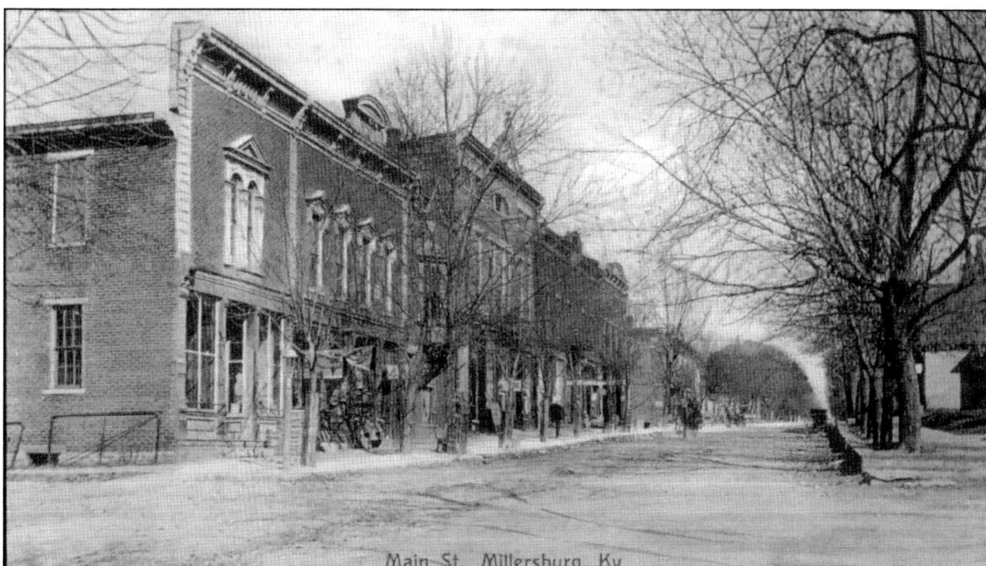

View of Main Street Millersburg Taken Around 1900. This postcard view is interesting for several reasons. It shows a commercially vibrant downtown in Millersburg and it also shows in the background what looks like trees in full leaf in the middle of winter— obviously an addition by the artist who colored the black and white photograph. Millersburg was once an important town with a strategic location straddling the Limestone Trail that stretched from Maysville to Lexington. The town even played host to royalty in 1825 when the Marquis de Lafayette and Louis Philippe, later to be King of France, spent the night at the St. James Inn.

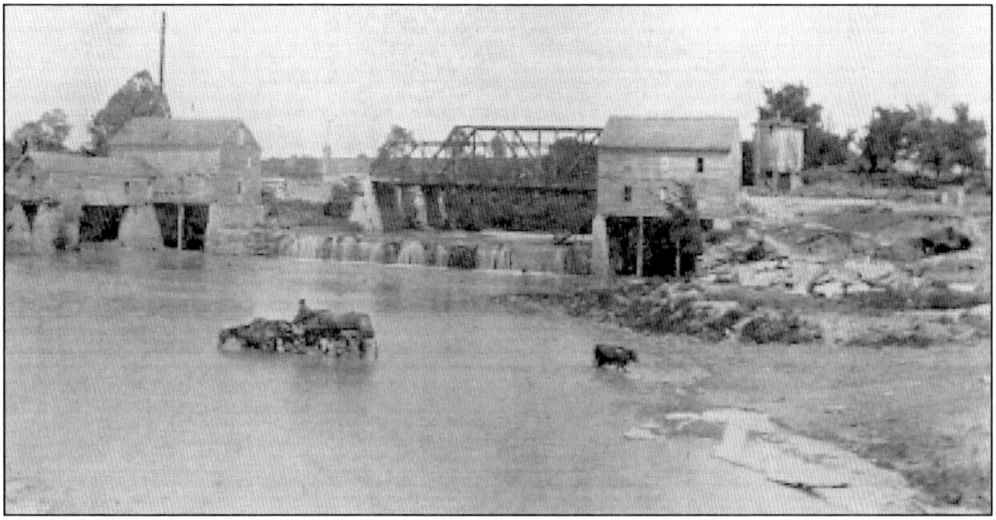

Two Mills on Hinkston Creek in Millersburg. John Miller and his brother, William, built the mills before 1800. By the time this photo appeared in a 1902 publication, the mills were long closed. According to the editor of the piece "These mill sites have, unfortunately for the community, been practically unused for a number of years, but we understand that they will soon be on the market." That turned out to be incorrect.

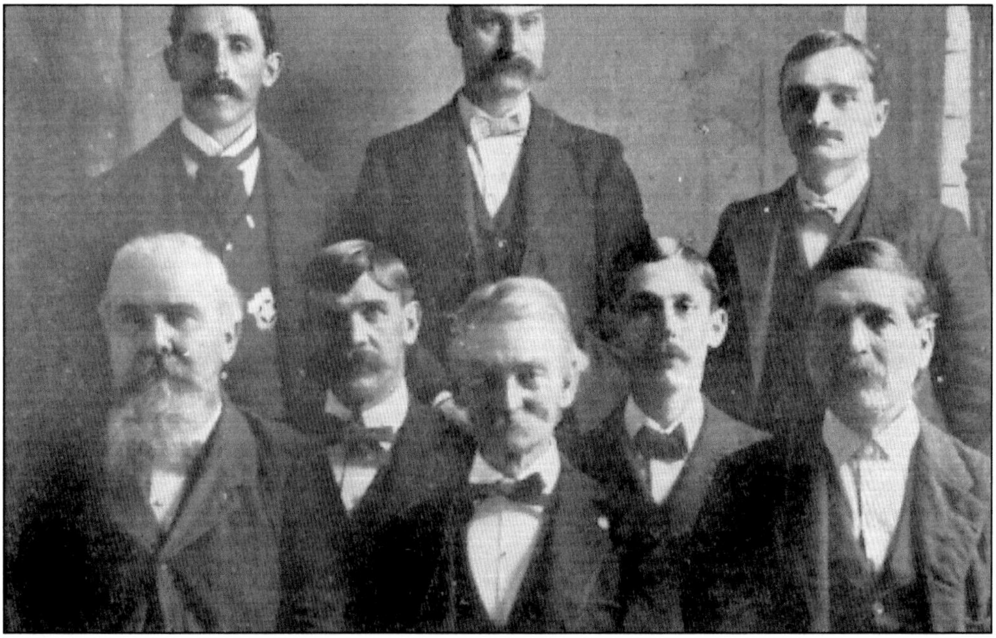

1902 Millersburg City Officials. Shown from left to right are (front row) William Carpenter, J.H. Warford, and Levy Trotter; (center row) W.D. McIntyre, F.B. Vimont; (back row) Henry Bowlin, C.E. Howard, and Edward Ingels. McIntyre served one term as mayor of Millersburg, which was much more important commercially before ease of transportation spelled the end for many local businesses. The town was on the railroad line and residents could travel by train across the county or across the country.

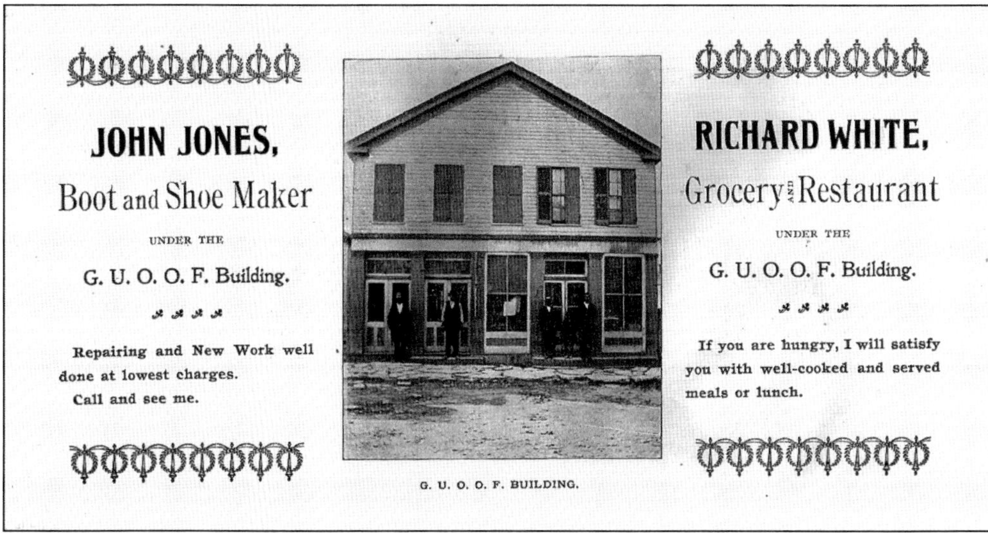

AFRICAN-AMERICAN MERCHANTS IN MILLERSBURG. There were many black families living in Millersburg in this era, and several of the black-owned or operated businesses ran advertisements in an early Millersburg publication. The building shown belonged to the Grand Union Order of Odd Fellows (GUOOF), a black fraternal organization. The ground floor was used by John Jones, boot and shoe maker, and Richard White, who had a grocery and restaurant.

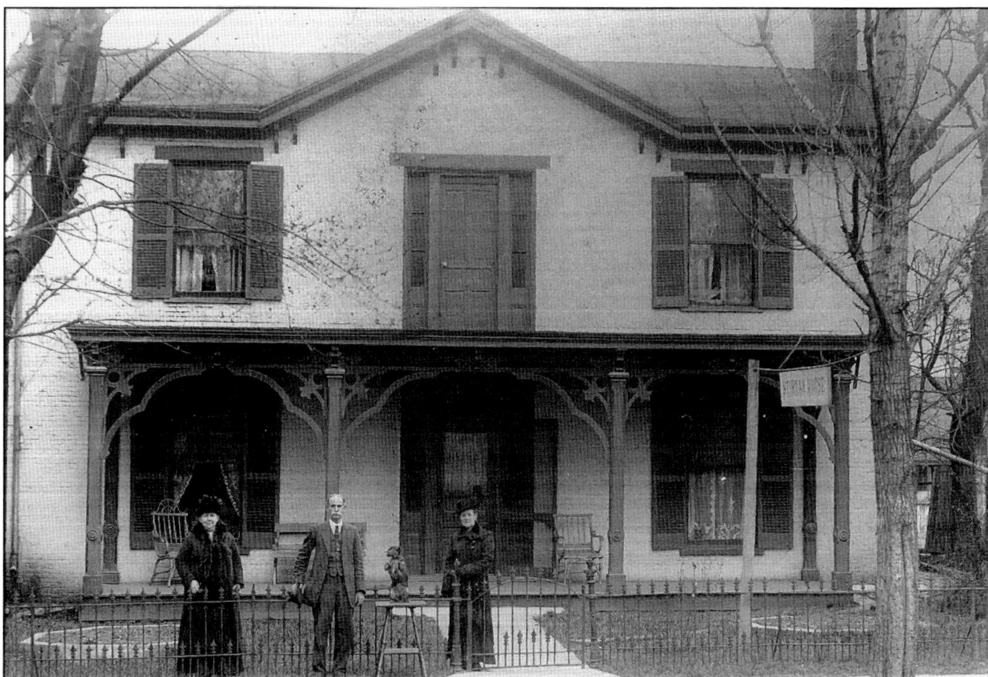

BEEDING HOUSE IN MILLERSBURG. In the late 1800s and early 1900s, commercial men had to travel to make calls in person on prospective customers. These commercial travelers would set up sample rooms to show their wares. The Beeding House (Elijah Thomas Beeding, proprietor; H.S. Stitt, clerk) had sample rooms and an attached livery stable. Notice the dog on the table.

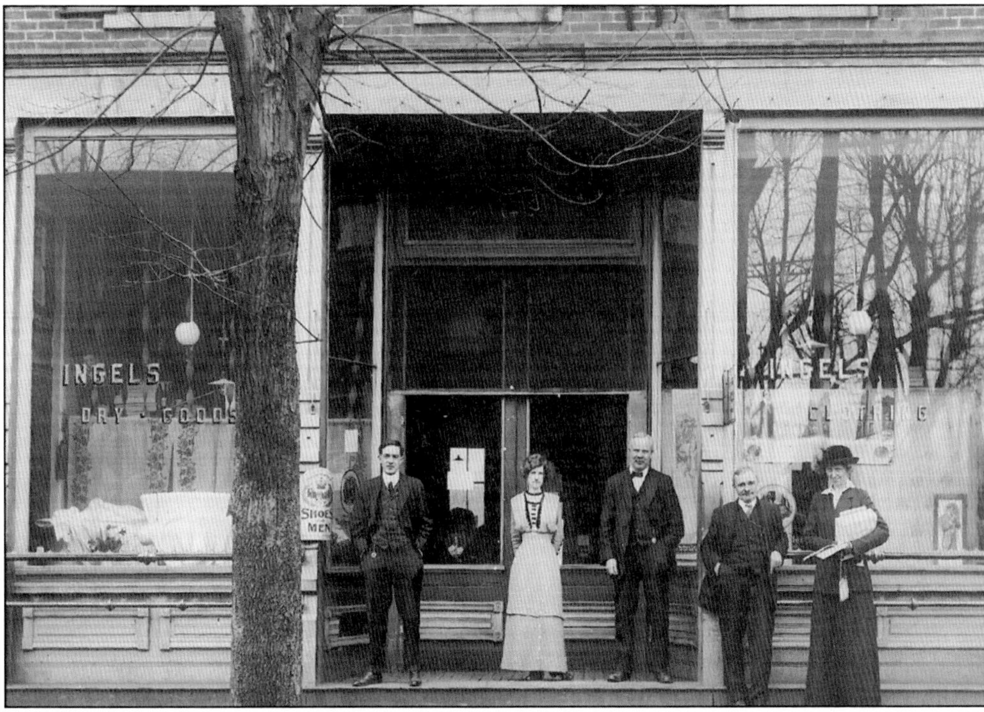

INGELS DRY GOODS & CLOTHING STORE. Shown in this photo, at the extreme right, are Edward Ingels and his wife, Mamie. Several members of the Ingels family were associated with this Millersburg store which carried hats, boots, shoes, notions, and material and patterns for women's dresses. In addition, gentlemen could get suits made to order at the store.

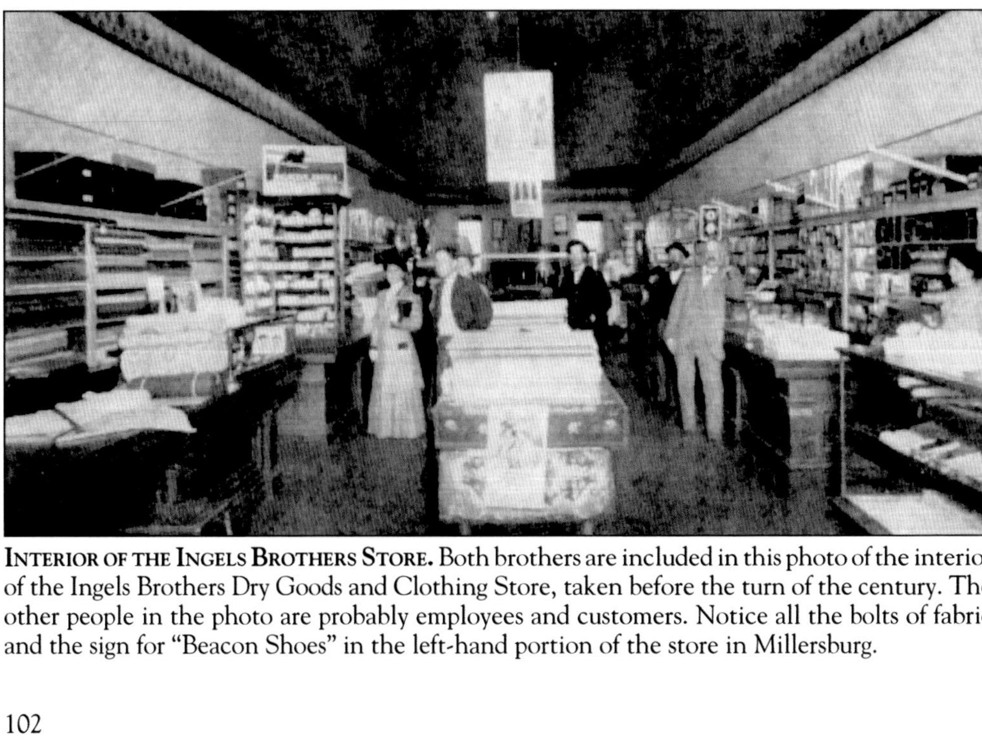

INTERIOR OF THE INGELS BROTHERS STORE. Both brothers are included in this photo of the interior of the Ingels Brothers Dry Goods and Clothing Store, taken before the turn of the century. The other people in the photo are probably employees and customers. Notice all the bolts of fabric and the sign for "Beacon Shoes" in the left-hand portion of the store in Millersburg.

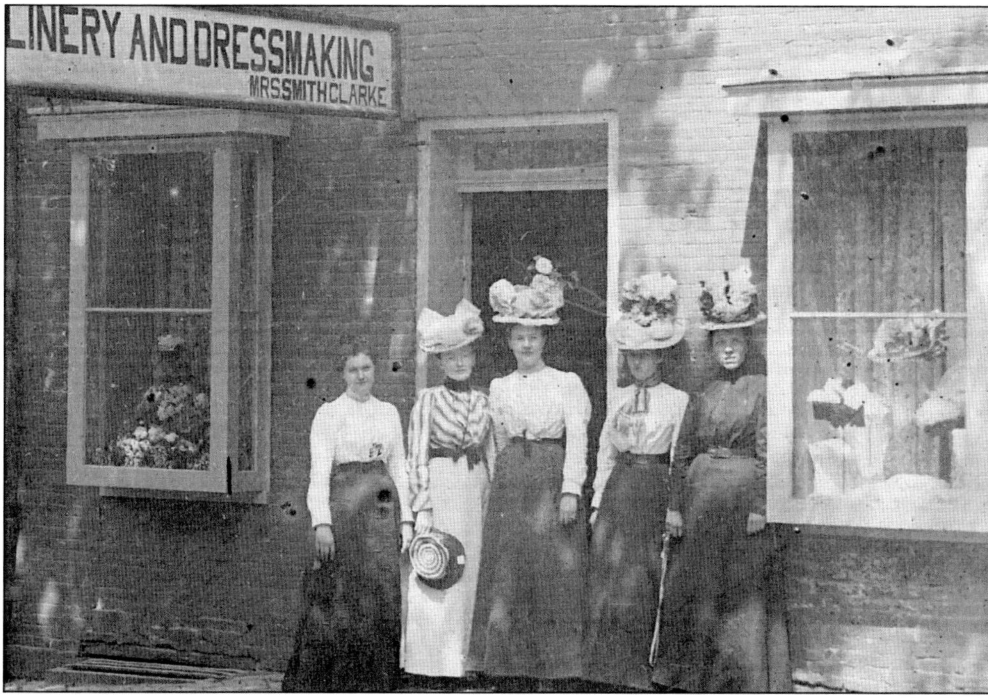

Mrs. J. Smith Clarke, Milliner and Dressmaker. Mrs. Clarke, who had a shop on Main Street, believed that being well dressed included a stunning hat. An ad she ran in 1902 said, in part, "Has on hand for the inspection of the ladies the latest and prettiest creations in the way of Bonnets and Hats, both trimmed and untrimmed. If you wish to feel satisfied that you are wearing the proper thing, give her your orders."

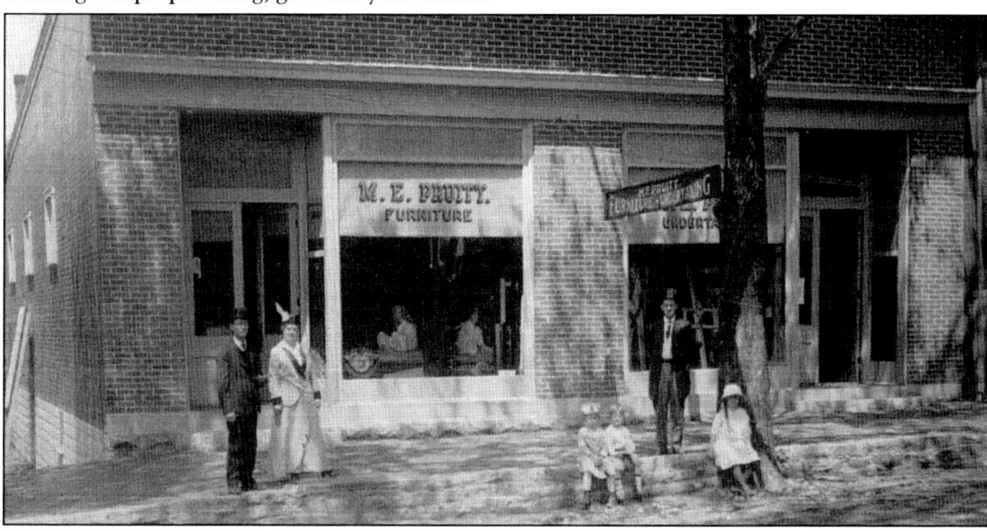

M.E. Pruitt Furniture and Undertaking in Millersburg. This photo, taken in 1916, shows the premises split between the two Pruitt family businesses. Both enterprises utilized woodworking expertise and the combination of the two was also seen in Paris where John Hinton had a large furniture store on the corner of Sixth and Main and was also an undertaker. The Pruitt Funeral Home is one of the few Millersburg businesses from this era that survives today.

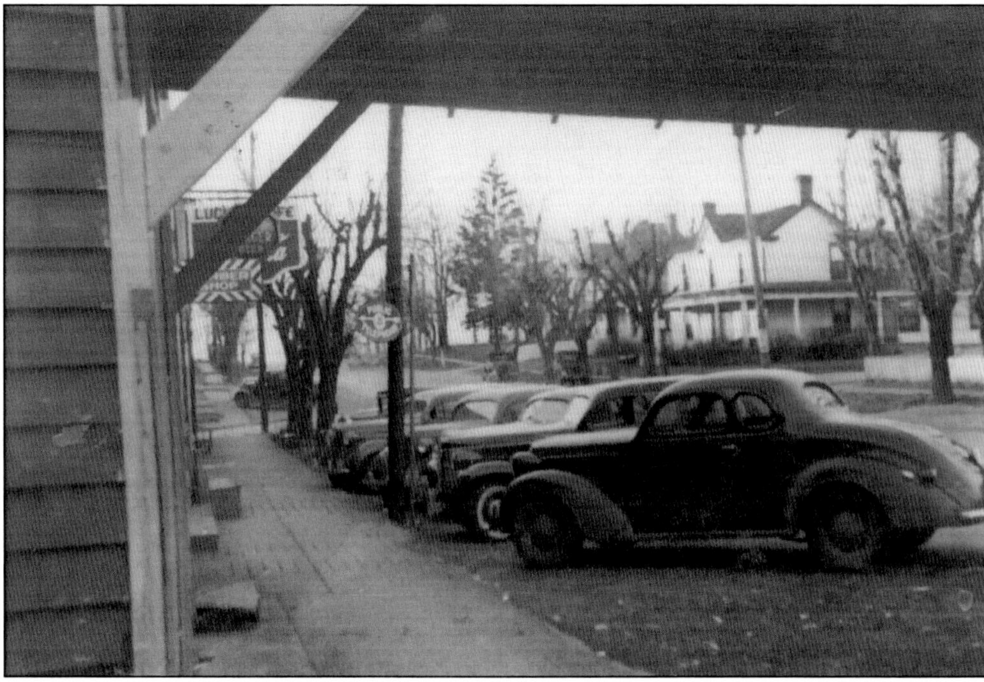

NORTH MIDDLETOWN MAIN STREET. Once Called "Swinneytown" in honor of an early settler, the community is located 10 miles east of Paris; it offered a range of businesses to its citizens early in the 20th century so that the trip into Paris was needed only occasionally. Among the businesses that were once a vital part of the North Middletown Community were the Cline House Hotel, the Patterson Institute (which became the Kentucky Classical and Business College), and a newspaper, *The North Middletown Advocate*.

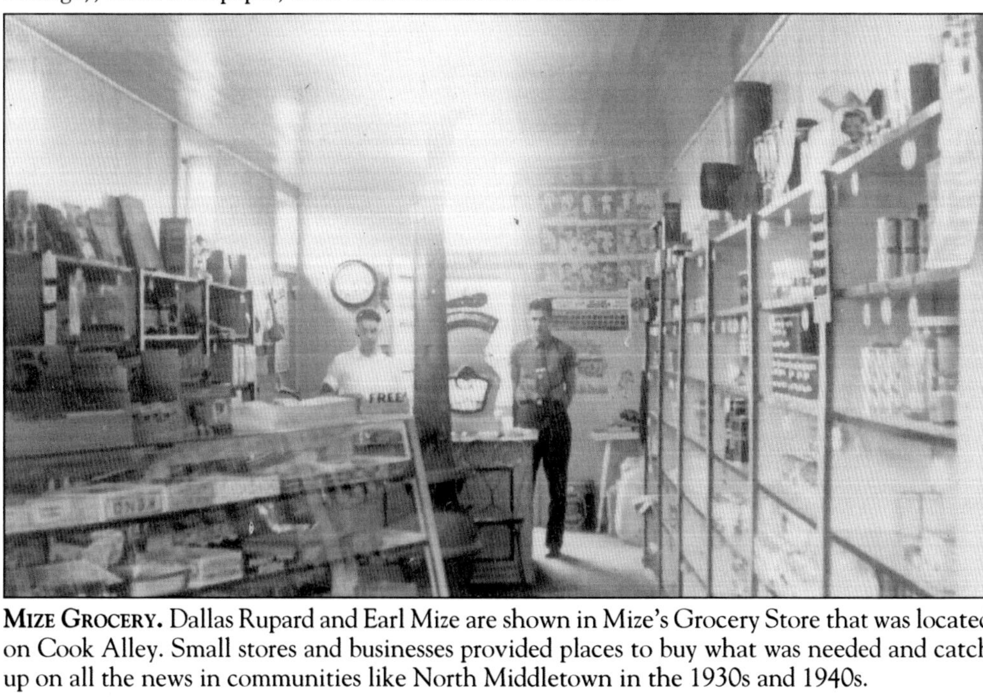

MIZE GROCERY. Dallas Rupard and Earl Mize are shown in Mize's Grocery Store that was located on Cook Alley. Small stores and businesses provided places to buy what was needed and catch up on all the news in communities like North Middletown in the 1930s and 1940s.

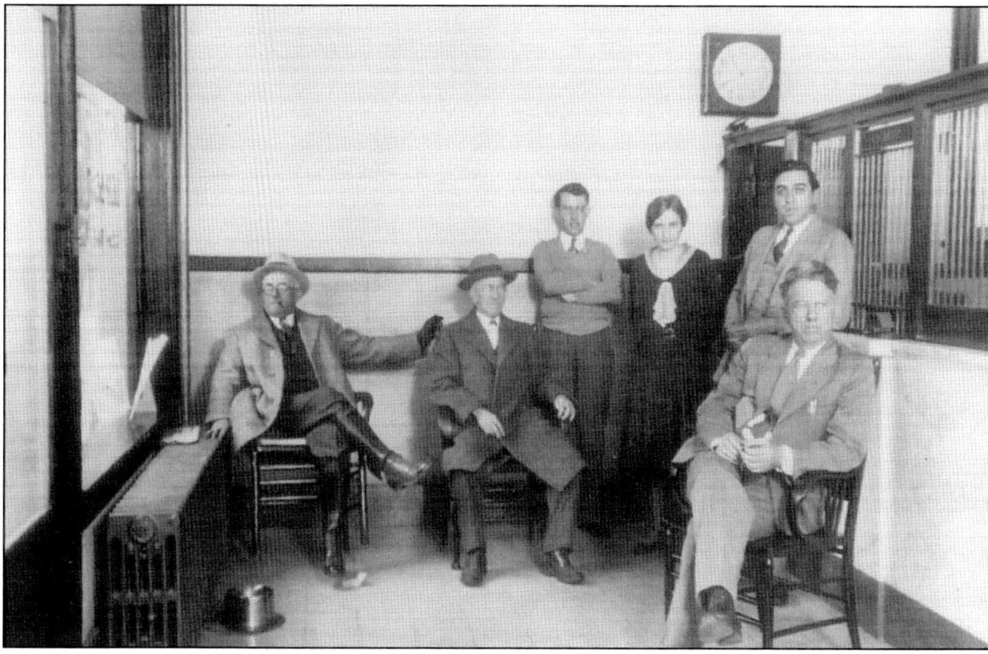

North Middletown Deposit Bank. This bank provided a strong financial base for decades. Shown from left to right are Henry S. Caywood, A.G. (Allie) Jones, Harry See, Mrs. Russell Summay, Russell Summay, and John Willie Jones. John Willie Jones was for many years the president of the Burley Tobacco Grower's Cooperative Association and Allie Jones was a noted breeder of fine saddle horses. He owned Bourbon King, a well-known, champion, five-gaited saddle horse.

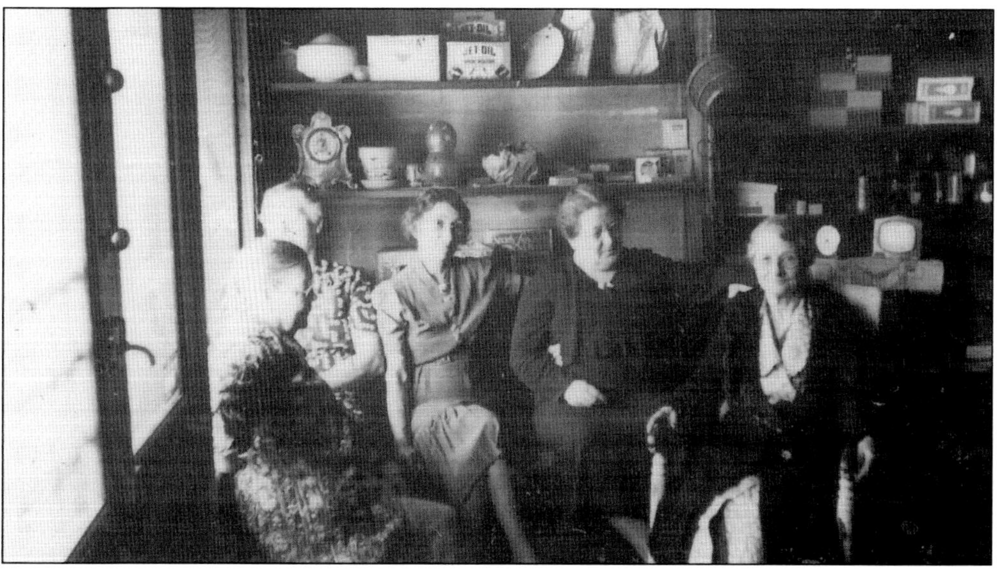

Passing Time at Mrs. Belle Mitchell's Store. The store was located on Main Street in North Middletown. Shown from left to right are Belle Mitchell, Sally Hamilton, Lula Formann, Elm Rash, and Lucy Day. Time seemed to move more slowly in the small towns in Bourbon County before 1940. Try to imagine five women sitting down at Wal-Mart today to catch up on the local happenings.

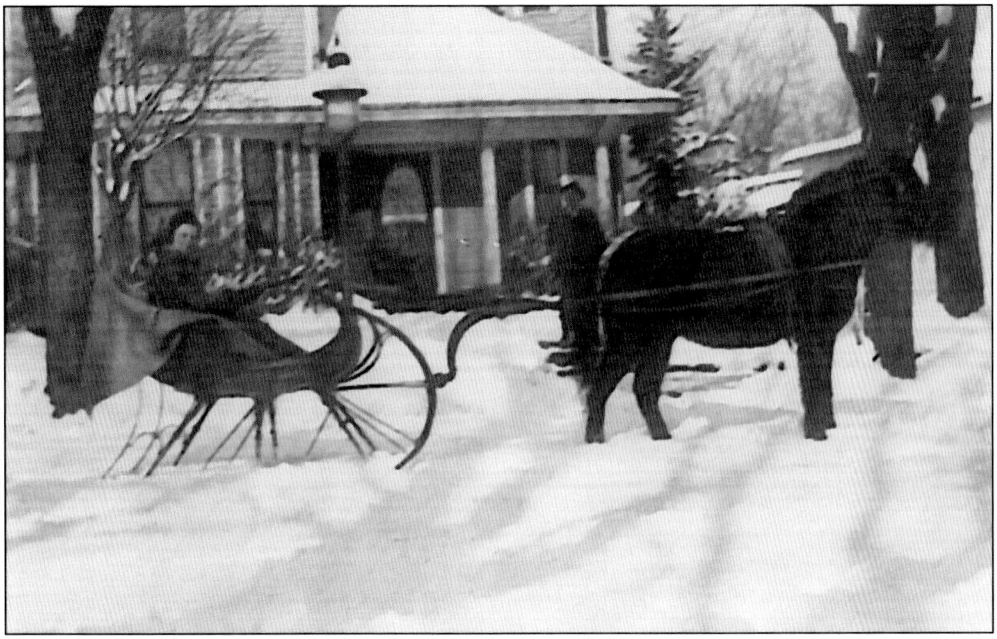

WINTER 1935–1936. This horse-drawn sleigh was probably pulled out of a shed to help navigate the snow-covered roads that winter. The sleigh is shown in front of the John Skillman house in North Middletown, which was built about 1910. According to newspaper reports, January 1936 was a record cold month with temperatures ranging from 16 to 20 below zero for several days.

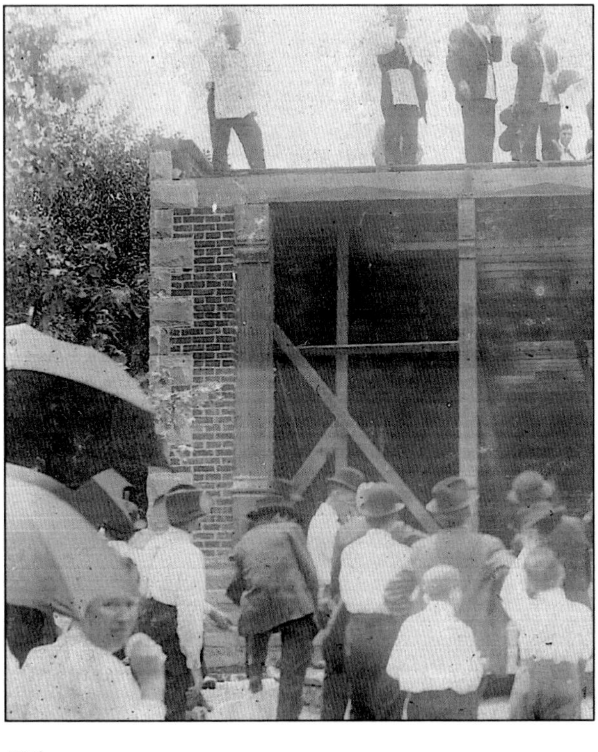

LITTLE ROCK BUILDING. This building combined a bank on the first floor with a Masonic Hall on the second. The photo shows Masons possibly laying cornerstone for the second floor of the building that was their Masonic Hall. It was constructed in 1909 for Hope Lodge, No. 246, organized in 1850. The Little Rock Bank closed in the 1920s and the first floor was later occupied by a general store.

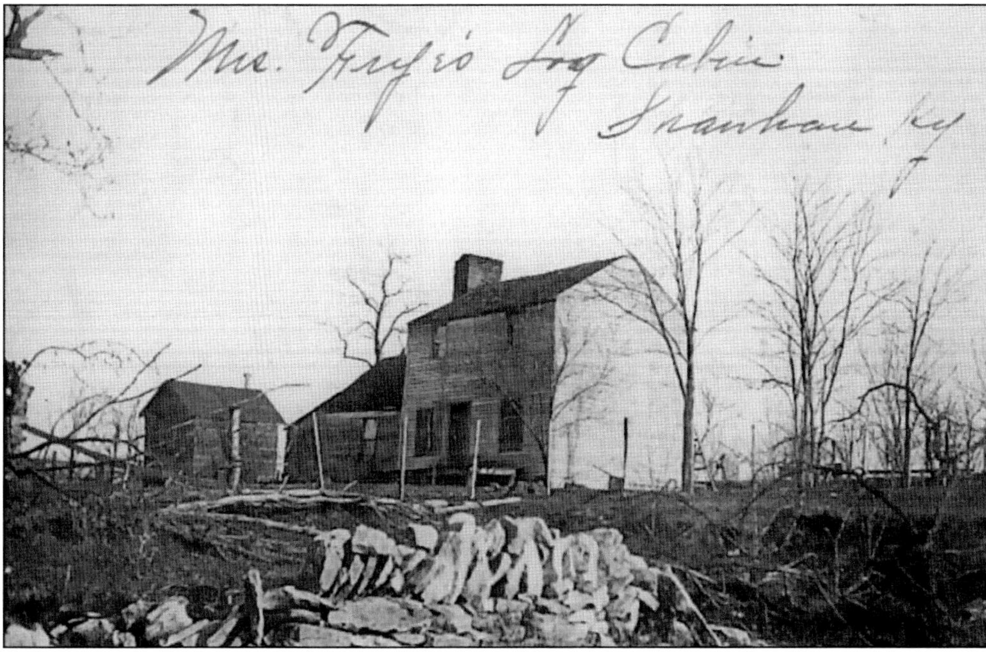

Mrs. Frye's Log Cabin, Shawhan, Kentucky. The photo shows a weatherboarded two-story log home which has a one-story log wing. Also shown is the log outbuilding and part of a rock fence in the foreground. Limestone rocks that were cleared from fields were often used to build rock fences at many early farms in this part of Kentucky.

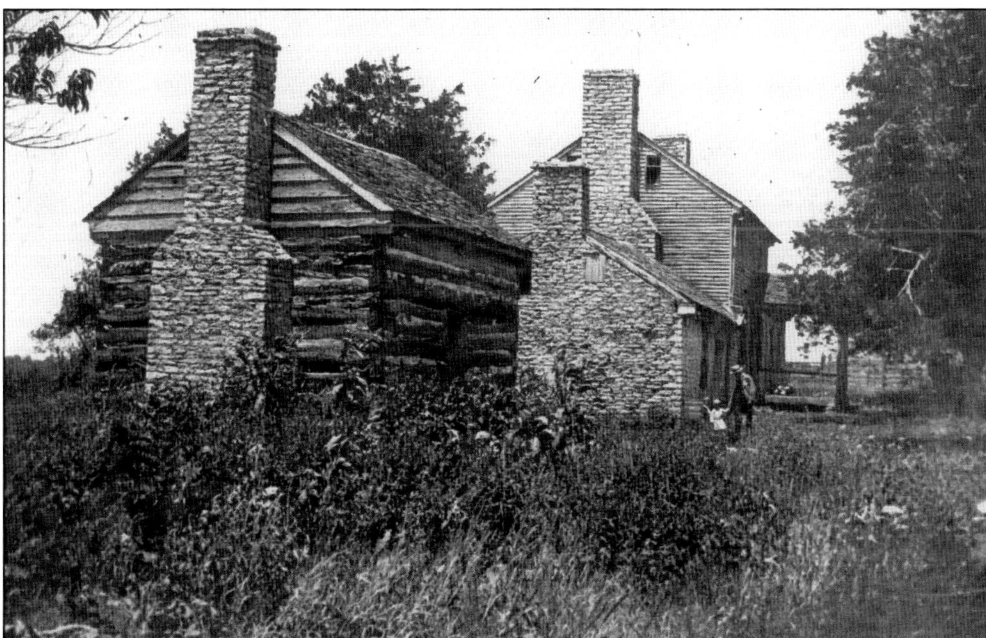

Early Home Near Ruddles Mills. This photograph of the Joseph Stephens House on the Ruddles Mills-Cynthiana Road shows a man and two children in the yard of the home built around 1786. The area around Ruddles Mills was one of the first areas of Bourbon County occupied by settlers in the late 1700s.

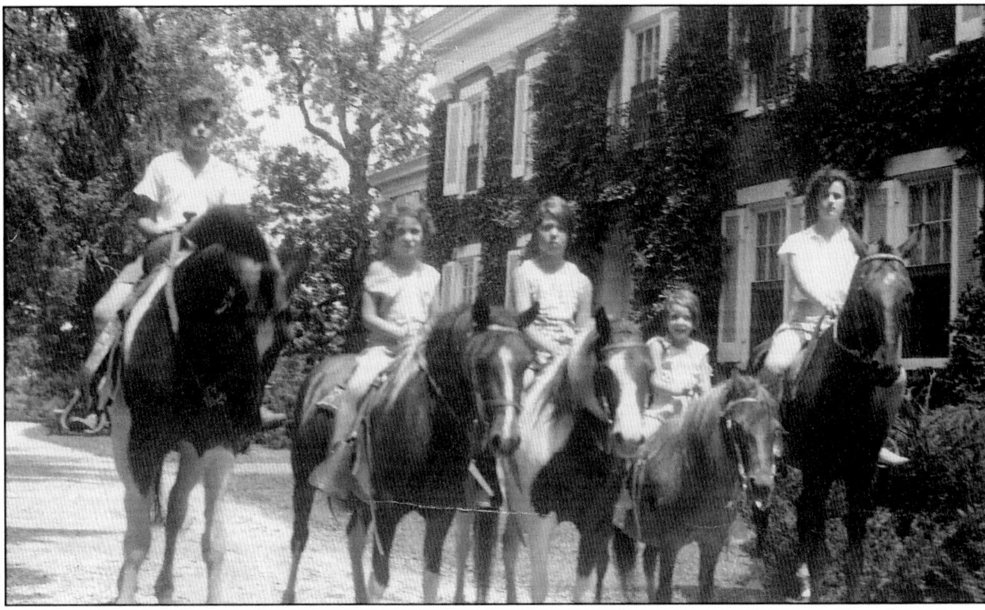

Children on Horseback. Each child seems perfectly matched to his or her steed in this photo. Three Clay children and two of their cousins were photographed on horseback (or pony back) in front of Runnymede on the Paris-Cynthiana Road. Shown from left to right are Catesby Clay, Mary Jane Dushane, Patricia Dushane, Amelia Clay, and Agnes Clay. On the other end of the equine spectrum from children's ponies are the three Kentucky Derby winners that have been bred at Runnymede.

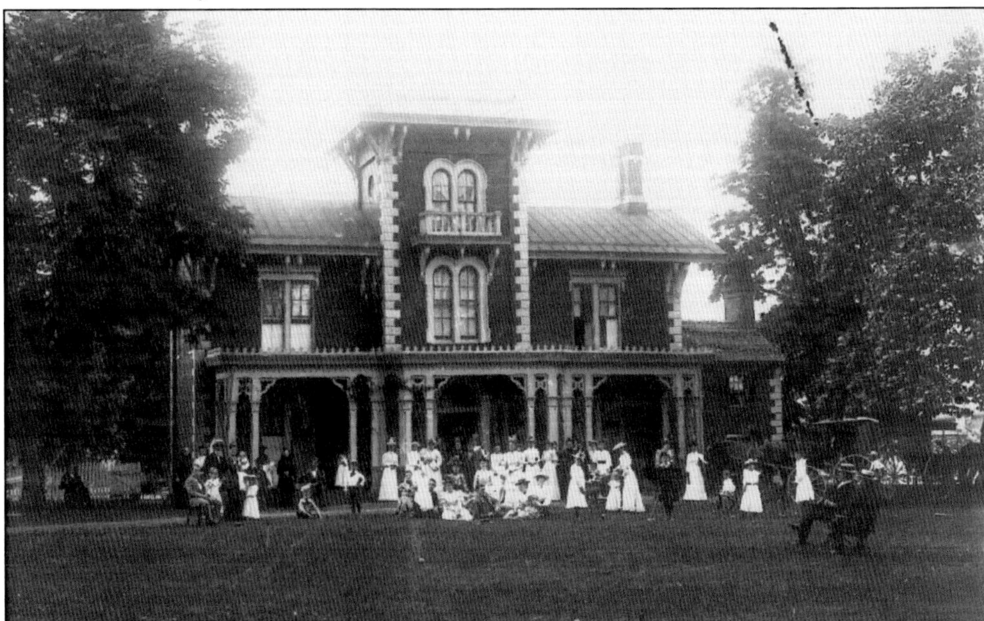

Large Crowd Turns Out for Croquet. One way to spend a summer afternoon is to enjoy a spirited croquet game. It looks like there were a number of children along with their mothers, fathers, and nannies gathered on this day to do just that. We have been unable to identify the house and suspect that it is no longer standing.

John Simpson. Shown in this photo taken before 1920, Simpson worked on the Clark farm near Little Rock for many years. Behind him can be seen the bell used to summon everyone for lunch. Most farms produced much of the food to feed those that lived and worked on the farm. This involved butchering and processing meats, gathering eggs, milking the cows, churning the butter, and canning the produce from the garden and the orchard.

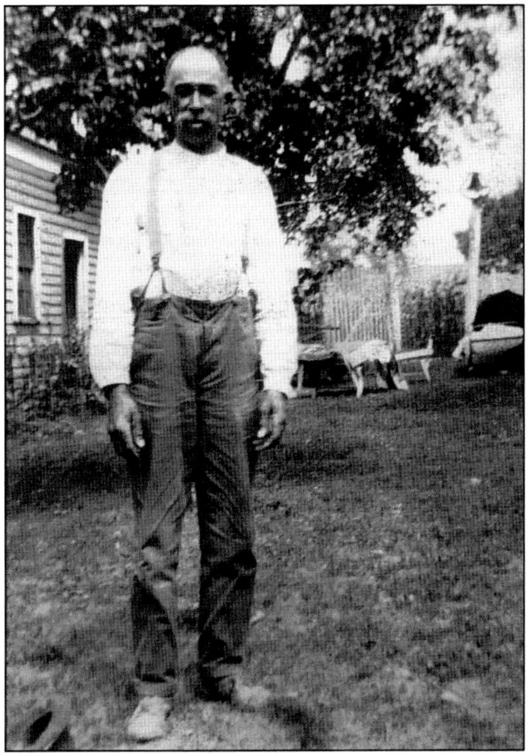

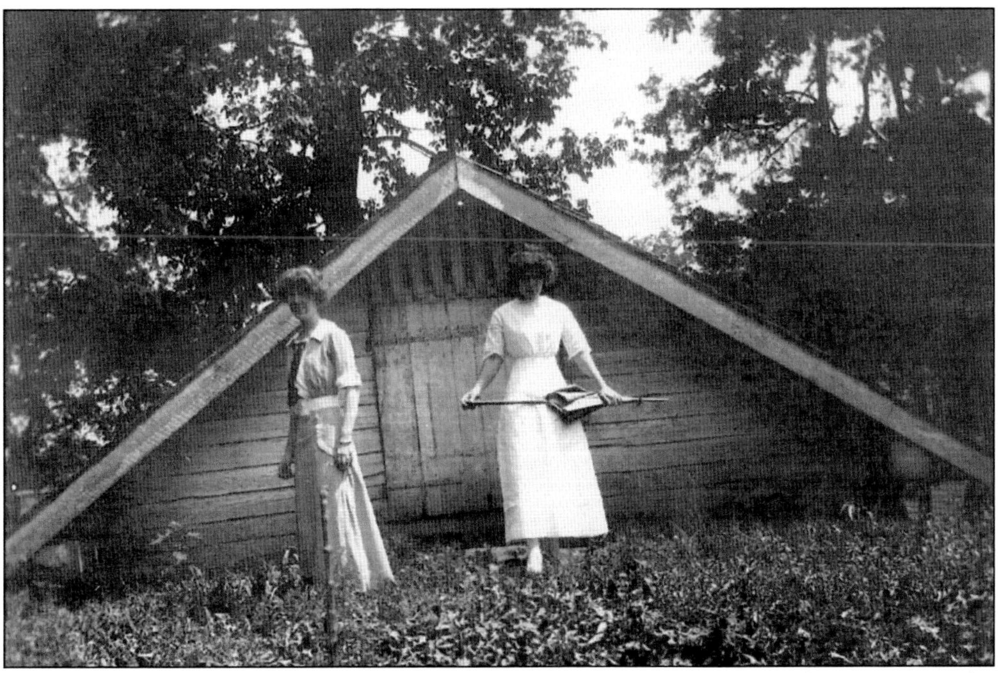

Welcome Relief on a Warm Afternoon. These two ladies are shown making a visit to the icehouse. Large blocks of ice were cut in the middle of winter and packed in straw in an icehouse, which was partly underground. Perishable items that needed refrigeration could then be stored. In towns, the iceman would deliver block ice used in early refrigerators or iceboxes.

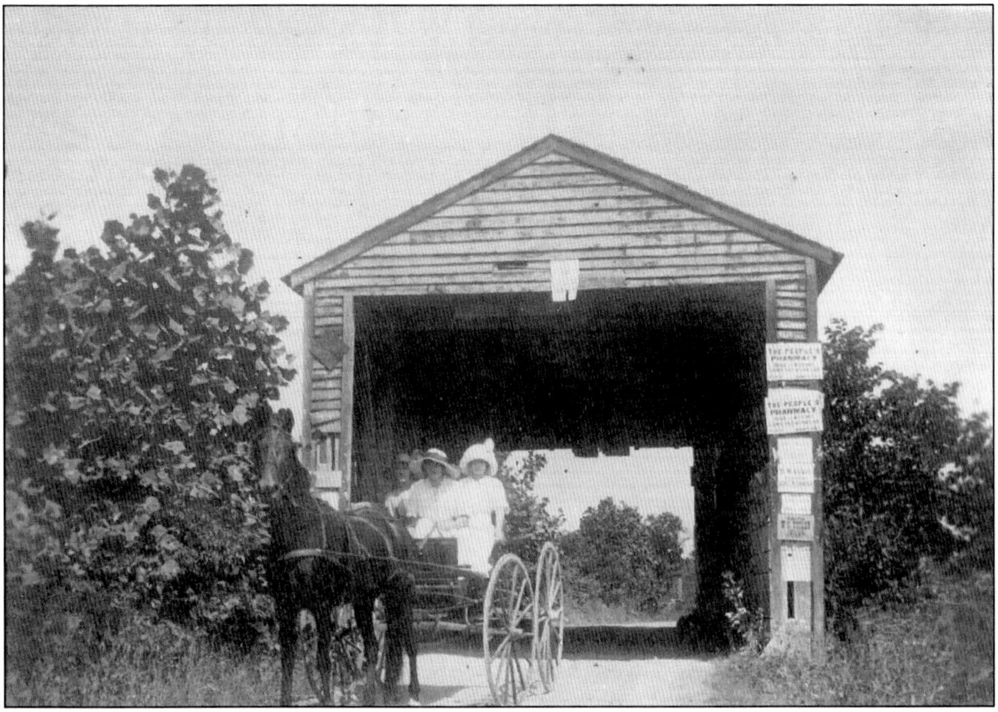

In the Good Old Summer Time. That was the scrapbook label under this photo of three girls shown in their buggy just after they came through one of the covered bridges that used to span the creeks on the Paris-Winchester Road. The bridge pictured is believed to have crossed Kennedy Creek. One of the girls is Francis Clay Batterton. Notice all the signs on the covered bridge, which often served as early billboards.

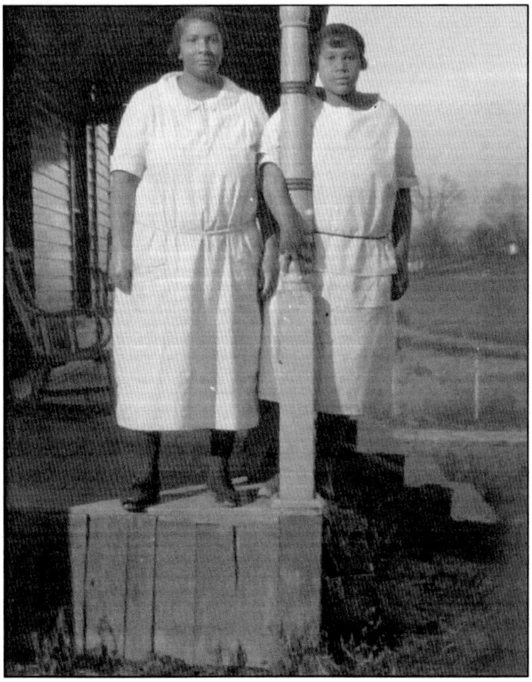

Mother and Daughter Portrait. This unidentified pair looks like mother and daughter and is shown on the porch of their rural home. Porches provided a comfortable place to sit during three seasons of the year. The best place to sit in the winter was as close to the fireplace as possible. After the Civil War, many African Americans purchased farms and by the late 1870s, black farmers owned more than 5,000 acres of farmland in the county.

STILES USED TO SURMOUNT STONE FENCES. Mary Emma Clark demonstrates the correct way to use a stile—a set of steps built into a rock wall—in this photo taken in 1921 near Little Rock. The use of stiles allowed for the passage of pedestrians but not livestock.

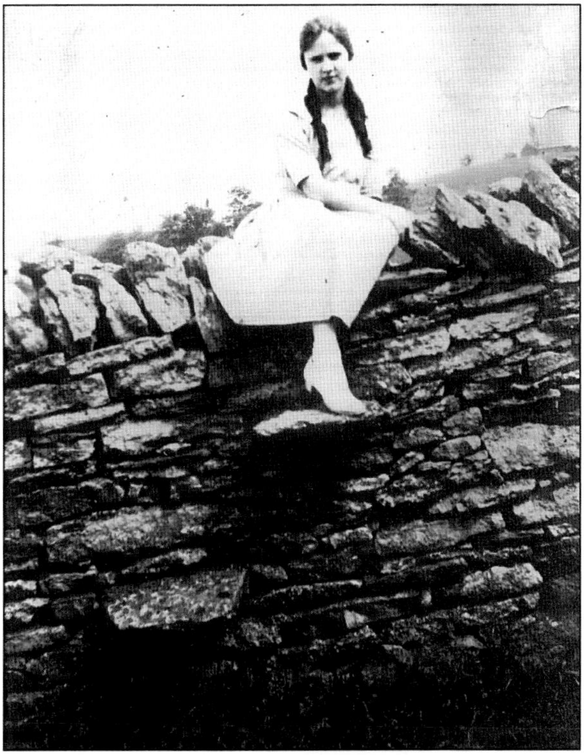

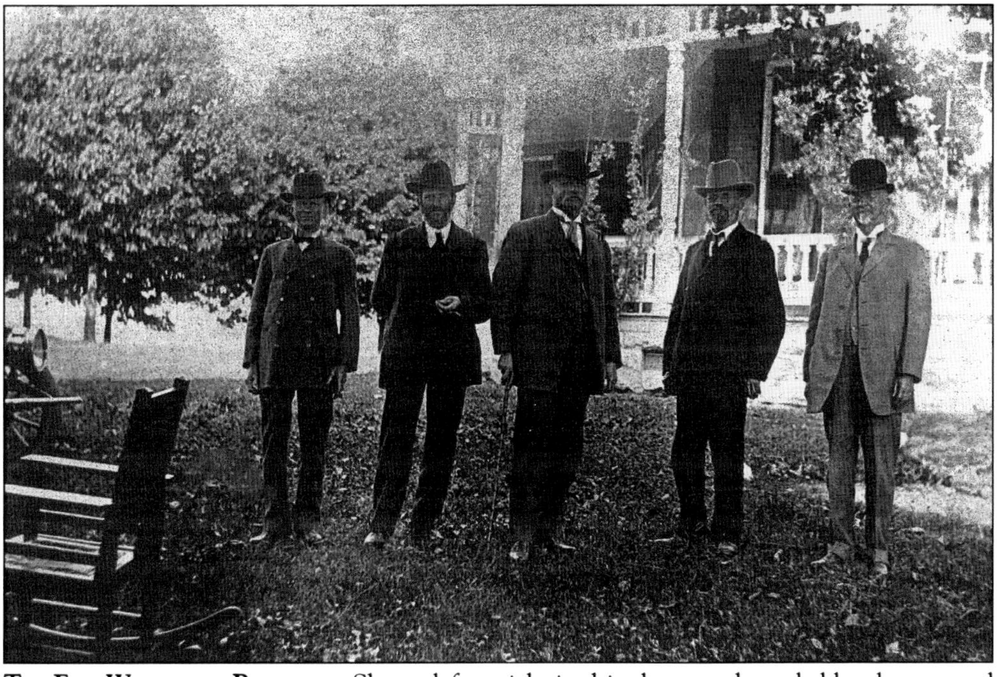

THE FIVE WOODFORD BROTHERS. Shown left to right in this photograph, probably taken around 1917 or 1918, are Ben, John T., Catesby, Henry, and Buckner Woodford. There were also four sisters in the family—Sally, Mary Letitia, Betty, and Maria Woodford. Hundreds of people still living in Bourbon County are descended from this generation of Woodfords.

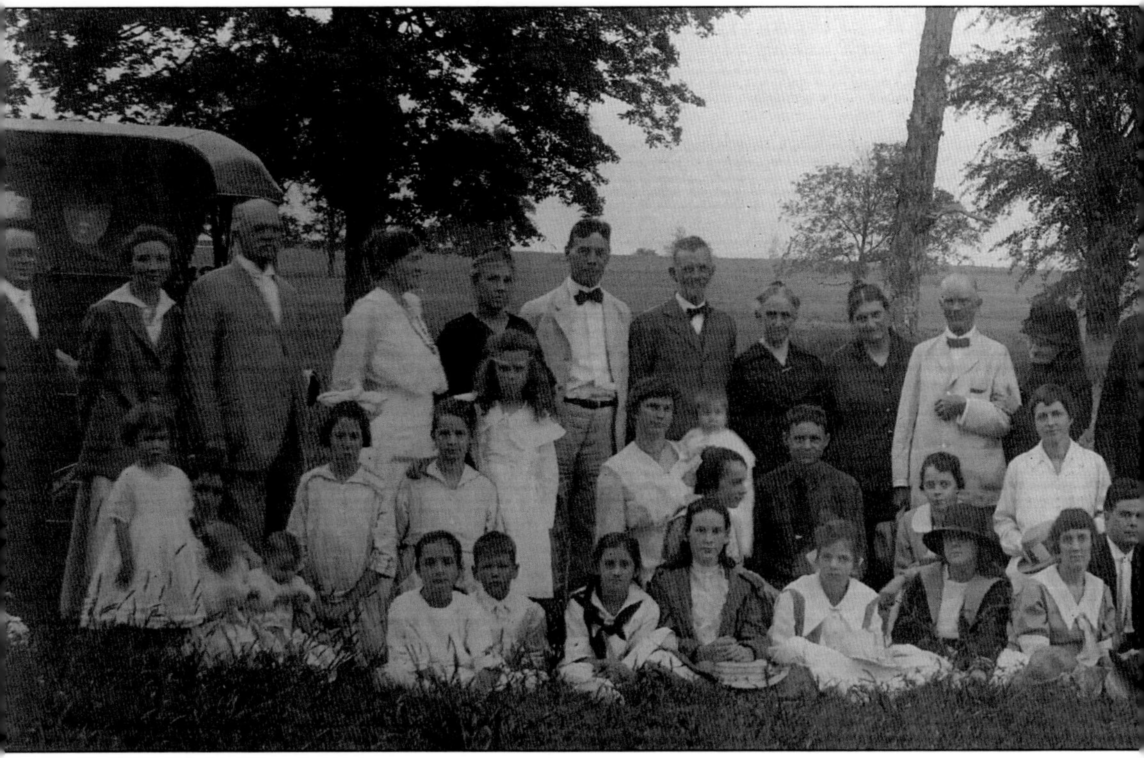

FAMILY REUNIONS IN BOURBON COUNTY. This Woodford family reunion was held around 1917. Shown from left to right in the back row are John Spears, Sally Lockhart Spears, Catesby Woodford, Amelia Woodford, unidentified, James Dodge, John T. Woodford, Nannie Chenault Woodford, Alice Brooks Woodford, Ben Woodford, Sally Woodford Spears, Col. E.F.

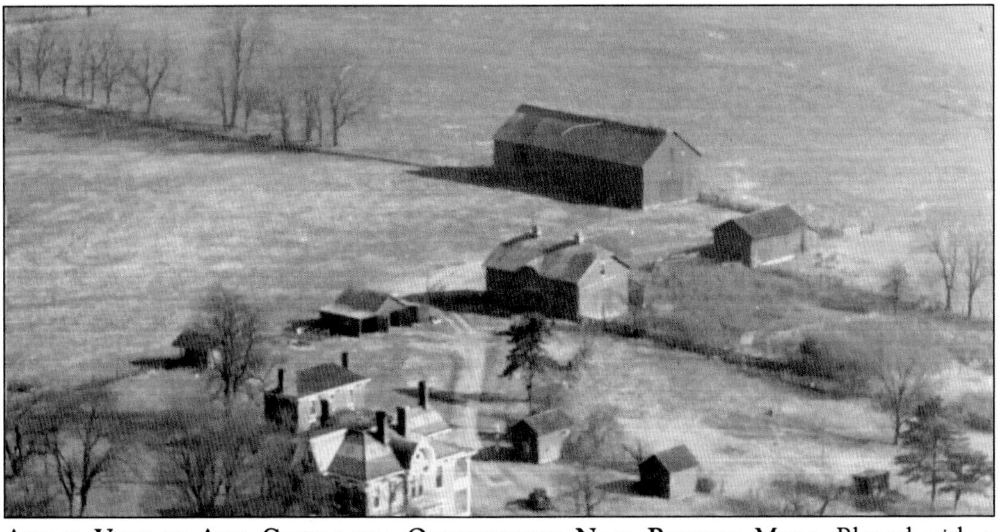

AERIAL VIEW OF AIRY CASTLE AND OUTBUILDINGS NEAR RUDDLES MILLS. Blessed with a lovely name, this photo shows another advantage this property had—the fact that many of the outbuildings long gone on other rural properties are still intact here. This includes the two-story servants' or tenant house behind the main house; an unusual two-story brick horse barn; and several smaller outbuildings.

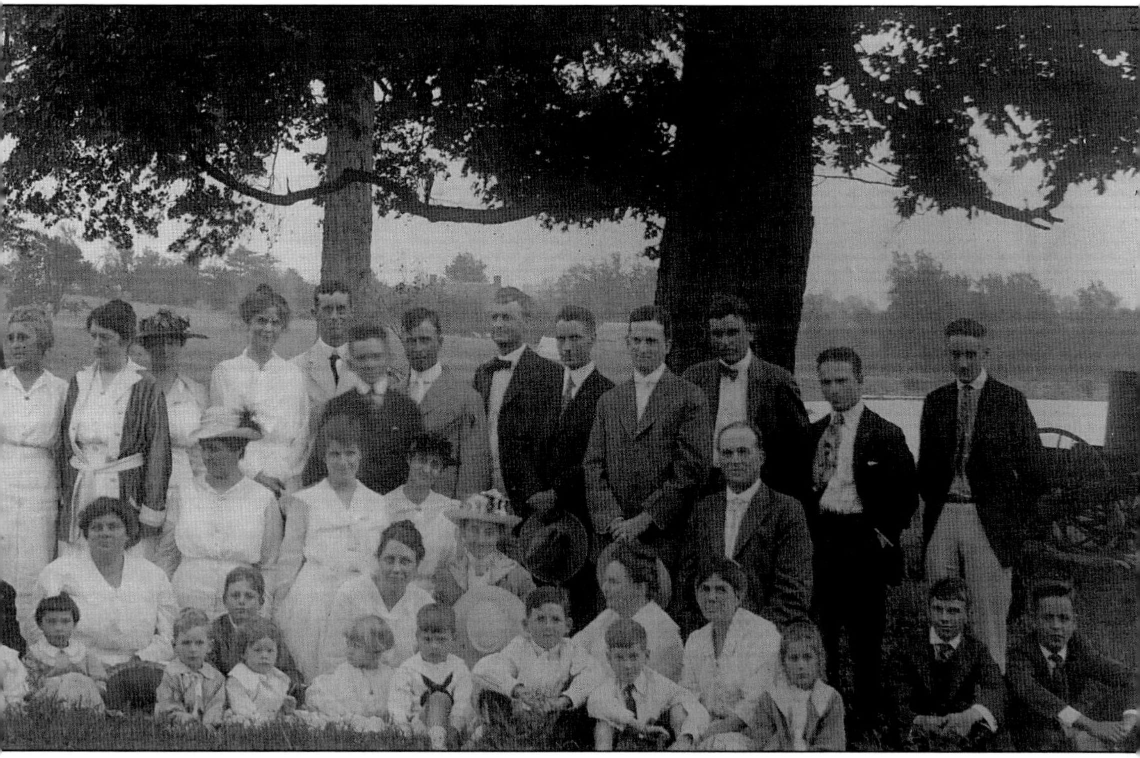

Clay, unidentified, Bessie Woodford Clay, Minnie Horton Woodford, Mary Spears, Keith Spears, Woodie Gay, Catesby Woodford, Woodford Spears, William Woodford, Buckner Woodford, Jr., Chenault Woodford, John T. Woodford, and Charles S. Spears.

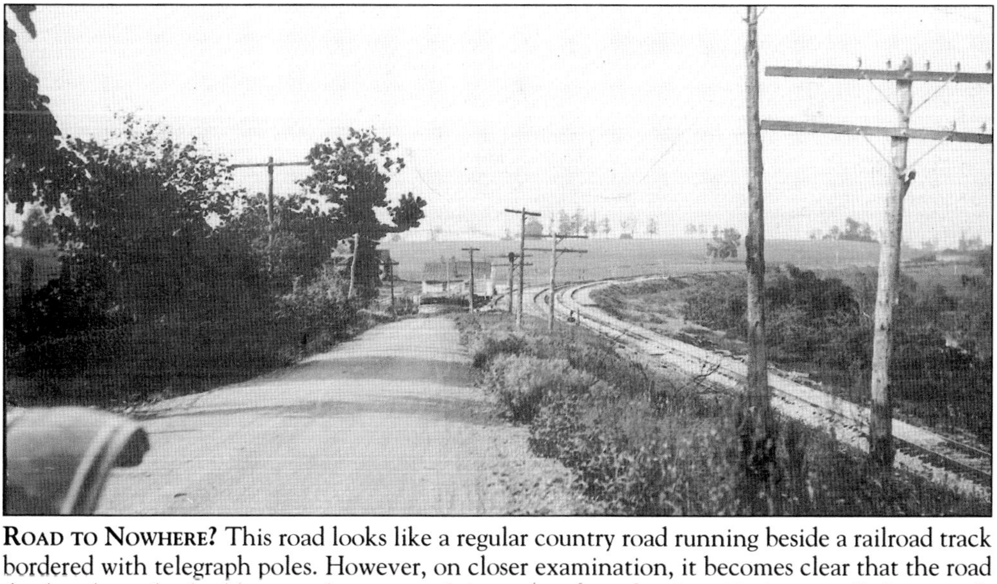

ROAD TO NOWHERE? This road looks like a regular country road running beside a railroad track bordered with telegraph poles. However, on closer examination, it becomes clear that the road dead-ends at the building in the curve of the railroad tracks. It is likely a small depot with wooden chutes that were used to place livestock onto the train cars so that farmers didn't have to drive their animals all the way into town.

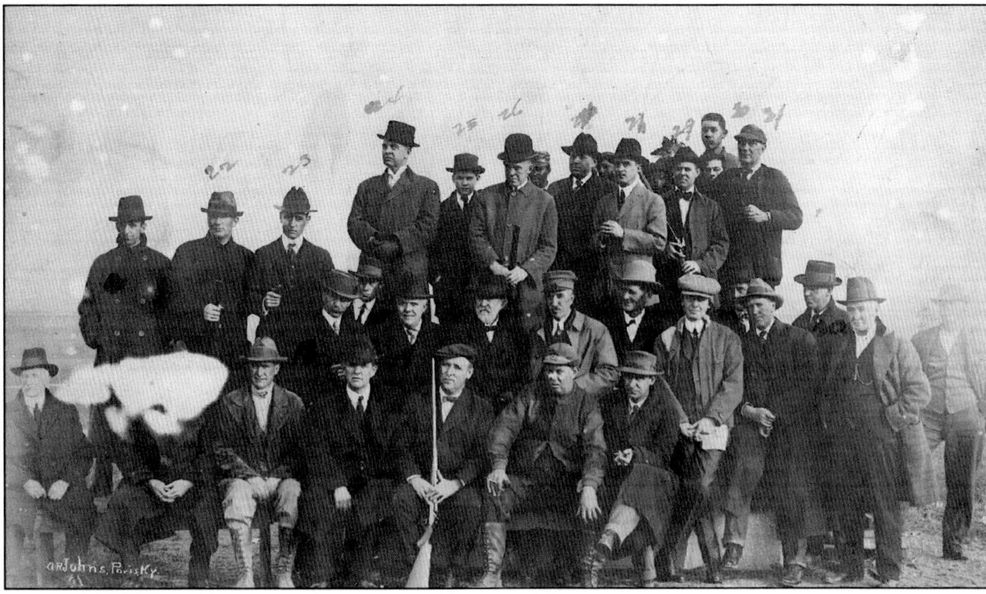

Early Bourbon County Gun Club Attracted Sportsmen. Hunting and fishing have long been popular pastimes for the masculine branch of the Bourbon County population. In 1915, Catesby Spears, T. Henry Clay Jr., and William B. Ardery organized the Bourbon Fish and Game Club. For many years, the group held an annual fish fry and barbecue that attracted hundreds.

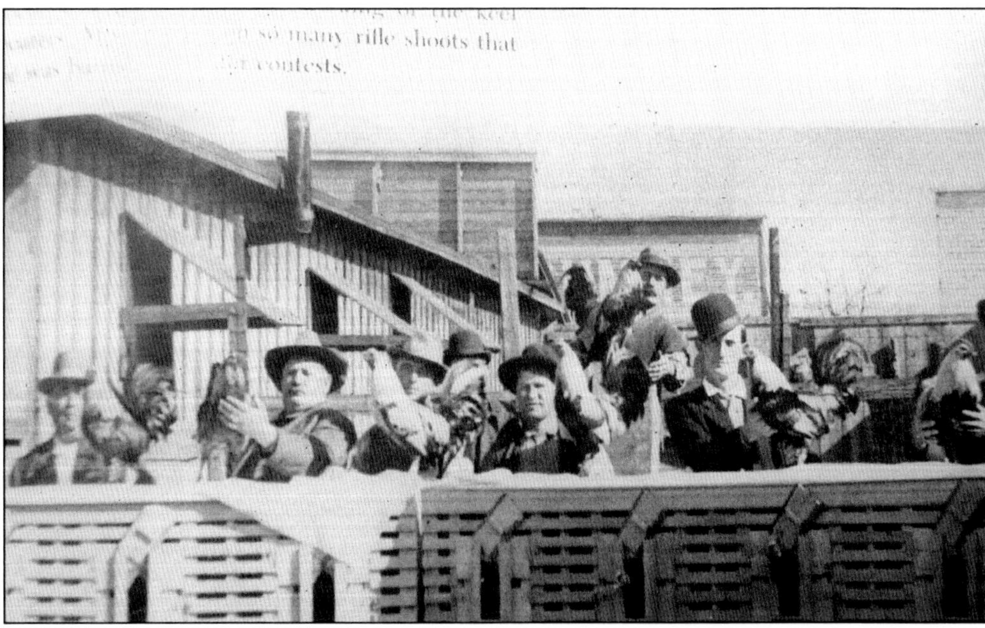

Proud Bourbon County Cockfighters. Before they were raising Thoroughbred horses or pedigreed sheep and cattle in Bourbon County, they were probably breeding fighting gamecocks. Game fowl were packed over the Cumberland Gap by some of the earliest settlers. George Washington, Thomas Jefferson, and many of Kentucky's leading citizens were devotees of the sport. Fighting game birds in Bourbon County was popular up into the 1950s. Today, people raise the colorful birds merely for their appearance.

Eight

FASCINATING FACES

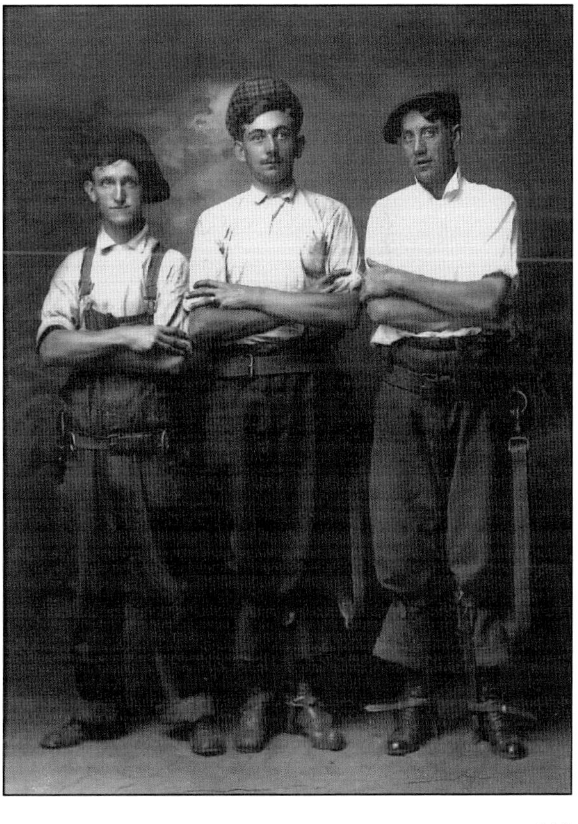

LINEMEN FOR THE COUNTY? In selecting images to include in this book, we came across so many interesting faces and individual stories we could have produced a work of nothing but those. In this short chapter we included some of our favorite faces and stories. The stories of these three men who posed at a photographer's studio at the turn of the century is really unknown to us other than they were linemen for a telegraph, telephone, or possibly electric company. This we can tell by the climbing straps and pole spurs they are wearing. But their faces, to us, are fascinating.

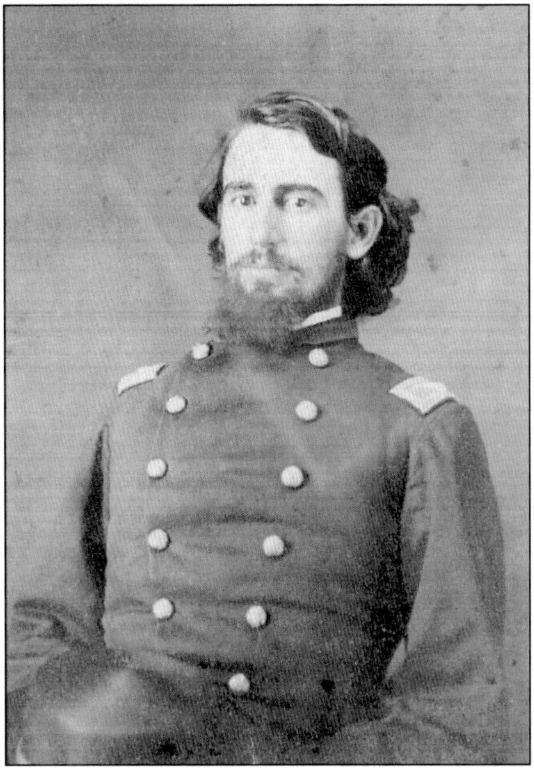

Gen. John T. Croxton. Born in Bourbon County in 1837, Croxton graduated from Yale, practiced law in Paris, and reportedly was one of only two people in the county who voted for Lincoln in 1860. He joined the Union Army with the rank of lieutenant colonel in the 4th Kentucky Mounted Infantry (as pictured here). Croxton served with great distinction in several major battles. At the end of the war he held the brevet rank of major general.

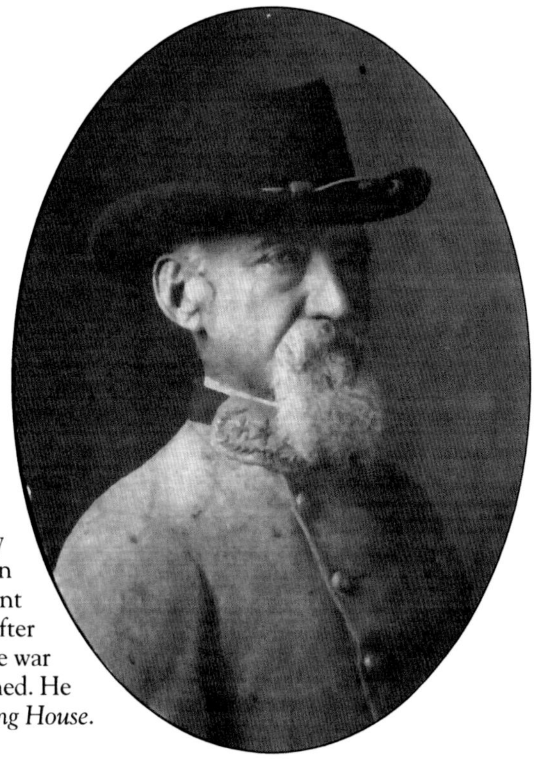

Lt. James R. Rogers. Born in 1838 on Cane Ridge in Bourbon County, Rogers helped raise a company of the Third Kentucky Mounted Rifles for the Confederate Army in 1861. He was promoted to brevet lieutenant for gallantry during a behind the lines raid after the battle of Chickamauga in 1863. After the war he returned to the Cane Ridge area and farmed. He also wrote the history *The Cane Ridge Meeting House.* He died in 1920.

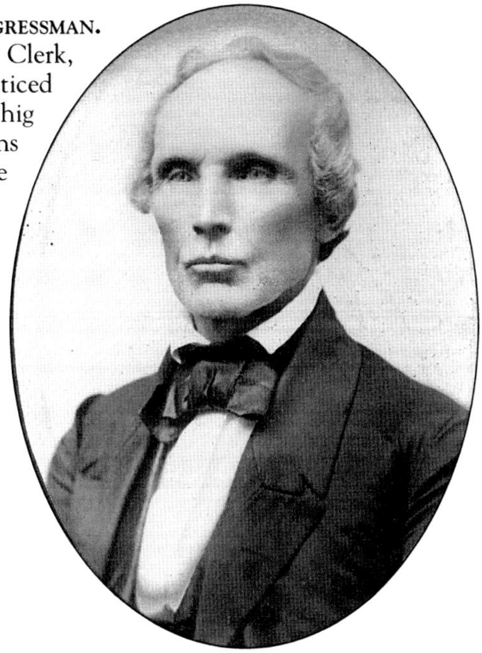

GARRETT DAVIS, U.S. SENATOR AND CONGRESSMAN. Born in 1801, he served as Bourbon County Clerk, was admitted to the bar in 1823, and practiced law in Paris. Davis served in Congress as a Whig from 1839 until 1847. He declined nominations for governor and the presidency from the American Party ("Know Nothings") in 1856. Davis opposed secession and was elected as a Unionist to the U.S. Senate in 1861. He was re-elected as a Democrat in 1867 and served until his death in Paris in 1872.

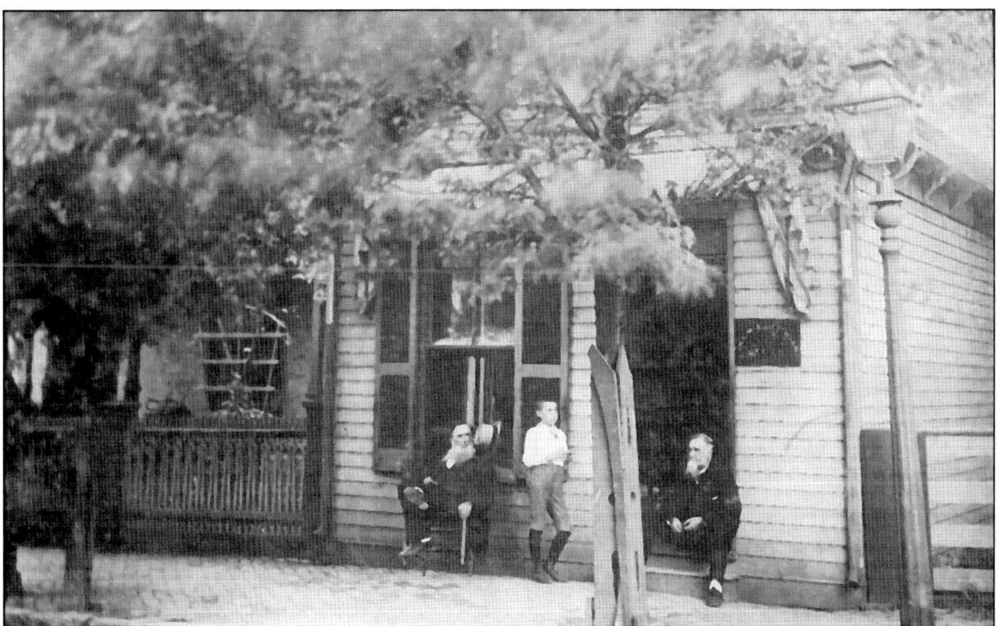

FITHIAN BROTHERS—DIVIDED BY WAR BUT CONTINUED MEDICAL PRACTICE IN PEACE. Dr. Joseph Fithian (left in chair) and Dr. Washington Fithian (in doorway) are seen outside their Pleasant Street office with Washington's grandson, John Peck. When the Civil War began, Wash donned the gray uniform and Joseph the blue. When the war was over, according to family tradition, both came back to Paris, reopened their joint practice, and never mentioned the war to each other.

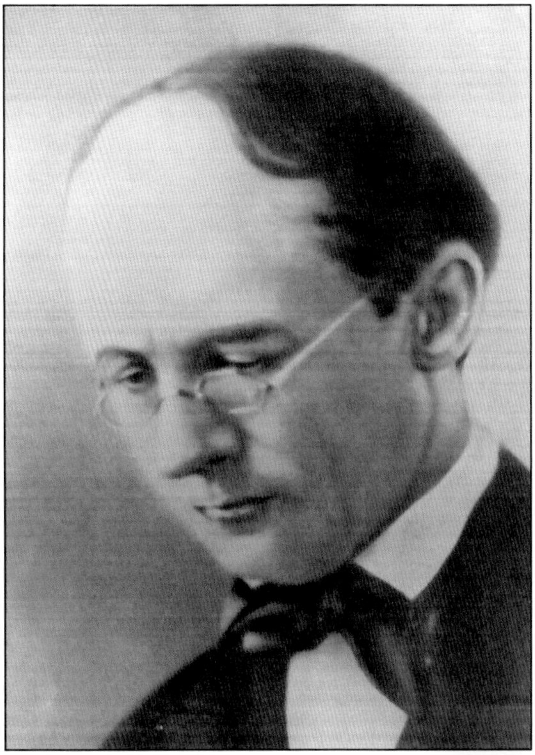

William Holmes McGuffey. In 1823, McGuffey set up a school in Paris in a dining room with seven pupils during a break in his college education at Washington College in Pennsylvania. The enrollment grew steadily to 40 students and the school moved to a more traditional location. McGuffey graduated from college in 1826 and began creating his "eclectic" *McGuffey Readers* in 1833.

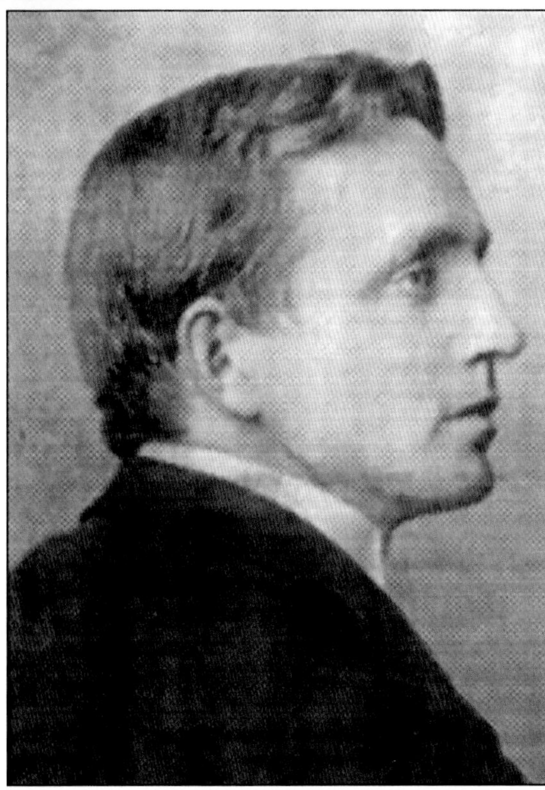

John Fox Jr.—First U.S. Novelist to Sell a Million Copies. Fox was born in Bourbon County in 1862 and educated at his father's Stony Point Academy, a noted private school in Bourbon County from 1862 to 1890. Fox graduated from Harvard in 1883 and, after a short career as a journalist, began writing fiction. His novel, *The Little Shepherd of Kingdom Come*, was published in 1903 and sold more than one million copies.

FANNIEBELLE SUTHERLAND. Mrs. Sutherland had a private elementary school on Main Street in Paris from 1910 to 1924. In 1924, she was appointed to fill an unexpired term as Police Judge and was the first woman in Paris and one of the first in the state to hold that position. She was then elected to a four-year term as Police Judge that ran from 1926 to 1930. Mrs. Sutherland also served as the president of the Kentucky Federated Women's Club.

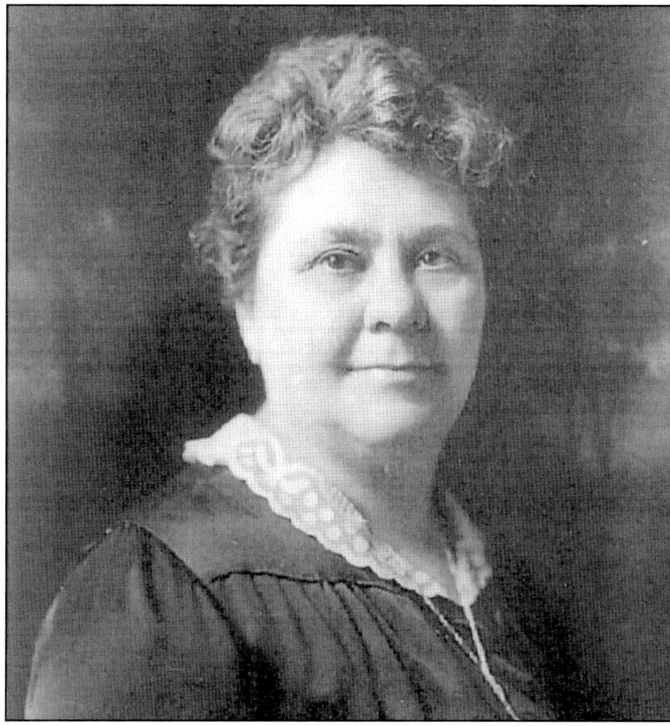

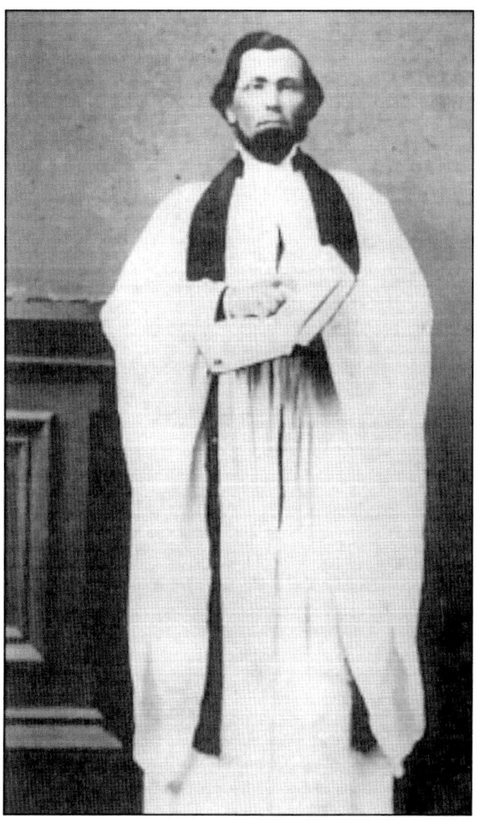

REV. AMOS CLEAVER, FIRST RECTOR OF ST. PETER'S EPISCOPAL CHURCH. The first Episcopal service held in Paris was in 1815. Two years after the Diocese of Lexington was formed in 1829, Reverend Cleaver, an Englishman, came to Paris to organize St. Peter's. He established a female academy, then began raising money for construction of the church. It is recorded that Cleaver helped in the construction by bringing sand from Blue Licks on pack horses to mix the mortar.

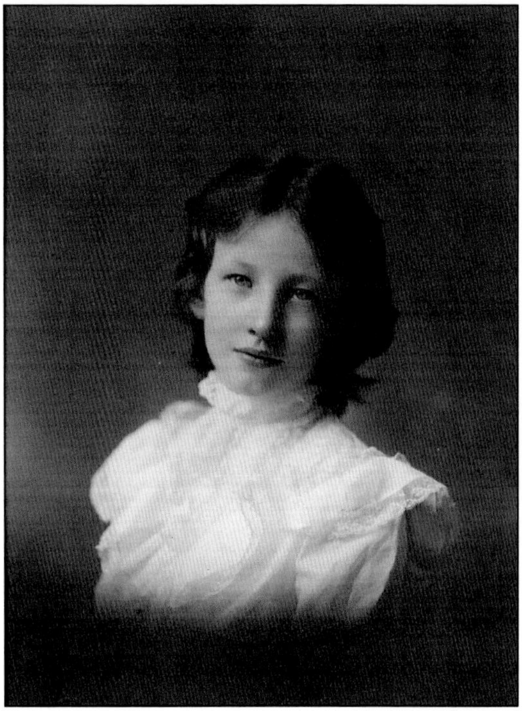

Edna Talbott Whitley—Bourbon County's Most Noted Local Historian. This photo shows Mrs. Edna Talbott Whitley as a child—before she began her long career as a "historical detective," searching out clues in mountains of yellowing documents to help trace the identity and history of the people and structures that were the focus of her research. She wrote a weekly newspaper column for many years in addition to several books.

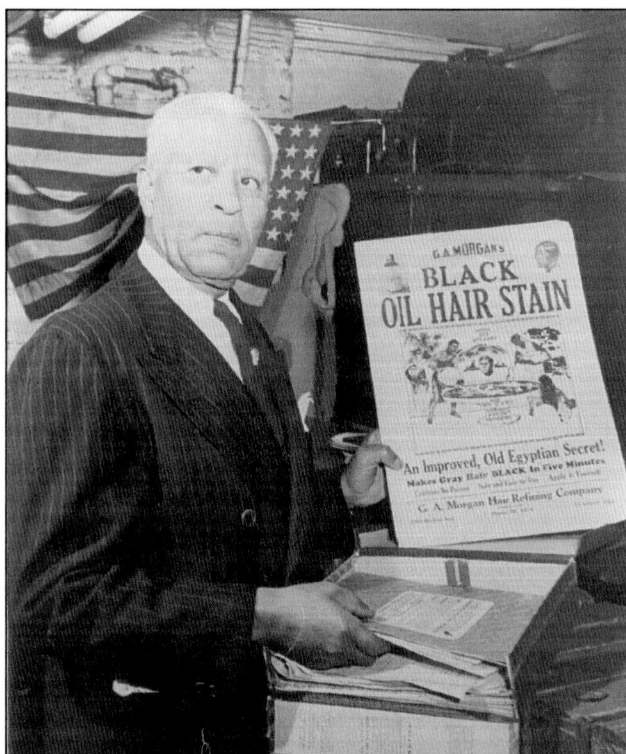

Millions Helped by Inventions from the Creative Mind of Garrett Morgan. Garrett Morgan was born in Bourbon County in 1877 in Claysville —a small African-American community on the outskirts of Paris. His parents had been slaves, but Morgan's mind knew no bounds. He invented the gas mask and the tri-color traffic light—inventions that affect millions. In addition, he invented hair products and this photo shows him with a poster touting the advantages of one of those products.

Nine

TRAINS, PLANES, AND AUTOMOBILES

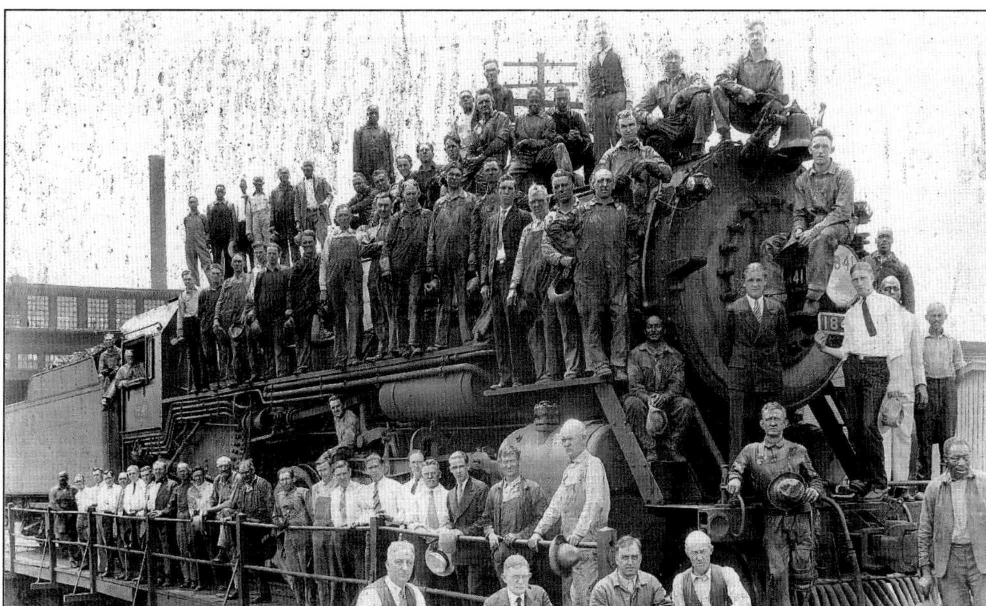

RAILROAD ROUNDHOUSE AND REPAIR YARDS. In 1905 the L&N Railroad expanded their shop facilities in Paris and began construction of a large brick round house and turntable for engines. The shops would soon be running three shifts a day, seven days a week, with a schedule employing more than 200 men. Probably pictured here in the mid 1920s is one of those shifts along with the office staff. They are proudly posing with a J-4-A steam locomotive, one of the largest and most powerful freight pullers of the time. It was used to haul coal out of the mountains on the Cincinnati to Corbin line.

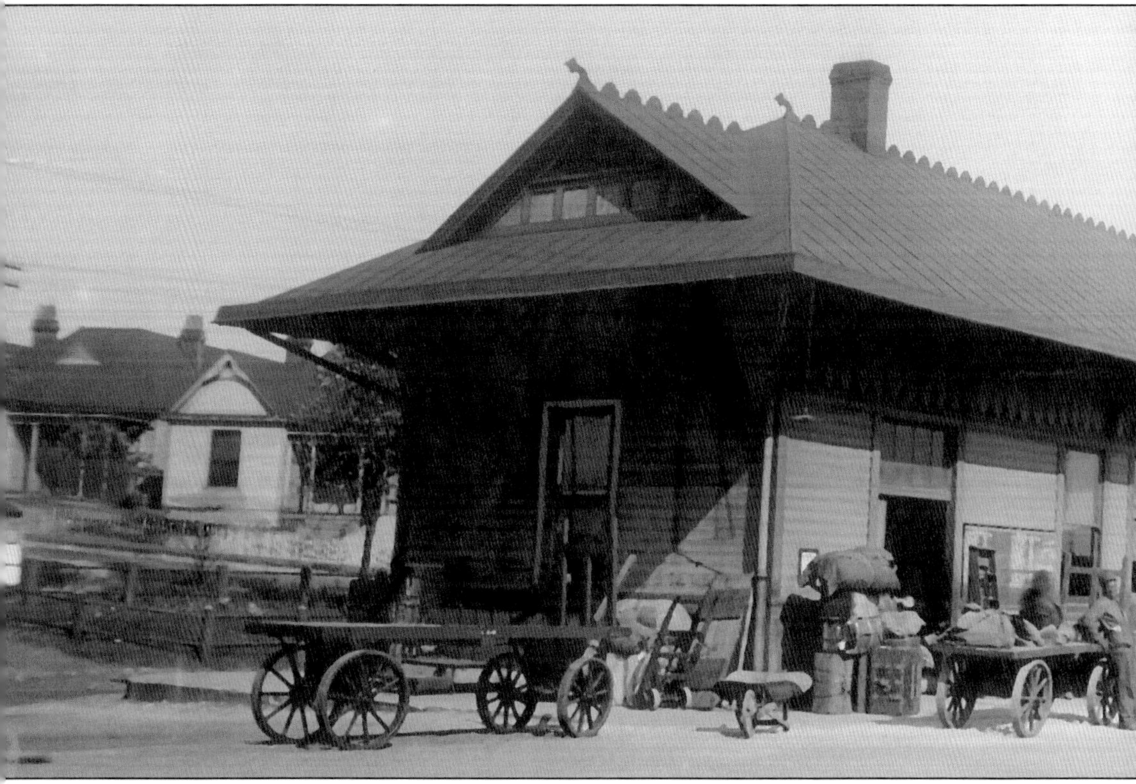

L&N Depot—Paris's Portal to Outside World. The first railroad came to Paris from Lexington in 1853. The depot seen here was built in 1882 by the Kentucky Central Railroad and acquired by the Louisville & Nashville line when the former failed. This picture was

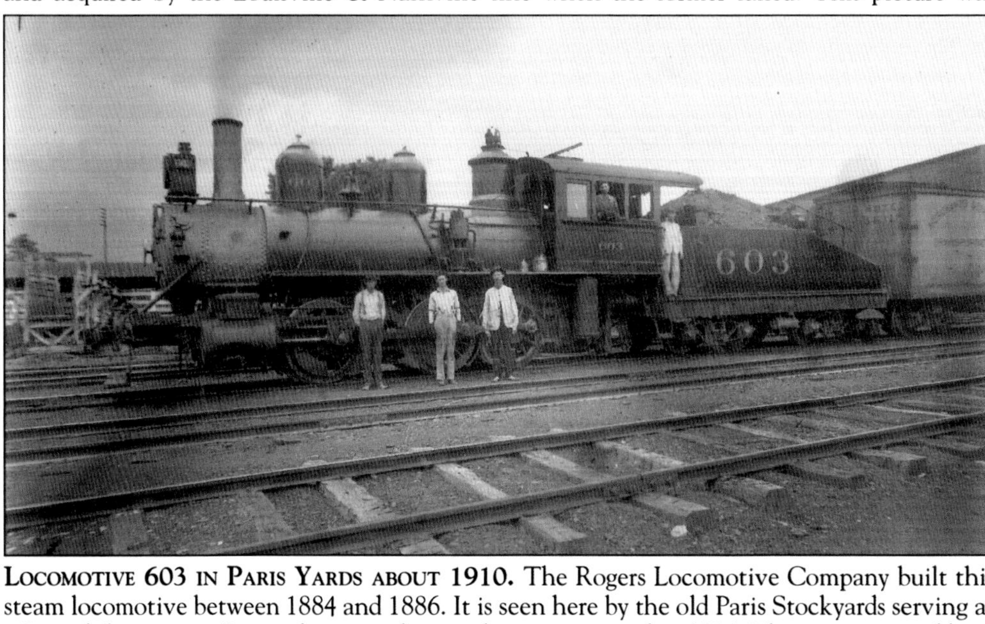

Locomotive 603 in Paris Yards about 1910. The Rogers Locomotive Company built this steam locomotive between 1884 and 1886. It is seen here by the old Paris Stockyards serving as a "switch locomotive"— a job it served at until it was scrapped in 1924. The crew pictured here would have typically included flagman, brakeman, conductor, fireman, and an engineer.

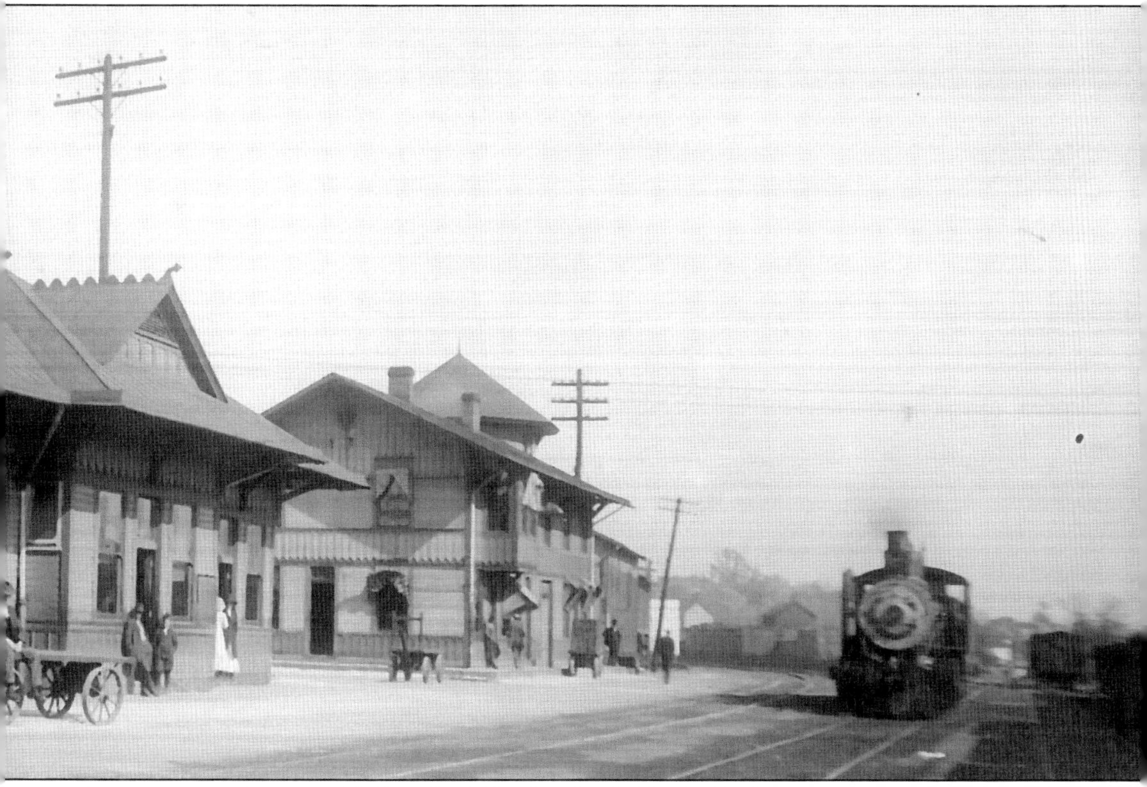

taken sometime between 1901 and 1910 after the L&N build the two-story station master's building seen beyond it. Generations of Bourbon Countians went off to school, new careers and even to fight wars from this spot—the luckiest ones got to return.

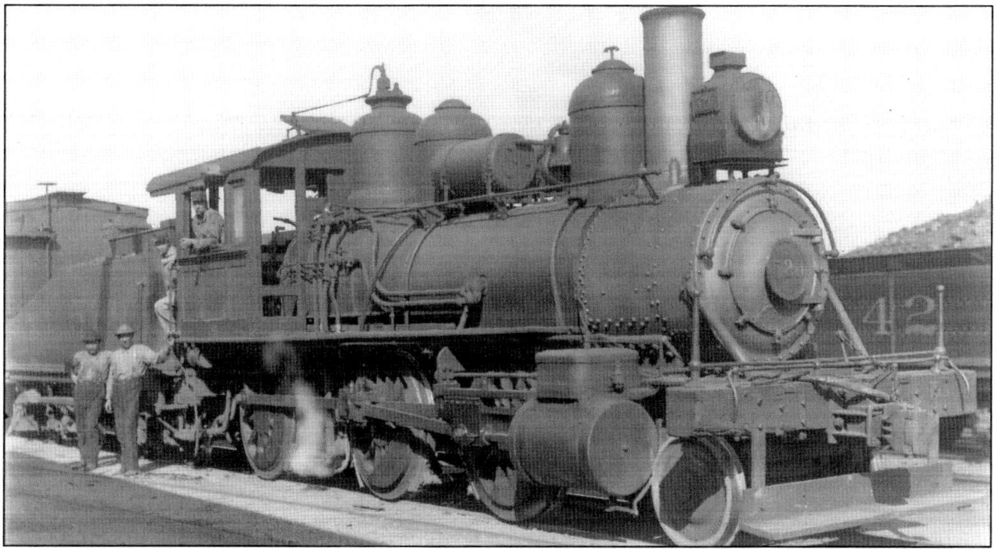

Locomotive 520. This steam locomotive served in the Paris switching yards from the late 1920s to the 1950s. Many of the crews and workmen on the railroad were Irish immigrants who lived south of the yards in an area known as "Irishtown." Their influence on the town's culture and politics was felt almost immediately.

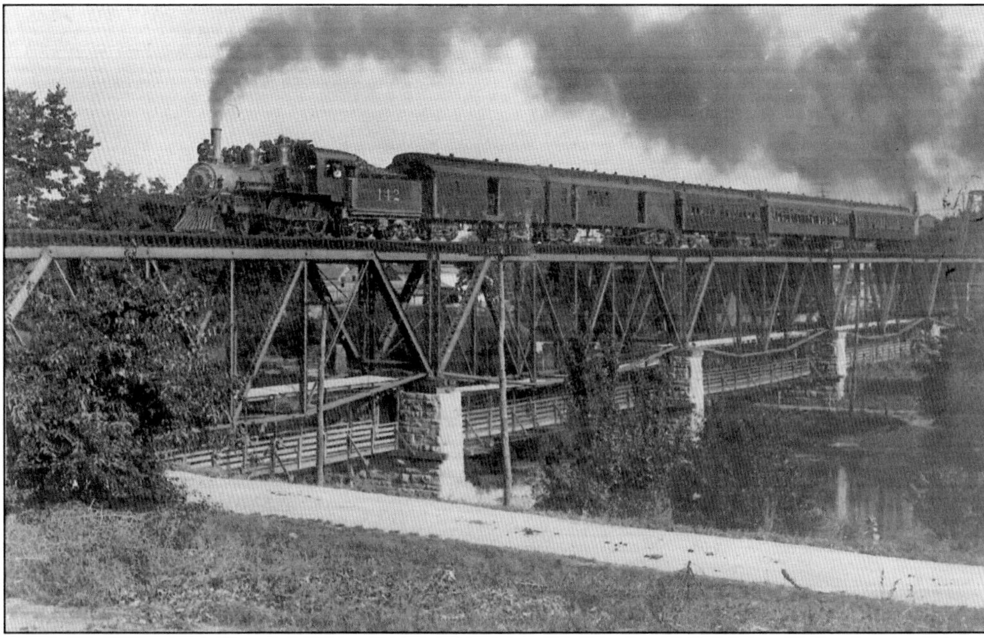

TRAIN FROM MAYSVILLE CROSSING STONER CREEK. Billowing a long plume of coal smoke, Locomotive 142 is seen here pulling a train consisting of three passenger cars and two freight cars across the trestle crossing Stoner Creek about 1890–1905. The round trip between Maysville and Paris was probably made two or three times a day. One can see the pedestrian walkway beneath the tracks—a place you wouldn't want to be when the splinter-causing, ember-shooting train roared overhead.

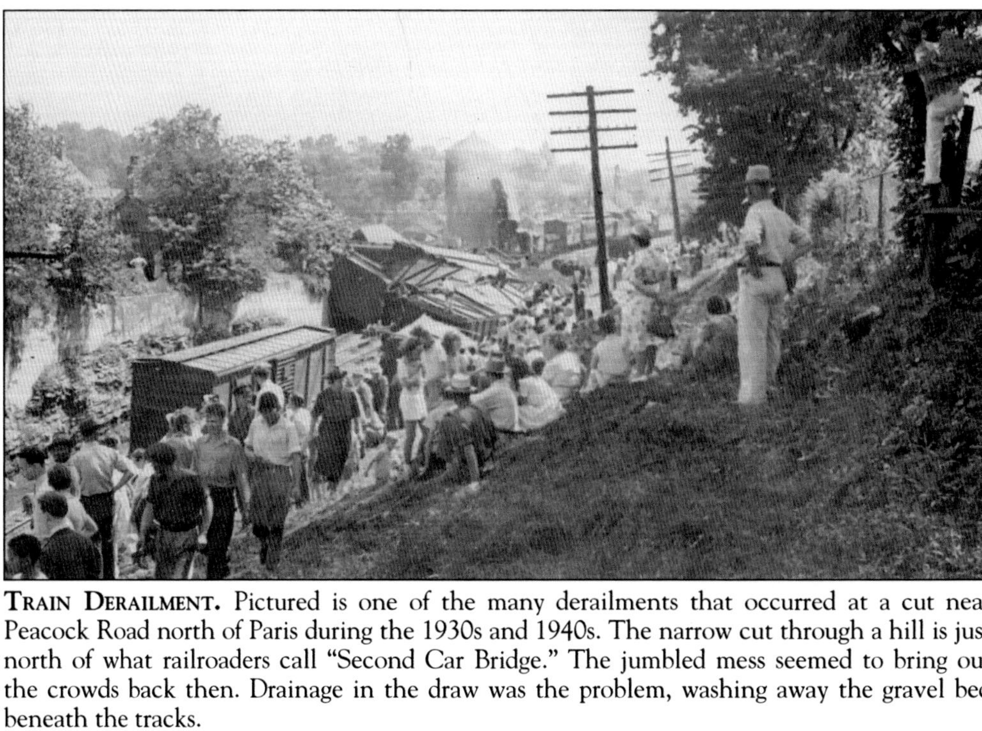

TRAIN DERAILMENT. Pictured is one of the many derailments that occurred at a cut near Peacock Road north of Paris during the 1930s and 1940s. The narrow cut through a hill is just north of what railroaders call "Second Car Bridge." The jumbled mess seemed to bring out the crowds back then. Drainage in the draw was the problem, washing away the gravel bed beneath the tracks.

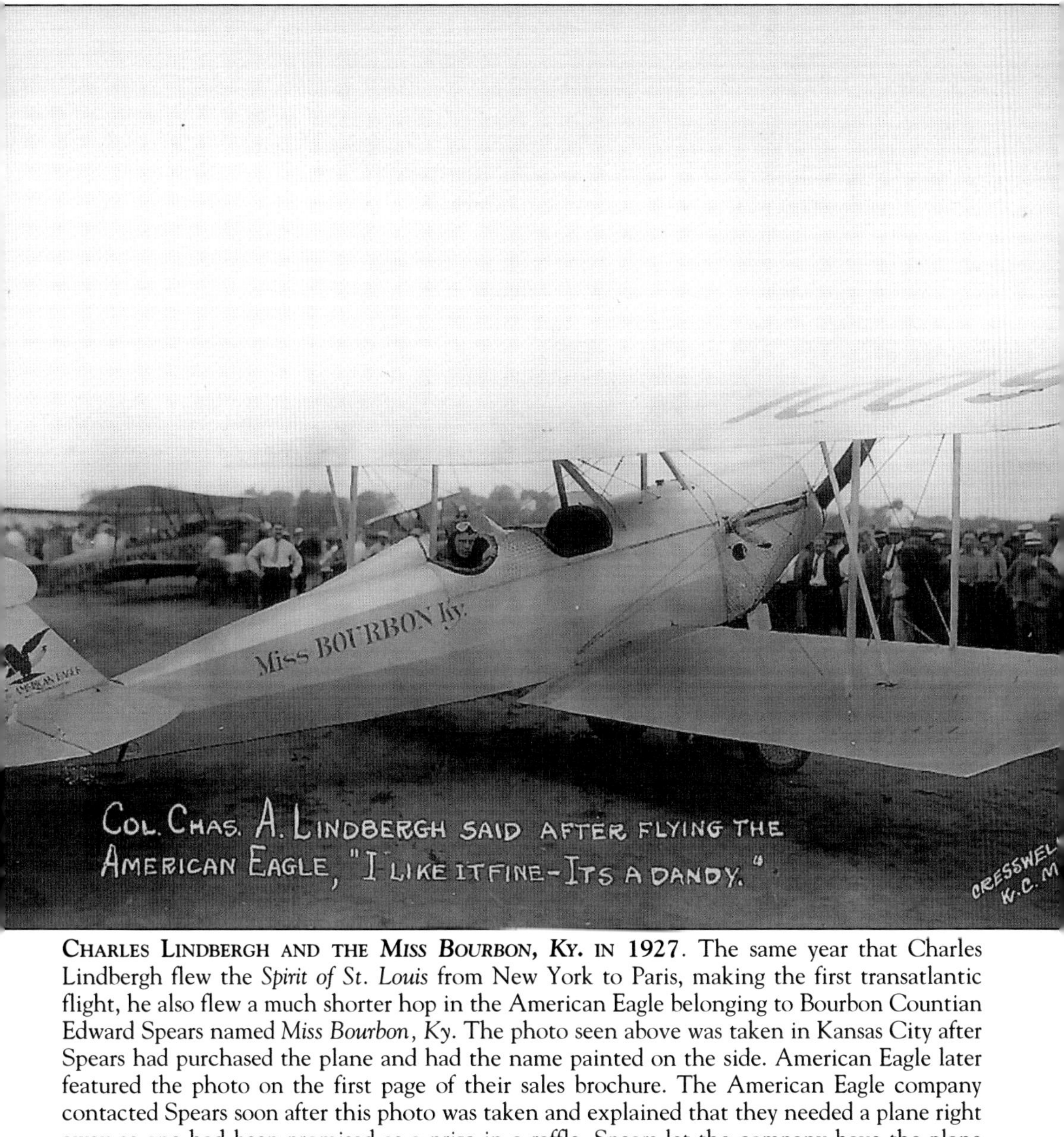

CHARLES LINDBERGH AND THE *MISS BOURBON, KY.* IN 1927. The same year that Charles Lindbergh flew the *Spirit of St. Louis* from New York to Paris, making the first transatlantic flight, he also flew a much shorter hop in the American Eagle belonging to Bourbon Countian Edward Spears named *Miss Bourbon, Ky*. The photo seen above was taken in Kansas City after Spears had purchased the plane and had the name painted on the side. American Eagle later featured the photo on the first page of their sales brochure. The American Eagle company contacted Spears soon after this photo was taken and explained that they needed a plane right away as one had been promised as a prize in a raffle. Spears let the company have the plane back as he hadn't yet finished his flying lessons and got a brand new *Miss Bourbon, Ky.*, in a few weeks but this one had not been flown by Lindbergh.

Bourbon County Airport. Doug Wilson, one of the driving forces behind the establishment of the Paris Airport on a flat grassy tract of land on the Ruddles Mills Road, is shown at the field with two of the planes. Ben Gorham was the area's first commercial pilot and charged daring residents a dollar for a short flight around the area to see local landmarks. During World War II, the airport was used for testing parachutes by the Irvin Air Chute Company, Inc. of Lexington. After the war, the airport was designated by the government as a certified landing area and C.M. Wasson of Little Rock was hired as instructor pilot and field manager. The airport opened in 1940 and closed in 1951.

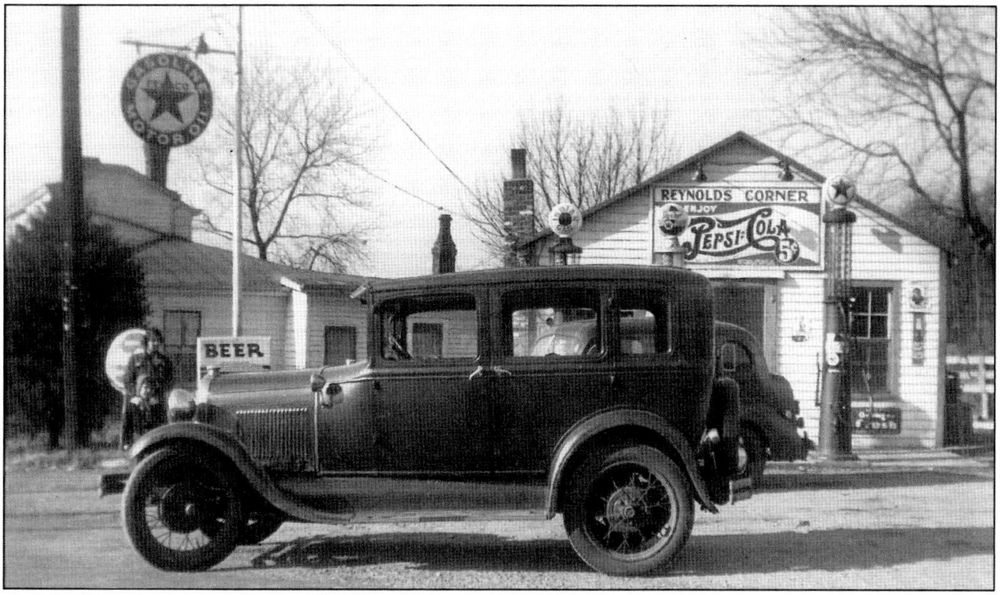

REYNOLD'S CORNER. They offered Pepsi-Colas for 5¢ and Texaco Gasoline for probably not much more a gallon. Reynolds Corner was located on the Paris Pike and was a favorite place to get a cold drink, a great sandwich, or to fill up the car on the way to Lexington. Notice the glass-topped gas pumps—consumers pumped the gas up into the glass section, which was marked off into gallons, and then let it flow back into their tank.

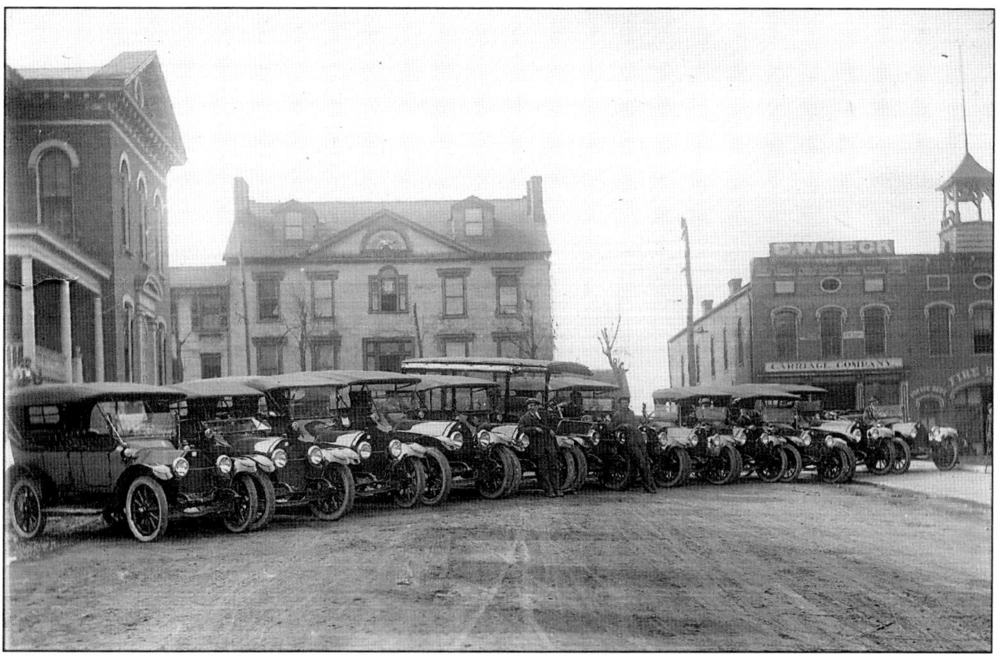

SHOWING OFF THEIR "HORSELESS CARRIAGES." We had an earlier photo in the book that showed this area filled with men and their steeds. This later photo shows some men exhibiting their new "horseless" machines. The fact that this was very early in the history of the automobile is obvious from the types of cars on display and because the building in the background next to the fire station is still the C.W. Heck Carriage Company.

ACKNOWLEDGMENTS

We would like to thank everyone who loaned their photographs for this book. We started out thinking that 200 photographs taken between 1860 and 1940 would be hard to find and ended up having to return more than we used. We wish we could have run all of them and appreciate the effort that many people have taken to preserve and share these priceless local images.

Tug Wilson loaned us a large group of glass negatives with images that had not been seen for many years. The experts at the Kentucky History Center printed the photos from these negatives and many were used in this book. In addition, the photo collections at the Hopewell Museum, the Kentucky History Center, and the photos collected by Historic-Paris Bourbon County and Nannine Clay Wallis proved invaluable. We hope that anyone with old photographs would consider donating them to either the Kentucky History Center or the Hopewell Museum, or both. Keep in mind, too, that we hope to do a second book sometime in the future—picking up in 1940 and continuing to the present.

Finally, we want to thank the many individuals who took the time to pass along information on different subjects, scoured attics and basements for photographs, and helped in many other ways, including: Betsy and Ted Kuster, Bobby Shiflet, Betty Witt, Clara Watson, Raymond Vanhook, Charleen Tate, Mike Horne, Tom Kincaid, Kenney Roseberry, Biz and Catesby Clay, Bill Bryan, Ann Butler Burroughs, Karl Lusk, Jr., Amos Penney, Sr., Everett Garrison, Steve Spears, Sr., Charles Ramey, Kevin Crump, Jacquie Nichols, Catherine Lytle, Lucy Cooper, Richard Eads, Sherry Rankin, Donnie Foley, Bessie Hunt, Mary Winter, Bill Bright, Tom Dailey, Mary Louis Evans, Jim Ginter, Mary Wilder, Mike Withrow, Dudley Forsythe, Jean Wallen, Edith Beeding, Patsy Baldwin, Patty and Jeff Layson, Jim Friess, John Sosby, Jerome Harney, Corky Carlisle, James Pruitt, Patty Biddle, Pat Simpson, Elizabeth Danforth, Norma Adair, Price Huston, Brenda Childers, Betsy Kephart, Mary E. Winter, Bill Bright, Allison Weber, Bruce Brown, Cathy Carter, Edna and Basil Hayden, and Eva Rice.

There are also a couple of people who are no longer with us, but whose influence was evident in this book: Mrs. Edna Talbott Whitley was always a great historical resource and her written material continues to provide invaluable information; also Bud Watson who, with his wife Clara, collected historical photos at Watson's Laundry for years, serving as a mini-museum before the Hopewell Museum was born.

As can be seen from this long list, we had a large "quilter's circle" to help create and craft this quilt of images made as a gift to our community and we thank them all.